ANATOMY OF A CON ARTIST

ANATOMY OF A CON ARTIST

**THE 14 RED FLAGS TO SPOT
SCAMMERS, GRIFTERS, AND THIEVES**

JOHNATHAN WALTON

RODALE

New York

Rodale Books
An imprint of Random House
A division of Penguin Random House LLC
1745 Broadway, New York, NY 10019
rodalebooks.com | randomhousebooks.com
penguinrandomhouse.com

Library of Congress Cataloging-in-Publication Data
Names: Walton, Johnathan author
Title: Anatomy of a con artist / by Johnathan Walton.
Description: First edition. | New York, NY: Rodale, [2025] | Includes index.
Identifiers: LCCN 2025009016 (print) | LCCN 2025009017 (ebook) |
ISBN 9780593797167 hardcover | ISBN 9780593797174 ebook
Subjects: LCSH: Swindlers and swindling
Classification: LCC HV6691 .W36 2025 (print) | LCC HV6691 (ebook) |
DDC 364.16/3—dc23/eng/20250514
LC record available at https://lccn.loc.gov/2025009016
LC ebook record available at https://lccn.loc.gov/2025009017

Printed in the United States of America on acid-free paper

2 4 6 8 9 7 5 3 1

First Edition

BOOK TEAM: Managing editor: Allie Fox • Production manager: Richard Elman •
Proofreaders: Pam Rehm, Kimberly Broderick, Ruth Anne Phillips, Cameron Schoettle •
Indexer: J S Editorial, LLC

Book design by Debbie Glasserman

The authorized representative in the EU for product safety and compliance is
Penguin Random House Ireland, Morrison Chambers, 32 Nassau Street,
Dublin D02 YH68, Ireland, https://eu-contact.penguin.ie.

I wholeheartedly dedicate this book to the victims of scammers who stand up and fight back. It's a tough road to hoe to be sure—but it's the only way to stop these malevolent caricatures of human beings from hurting others.

CONTENTS

Introduction ix

1. THE 14 RED FLAGS CON ARTISTS WAVE 3

2. RED FLAG #1: "I JUST WANT TO HELP" 14
Queen of the Con I 24

3. RED FLAG #2: TOO KIND, TOO QUICK 33
Queen of the Con II 43

4. RED FLAG #3: DRAMA, DRAMA, DRAMA 48

5. RED FLAG #4: ISOLATION 59
Queen of the Con III 73

6. RED FLAG #5: "I'M BETTER THAN YOU" 85
Queen of the Con IV 93

7. RED FLAG #6: TECHNOLOGY 99
Queen of the Con V 108

8. RED FLAG #7: SCARCITY 114

9. RED FLAG #8: BEAK WETTING 122
Queen of the Con VI 129

10. RED FLAG #9: A GOOD DAY JOB 139
Queen of the Con VII 146

11. RED FLAG #10: WIRES 154

Queen of the Con VIII 161

12. RED FLAG #11: THEY MOVE AROUND A LOT 171

Queen of the Con IX 180

13. RED FLAG #12: STORIES FROM FARAWAY PLACES 186

Queen of the Con X 192

14. RED FLAG #13: TMI 196

Queen of the Con XI 203

15. RED FLAG #14: THE DALE CARNEGIE TECHNIQUES 209

Queen of the Con XII 213

16. WHAT TO DO IF YOU'VE BEEN CONNED 222

Acknowledgments 229

Index 233

INTRODUCTION

THE DAY I REALIZED I HAD GOTTEN CONNED AND LOST ALL MY MONEY, I WAS DEVASTATED. I went home and collapsed in my husband's arms. I didn't just cry. I wailed as the pain and regret washed over me like a slow-moving hurricane.

"How could I let this happen to us?" I sobbed over and over again. My tears drenched his neck. I was inconsolable.

"I'm a good person," I thought. Kind. Generous. I had gone out of my way to help people my entire life. How could *this* be happening to *me*?

At that point, I had no idea that there are in fact professional con artists everywhere: millions of them, living among us, wearing clever disguises. They're the new boyfriend or the new girlfriend in your life. They're the new co-worker or the new neighbor. They seem super nice and loving. They're charismatic and fun to be with. You don't know until it's much too late that they're setting you up to rob you blind.

Since realizing I was conned, I have read a ton of books and articles about con artists in a desperate attempt to understand what happened to me—and *why* it happened to me. And while most were somewhat insightful, they all painfully lacked firsthand knowledge. They were all so antiseptic and sterile—written by college professors and professional authors who "researched" the topic and "reported" what they found, citing tons of studies and scientific principles about the psychology of scams.

These books always seemed to be holding their subject at arm's length. The author of one bestseller casually admits that they have never been conned themselves and they don't know any con artists personally in their lives.

In all these accounts, the authors make it seem as if getting scammed is something that happens to "other people." Not them. They're much too smart for that.

Well, I've got news for these authors with zero experience getting conned. News from the front lines. News from the trenches.

Con artists don't actually "outsmart" you. Con artists "out-feel" you. They use your emotions to gain entry into your life and make you care about them deeply, or care about whatever situation they've created out of whole cloth. And that's how they scam you—because once you're making decisions based on emotion, with your heart instead of your head, you'll make poor decisions, always. And they will get your money, eventually.

Reading all these books about con artists, I started to feel as if they were victim shaming to a certain degree. And as a victim, I suddenly felt as if all these authors were, like, *critics*.

An inspirational Teddy Roosevelt quote from a speech he gave in Paris back in 1910 would become my mantra:

> It is not the critic who counts; not the man who points out how the strong man stumbles, or where the doer of deeds could have done them better. The credit belongs to the man who is actually in the arena, whose face is marred by dust and sweat and blood; who strives valiantly; who errs, who comes short again and again . . . who spends himself in a worthy cause; who at the best knows in the end the triumph of high achievement, and who at the worst, if he fails, at least fails while daring greatly, so that his place shall never be with those cold and timid souls who neither know victory nor defeat.

Well, I am the man in that arena. My face *is* marred by dust and sweat and blood—because a con artist tried to destroy me. But I strove valiantly and managed to turn the tables. I put her in jail. And now my sole mission in life, to all who are reading these words, is to pull the curtain back and enable *you* to spot these soulless dregs of society, before they hurt you or anyone you love.

Also, most victims of con artists sadly aren't like me. Not to say that I'm better than anybody. I just don't have that *shame* thing going on. That shame thing really seems to shackle victims and keep them quiet. In fact, most people who get scammed don't tell a living soul about it— much less go to the police. And that not only enables the con artist to get away scot-free but also actually helps them scam other people— because no one's blowing their cover. No one's outing them. And more importantly, no one's stopping them.

Well, I wasn't like that. After I realized I had been conned, I told everyone and anyone who'd listen. And while I was summarily ignored in the beginning, eventually my con artist story exploded—especially after I got the woman who scammed me convicted by a jury of her peers and sentenced to five years behind bars.

My crazy quest of a story was picked up by newspapers and magazines worldwide. Heck, I even did a podcast about it called *Queen of the Con: The Irish Heiress.* And as soon as the first national news story chronicling what happened to me went public back in August of 2019, I started getting contacted by hundreds of victims of *other* con artists all over the world, asking me for help and advice on how to bring to justice the con artists who had dared to mess with their lives.

They desperately wanted what I had. And I desperately wanted to give it to them.

Sometimes I'd just have a phone call or a long text exchange with a victim explaining how to file a police report. Other times I'd advise them on what to do after police turned them away—because police had turned me away too, and I had figured out a way to effectively push back and change their minds. Or I'd work with victims on how to make their case "sexy"-sounding enough to get investigated by authorities. It turns out, pitching a criminal case to police is a lot like pitching a television show to a network executive.

By the way, I'm actually a TV producer. More on that later.

When you go to the police, it doesn't matter how hurt you are or how much money was stolen from you—they don't care. You're not dead. You're not bleeding. They're dealing with a lot of people who are. So crying and being overcome with emotion as you try to explain what happened to you turns them off immediately.

You have to be able to "sell" what happened to you in a sexy but clear sentence. Then you have to be able to elaborate—unpacking all the evidence you have—in an unemotional and compelling paragraph. And *then* you have to quickly present the evidence you have, in a Vanna White / *Wheel of Fortune* kind of way.

You have to hook them. And I'm going to show you how to do that.

Some con cases that I work on I get deeply invested in, emotionally and financially. Those cases usually involve a devastated widow or an elderly victim who got scammed out of all their money by a clever con artist, someone they swore they knew and definitely loved. It breaks my heart and gnaws at my soul. And it makes me really angry.

When I was struggling to get justice in my case, I felt that the system just didn't care. I've since learned that's not exactly true. The system wants to convict con artists, absolutely. But it's extremely difficult to prove those cases in court "beyond reasonable doubt." That's the legal threshold. And the system has a penchant for shunning difficult cases.

Let's face it. We all want "wins" in life. Whether we're athletes or stockbrokers or salespeople, we all want to rack up as many wins in our chosen profession as we can. Prosecutors working within the confines of the criminal justice system are no different.

But that system will never tell you what I will: that the onus for getting justice *is 100 percent on you—the victim.*

Yes, con artist cases are complicated, and they can be tricky to lay out for a jury. But at their core, they're quite simple: the con artist lied to you to trick you out of money. And as a victim trying to appeal to police or prosecutors, you need to be laser focused on all the physical evidence, all the circumstantial evidence, and all the witnesses that prove (1) you were lied to and (2) money was taken from you based on those lies. *Because that is the crime.* Everything else is just a red herring.

It's easy to get caught up in all the crazy stories the con artist told you to get your money. And it's easy to let those stories distract you and authorities and a jury from homing in on the crime. But the stories themselves are almost irrelevant, because they're not true. And the fact of the matter remains: They lied to you to steal your money. That is felony grand theft (also called grand larceny in some states) by inducement or by false pretense or by trickery. It's punishable by years behind bars.

In the midst of investigating *hundreds* of con artist cases, I had an epiphany. I felt as if I'd been staring at one of those 3D puzzle pictures for the longest time and seeing nothing when all of a sudden an amazing image emerged. It dawned on me that all the techniques that the con artist who sucked me into her world used to scam me were identical to the techniques being used on victims who were reaching out to me for help. Literally identical.

It became clear to me that there are a dozen or so *red flags* or *signs* that a con artist is in your midst—or worse, has penetrated your social circle and gained entry into your life. Certain "tells," if you will. They're easy to spot if you know what to look for, especially as they compound. But they're much easier to miss if you don't.

That's why I'm writing this book. I want to teach you what the signs are that you're meeting a con artist for the first time. I want to give you the tools to spot the con man or con woman in your life before they rob you—not just of your money but of your soul and your peace of mind and your innate ability to trust anyone ever again. The toll a con artist takes on you isn't just financial. It's so much more than that.

One of the biggest mistakes people make—it certainly was the biggest mistake I made and it led to my getting conned—is to believe that con artists aren't real. "The greatest trick the Devil ever pulled was convincing the world he didn't exist," the old adage goes. Replace "Devil" with "con artist" and that statement becomes even more true.

I mean, yes, we all know there are scammers out there. And that's the problem: We think they're "out there." They're the people calling you up on the phone and pretending to be a relative who needs money in the form of a Walmart gift card. They're the Nigerian princes sending you emails offering to transfer inheritance money. They're those sketchy characters who approach you at the gas station or convenience store, trying to solicit money from you with their fabricated stories of woe.

We are all operating on this false belief that con artists aren't people in our lives right now—people that we *know*. But the truth of the matter is, a con artist could be scamming your best friend or your cousin or your mother or *you* right now, and you won't realize it until it's much too late.

One of my favorite movies of all time is *Dirty Rotten Scoundrels,* starring Michael Caine and Steve Martin. It came out in the late 1980s and I've seen it a hundred times. It's just that good. Martin and Caine play a couple of professional con men who scam wealthy women on the French Riviera out of untold fortunes. They inject themselves into these women's lives by pretending to be doctors or aristocrats or war veterans. It's such a funny and exceptional movie.

But for me, *Dirty Rotten Scoundrels* ultimately proved to be dangerous, because it severely misled me and misinformed me by making light of a horrendous reality. Never for a second did I believe any of the characters in that film were based on real people. I foolishly thought con artists like that were just ne'er-do-wells you'd see on the big screen.

Not your friends in real life. Not the people you *know*. And certainly not the people you love.

And this perverse misunderstanding was to my own detriment. The woman who scammed me (and dozens of others) convincingly pretended to be Irish royalty for years. She had all the props and accoutrements too. It's like she was playing the lead character in a con movie that I was unwittingly cast in. Never for a second did I think she wasn't an Irish heiress—until it was all over and I went bankrupt.

I had no idea back then that there are people in the world who will fictitiously insert themselves into your life, into your psyche—*for years*—lying in wait for just the right opportunity to steal from you. These are people you swear you know, people you love, people you have a relationship with. And it's all fake—on their part at least. I mean, it was all real for me, until it wasn't.

And the red flags that could have alerted me that the woman who scammed me was a professional con artist were there from the very beginning, waving briskly in the wind. But I didn't notice them.

No one did.

ANATOMY OF A CON ARTIST

1. THE 14 RED FLAGS CON ARTISTS WAVE

I'VE SPENT YEARS ANALYZING THE RED FLAGS CON ARTISTS UNINTENTIONALLY WAVE THAT signal who they are. I've given them names. And throughout this book, I will show you how they appear in real life—in every single con. That way, when you see them waving from a distance in your own life, you will cross the street and avoid getting scammed. Or you'll be able to point them out to a loved one who's in the crosshairs of a con artist.

Red Flag #1: "I Just Want to Help"

I've been fortunate enough to spend some time interviewing former FBI criminal profiler Candice DeLong—a truly amazing woman. She taught me about the concept of a "rescue merchant."

A lot of con artists are what the FBI calls rescue merchants. They suddenly show up when there's a problem or a disaster or unrest. Regular people would flee these dire situations, but professional con artists gravitate toward them. They've learned that if they can offer a solution to a major problem someone's having (or what seems like a solution but is really just a lie), the person in trouble will focus exclusively on the offered solution, and it'll blind them to everything else—ultimately enabling the con artist to scam them.

The woman who scammed me, Mair Smyth, was a rescue merchant. She showed up at a time of turmoil in the community where I live and she offered a solution. And we all fell for it, hard.

Admittedly, I fell harder than most. Her solution was her "in," and it worked like a charm.

You need to be suspicious of a stranger who suddenly shows up offering to help. Your inclination is to like them (even love them!) and be grateful to them. But those are the precise feelings a sophisticated con artist will weaponize against you in order to bleed you dry.

Red Flag #2: Too Kind, Too Quick

You meet someone new. It could be a new boyfriend or new girlfriend, a new co-worker or a new neighbor. They're so kind, so thoughtful, so sweet. They're always paying for meals, giving you gifts, going out of their way to be as kind as possible. You can't help but like them—or even love them, on a truncated timetable, because they seem like the nicest person you ever met.

That is a major red flag.

The thing you need to keep in mind is that love is the most powerful force in the universe. I'm not waxing poetic here. It's just a fact of life. You will do anything for the person you love. People kill for love all the time, die for love all the time. Professional con artists know this, and they rely on it. They trade on it. It's how they get you to do what they want you to do.

When a con artist meets a new mark, their mission is to get that mark to love them—or love "the cause" they've invented for the mark. That's because when you're making decisions based on love, they win. You'll give them your money, your property, your treasured items. It happens thousands of times every day.

Red Flag #3: Drama, Drama, Drama

Once a con artist has gained your love, your admiration, and your trust, the drama starts.

Look, bad things happen to people all the time. People get cancer, have a death in the family, have a major car accident, have an angry brother or sister or cousin trying to "get" them. But all these bad things don't happen to the same person at the same time—unless they're a sophisticated con artist trying to distract you and trying to influence you.

Also, if you happen to have any drama whatsoever in your own life already, they will use that drama to manipulate you. If you have a crazy boyfriend stalking you, the con artist will tell you they saw them drive by your house yesterday.

Mair apparently "roofied" one of her other victims whom she met up with at a Los Angeles bar one night. Then she pretended she had gotten "roofied" too. This terrifying experience bonded the victim to Mair very quickly, in a way nothing else could have. It was a trauma bond, and it was powerful. Ultimately, it helped Mair scam that victim out of thousands of dollars. Drama in and of itself is not a red flag, but drama mixed with the other red flags is an absolute indicator that you are in the midst of chaos being deliberately created by a sophisticated con artist.

Red Flag #4: Isolation

This one's a biggie. For a con artist to successfully scam you, they need to be able to lure you away from people who might talk you out of going along with their scam. And it's remarkably easy to do.

Mair tricked me into believing that my neighbor was a criminal on the run from authorities. So I avoided her. She then convinced my neighbor that I was mentally ill and violent. So my neighbor avoided me. That way she could scam us both using different stories, and we were none the wiser until months later when I started my investigation. Even then, this neighbor was hard to get ahold of. She was actively avoiding me. She blocked my cellphone number and blocked me on social media. She was clearly terrified of me. I had to create a new email address to send her court records and criminal background checks so I could prove to her that Mair was the evil one here. Then I had to get other victims I had discovered to call this woman and explain to her that they had been victimized by Mair as well. That did the trick. But it took longer than it should have.

Anyone telling you not to talk to this person or that person is about the biggest red flag there is. It's a very effective tool for a "working" con artist.

Red Flag #5: "I'm Better Than You"

Most con artists are narcissists. They care only about themselves. They are incapable of caring about anyone else.

But they're really great at faking it. When you first meet them, they seem to care about you and about a lot of things, and they appear to be kind, generous, and loving people. But that is only an act—one that they have perfected over the course of their entire lives.

Likely when they were children, social cues and dropped-jaw reactions from others taught them at a very young age that something was inherently wrong with them. Something was "off" or different. They weren't like their peers. They were cold and they seemed uncaring. People didn't like that and didn't like them. But to their credit, con artists are super smart and quick studies. Over the years they cleverly learn how to cover up and compensate for their personality deficits. So by the time you meet a con artist in adulthood, they're a perfected apparition of everything they've learned they need to be to impress you, or anybody. Then the scam is on.

A professional con artist wants you to be impressed by them. They *need* you to be impressed by them. In fact, their con relies on it, because you need to think the world of them in order for their confidence tricks to work on you.

So after they get you to like them—or, God forbid, love them—they have to get you to respect them and ideally be in awe of them. To achieve that, they'll essentially brag about themselves. Backdoor brags. Front door brags. They'll show off. They'll paint a picture for you that they are the wealthiest, or most talented, or most connected person you ever met. They want you to feel lucky or blessed to know them, because that feeling goes a long way in gaining your confidence in them and paving the way for them to get their hands on your money.

It's worth noting here—and forgive me if you know this already—that the term *con artist* is actually short for *confidence artist*. These people are brilliant at engineering ways to gain your confidence so they can have their way with you and your bank account.

Red Flag #6: Technology

How many times has someone held up their cellphone for you to see and said, "Look what this guy/girl/my cousin/boss/parent just texted me"? Did you ever think this person had created a fake online texting account so they could text *themselves*—as these various characters—to trick you into believing a story?

How many times have you spoken to someone on the phone claiming to be your landlord, or someone calling from the phone company or the electric company? Did you ever for a second think that it wasn't any of those people, that it was actually someone you knew who knew you really well and was calling you using a voice-changing app on their phone to disguise their voice to get you to believe whatever it was they were telling you while sounding like various other characters?

Today's working con artist relies heavily on technology. They'll show you text messages from someone that tell a story. They'll share with you emails from someone to back that story up. You'll even get text messages, emails, and phone calls from people who you believe are real. But they're not. They're all just clever creations of a professional con artist. These are things you never think about, but in this day and age you need to.

Red Flag #7: Scarcity

Maybe you've had the experience of shopping for a new car or a used car when the salesperson seemed to be offering you a great deal—but with a catch. You had to buy it now—or before Friday. Otherwise, this great deal would *end*. And it would be gone, never to be seen again.

It's a total scam. But it's also totally legal. It's called artificial scarcity, and it's a ploy that a lot of retailers use to hook you. But con artists love to use it as well because it's very effective.

I see it all the time with investment scams. The con artist says they can get you stock in a huge company before they go public next week. Well, obviously you need to get them the money before next week, right? And after the money changes hands, you will never see your money again.

I've also seen artificial scarcity used in some of the love scams I've investigated. By this point, the victim has fallen madly in love with the con artist. The con artist tells the victim that they're going off to Europe or Africa or some far-off locale. Soon after their supposed departure the victim gets the call that the love of their life (the con artist) is in the hospital in that country and needs emergency surgery (Red Flag #3: Drama, Drama, Drama). But for whatever reason, the con artist can't access their bank from there, and they need $100,000 to pay for the surgery or they'll die.

As the con artist relays this information, they parenthetically are suggesting to the victim, "Act now or my blood will be on your hands." And this is someone the victim loves who's been really good to them (Red Flag #2: Too Kind, Too Quick). So the victim quickly sends them money.

Red Flag #8: Beak Wetting

This red flag has a lot do with human psychology and the belief that a person's history is the best indicator of their future actions. That theory is mostly true. How someone has treated you in the past, through words or actions or both, will accurately indicate how they will treat you in the future—most of the time.

That's why dogs who are trained to sit will sit every time someone says, "Sit." In the past they were rewarded for that sit with a treat or with affection or both. Now they are expecting the same thing to happen every time. So, they sit.

It's also why Visa or American Express will issue you—or not issue you—a credit card based on your history of paying your bills on time. If you have always paid your bills on time, they will happily issue you a card and beg you, with ritzy promotions and free gifts, to use your new card as much as possible. But if you have a history of not paying your bills on time (or at all), they'll assume you won't pay for the charges you make with them either, so they won't issue you a card. Period.

Con artists know all of this better than most. And they strategically weaponize your belief and expectations in this "past as prelude" assumption against you. This is why, in the vast majority of investment scams and Ponzi schemes and in a lot of love scams, the con artist will actually give the victim a little money up front. They'll let them "wet their beak," as it were. Mair did it to me. And it was very effective, because she ended up taking me for nearly $100,000 by the time all was said and done.

Red Flag #9: A Good Day Job

This is only a red flag if a bunch of the other red flags are present—because we all have jobs, right? We all work. In fact, you'd probably be immediately suspicious of a new person in your life who didn't have a job. And a good con artist knows this.

Most professional con artists have, or have had at some point, a legitimate day job. They use the reputation of those jobs to give their lives and especially their scams the patina of legitimacy.

They're mortgage brokers. They work in the mayor's office. They're investment analysts. They're foreign exchange traders. They're luxury travel agents. They work for a giant cellphone company. You think, "There's no way they're a con artist. They have this amazing job." And that's their plan: for you to think that and let your guard down. But don't believe their lies. Their day job is just a cover, a side hustle. Their real job is conning you.

Red Flag #10: Wires

Never send wires. Class dismissed.

In a lot of cases when a con artist needs to get a large sum of money from you, they'll trick you into wiring it to them though your bank. And as many safeguards as banks have in place to protect your money, they're all useless if you're the one, of sound mind and body, consciously making the decision to wire money to someone or some entity.

Once you wire money to someone else's account, it's gone forever.

The reason con artists love bank wires is . . . they're instant. For the most part. And you can send any amount of money to anyone anywhere in the world in seconds. In nearly every con artist case that I have investigated, when a large sum of money changed hands, it was usually through a bank wire.

Don't. Send. Wires. Period. And if someone is asking you, let alone pressuring you, to wire money, take that as a sign to step back and reassess your situation. Because if *any* of these red flags are present in conjunction with the request for a wire? You're probably getting scammed.

Red Flag #11: They Move Around a Lot

Most professional con artists move around a lot. They have to, because eventually they get found out and can no longer scam where they're living. So they find a new place to live with a new set of potential victims.

I realize some people serve in the military or work in certain industries that require them to move around a lot. So that's not a red flag in and of itself. But if some of the other red flags are present, *and* the person moves around a lot, you can bet you're dealing with a con artist.

In fact, in a lot of con artist cases that I've investigated over the past few years, when I run background checks on these suspects, the list of their past addresses is very long—spanning multiple states and even multiple countries.

So when you meet someone new in your life and they have a history of living in a bunch of different places at different addresses—be on guard.

Red Flag #12: Stories from Faraway Places

Professional con artists like to snow you with details about faraway places. They'll tell you about stuff they claim they did in countries half-way around the world—places that are so far away from you it's impossible to check on whether what they're saying is true or false.

When a con artist is trying to trick you into believing in some dramatic story, you will be more likely to believe it if it supposedly happened years ago in, say, Australia or Japan than if it happened recently in your own town. The farther away from you the story takes place, in both space and time, the more likely you are to accept it as fact.

People telling stories about faraway places is not a red flag in and of itself. But if some of the other red flags are present when they unpack these exotic tales, you can bet you're listening to a real-life con artist. And my advice to you is to stop listening and run.

Red Flag #13: TMI

One effective trick a professional con artist will use on you is the TMI technique. They will share TMI (too much information) as a way of getting you to share TMI as well.

They'll be the first to confess a deep dark secret, which they will invent, in order to make you feel like you can trust them with *your* deep dark secrets. It's a way for a con artist to get close to you quickly. After all, when someone reveals something painful or embarrassing or personal about themselves to you and "trusts you" not to tell anyone, it's human nature to immediately feel you can trust them too. And your trust is what they need to con you. Sharing TMI is a powerful bonding technique that quickly engenders trust.

Further, this TMI technique will usually prevent victims from reporting the con artist to police. That's because, even though they've been scammed, the last thing in the world they want is for their con artist to tell police—or anyone—their deep dark secrets.

Red Flag #14: The Dale Carnegie Techniques

You know the famous book *How to Win Friends and Influence People* by Dale Carnegie?

Well, every con artist does. In fact, they all study that book obsessively. It's like con artist college to them. And they use those Dale Carnegie techniques on their marks very effectively.

During the four years I believed Mair to be my best friend (and this continues to sting and anger me), she conspicuously used my name on me *a lot* during conversations, over texts, and in emails. Stuff like "Listen, Johnathan, that's not what I want to do with my life," or "Johnathan, you expect me to pretend I don't know he's not leaving his wife?" or "You don't understand, Johnathan, I'm doing the best I can."

It always felt weird to me that she'd use my name so frequently in our exchanges. And I always noticed when she did it. But at the time I had no idea that she was employing a go-to Dale Carnegie technique from his book.

According to the book, "A person's name is to that person the sweetest and most important sound in any language." And Carnegie firmly believed that if you're trying to make someone feel noticed or important or valued and at the same time trying to get them to like you—say their name to them as much as you can.

That's just one of the Dale Carnegie tips that con artists use. Here are five other principles he lays out as tried-and-true strategies to get strangers to "like you" ASAP:

1. Become genuinely interested in other people.
2. Smile.
3. Be a good listener and encourage others to talk about themselves.
4. Talk in terms of the other person's interests.
5. Make the other person feel important.

I'm not saying Dale Carnegie is a con artist. But his groundbreaking book has certainly, albeit inadvertently, trained most professional con artists working today.

Obviously a single red flag on its own isn't a clear sign of present danger—except someone asking for a wire transfer—but as they compound, watch out and be aware!

My sincere hope is that by candidly sharing what happened to me and other victims in these pages, as excruciatingly embarrassing as it was to us, we can prevent it from ever happening to you or anyone you care about.

2. RED FLAG #1: "I JUST WANT TO HELP"

AS HUMAN BEINGS, WE INNATELY LOVE "HELPERS." AND WE ALSO ARE INNATELY DRIVEN TO help others. It's in our DNA. It's how society has advanced since the beginning of time. People help other people. Groups help other groups. Countries help other countries.

One of the things that has always moved me, sometimes to tears, is that frequently in the face of great tragedy, random people show up out of nowhere, and solely out of the goodness of their hearts and their earnest desire to be of aid and of service—they help. When there's a missing child last seen in the woods somewhere, overnight hundreds and hundreds of complete strangers assemble in search parties to find that kid. There's no financial gain in it for any of them—they just do it because they want to help.

When we're sitting on an airplane watching other passengers board and we notice an elderly person struggling to get their luggage in an overhead bin, 99.9 percent of us will jump up and offer to help.

When we're standing in line at the supermarket checkout and a mother of two ahead of us doesn't have enough money for all her groceries and is trying to decide what items she needs to put back, most people (myself included) will immediately offer to pay for the few things that that mother doesn't have the money for.

And that mother of two is eternally grateful for the help. So is the elderly person boarding that flight. So are the parents of that missing kid in the woods.

It's hard to not immediately like or even love someone who enters your life offering to help with whatever situation you're going through. Con artists know this better than most, and they weaponize it. They are perpetually searching for discord, for acrimony, for problems, for any situation where they can help or be perceived as "helping" by pretending to offer solutions. It gives them a plausible way in to their victims' lives and immediately engenders gratitude and trust from everyone around.

One of the more tragic cases of someone victimized by a con artist who offered to help is Erik Kramer. Erik reached out to me in 2020 asking for advice after reading about my own crazy con artist experience. The woman who scammed me got a foothold in to my life by offering to help. And the woman who scammed him did the same thing—multiplied by a thousand.

ERIK KRAMER WAS A QUARTERBACK IN THE NFL; BACK IN THE 1980S AND '90S HE PLAYED for some of the most storied football teams of all time, including the New Orleans Saints, the Chicago Bears, the San Diego Chargers, and the Detroit Lions. He had one hell of a professional sports career.

Erik's well-deserved transition into retirement was tragically interrupted in 2011 when his eldest son Griffen died of an accidental heroin overdose at just eighteen years old. Erik was devastated. "Losing Griffen was the biggest shock to my system that I ever encountered," he told me.

The pain of losing a child is immeasurable and it plunged Erik into a deep depression. Sadly, that pain was multiplied tenfold a year later, when his mother died after a long battle with cancer. And shortly after that, his father died of cancer too. The compounding trauma and depression was too much for him, and in 2015, at the age of fifty, he attempted to kill himself.

Erik shot himself in the head. And miraculously, he survived. The bullet somehow carved a path through his frontal lobe and exited out the top of his skull—missing certain arteries and certain parts of his brain where a hit would have instantly killed him.

Erik lived. But understandably, he had brain damage. He could still walk and talk and think and live a life—but doctors diagnosed him at the time as having the mental capacity of a six-year-old.

This ironically had some advantages. Erik's depression seemingly disappeared overnight. He became much more easygoing and agreeable. He seemed to almost enjoy life more and be happier. He'd sit in front of the flickering screen of a television for hours without getting up, without going to the bathroom, and without eating. It mesmerized him.

Left to his own devices, Erik was only capable of living in the moment. He could barely process complex concepts or make independent decisions. He mostly did what he was told, like a child. And he was very trusting of everyone.

He was a sitting duck for a professional con artist at this point. He just didn't know it. And how could he have? How could anyone have known what was about to happen?

Seemingly out of the blue, one of Erik's former girlfriends showed up: an attractive, blond, forty-two-year-old woman named Cortney Baird. Erik had broken up with Cortney two years earlier. Their relationship was toxic and unhealthy. And at the time of the breakup, Erik was glad to be free from her. But at this point in time, Erik had no memory of the breakup. And Cortney figured that out pretty quickly.

In the two years she'd been apart from Erik, Cortney had been arrested and charged with "obtaining a controlled substance via fraud" in Ventura County, about seventy miles northwest of Los Angeles. Cortney eventually pleaded guilty to a single misdemeanor, and the case against her was later dismissed after she paid restitution. But Erik was not aware of any of that.

Almost overnight, Cortney moved into Erik's life under the guise of "helping" him. She seemed so kind and loving and caring. She convinced all his friends and family (usually during dinners she'd host for them in Erik's home) that she really loved Erik and wanted to help him make a full recovery. And everyone bought what she was selling—at first.

As for Erik, his diminished mental capacity was not obvious to people. He could drive a car. He could play golf. He could hold a basic, friendly conversation, especially with strangers. He looked and acted normal by most accounts. But if you asked him for directions to the airport, he could not answer. If you gave him a detailed cake recipe and asked him to bake it, he wouldn't know how. If you asked him to read a newspaper article and then quizzed him on what he had just read, he would be at a loss. At the time Erik could do simple mundane things easily, almost by rote. But complex mental calculations, decision-making, and extrapolating were abilities his damaged brain did not possess. As a result, Erik usually just went along with whatever situation was presented to him by anyone, especially by Cortney.

To the casual observer, Cortney seemed like a godsend, an angel. She came off as being so kind and so sweet and so concerned for Erik's welfare. She seemed like she just wanted to help him.

Certainly there are people like that in the world. But there are also professional con artists who seem a lot like those *good* people—at first. And showing up out of the blue offering to help is a *major* red flag that con artists like to wave but that very few people seem to notice. It's how they trick you into liking them, loving them, and trusting them.

Cortney quit her office job and moved into Erik's home, where she completely took control of his care and his finances. She wasn't collecting a paycheck anymore and had no money coming in. And almost immediately, she started testing the waters. When she'd go to the supermarket or to the corner drugstore to buy things for Erik using his ATM card, she'd get a cash advance of a few extra dollars just to see if anyone was watching—$50 here, $50 there.

And no one noticed. Not Erik, not anyone.

As the months ticked by, Cortney got bolder and bolder, taking out even more money while using Erik's ATM cards and his credit cards. Then, all of a sudden, thousands and thousands of dollars were getting leached out of Erik's accounts on a weekly basis. And Erik was none the wiser.

One of Erik's sources of income at the time was a $4 million trust fund that would automatically transfer money into his checking account every month to pay his mortgage, car payment, and other living expenses. That monthly transfer also included an allowance of sorts that Erik was notoriously frugal with. He liked to save as much money as he could in that account. But suddenly Cortney started getting hundreds of dollars in cash advances every day using Erik's ATM card linked to that account. She forged checks from that account too.

Before Erik's suicide attempt, that account had had about $14,000 in it. But after Cortney entered the picture, that same account was overdrawn by $6,000.

And that was just the tip of the iceberg. After Griffen's death in 2011, a memorial fund was created and accumulated nearly $10,000. That money sat untouched for years. But in mid-2016, after Cortney got involved with Erik, the account was bled dry and overdrawn by $6.

Erik had no idea any of these withdrawals were happening. He was just going along with whatever Cortney said. He thought she was taking care of him. He trusted her implicitly.

But something unusual started happening, and it got the attention of Erik's childhood friend Anna Dergan, who frequently visited Erik at his home during his convalescence.

"Amazon boxes kept showing up at the front door. Piles of them," Anna said to me. "And Erik has a reputation for buying nothing."

In Anna's mind, these Amazon boxes were a bad sign. Even before the suicide attempt, when Erik was of sound mind, he rarely bought stuff on Amazon.

Anna was so alarmed by all the Amazon boxes being delivered on a daily basis that she started investigating. She surreptitiously got ahold of all of Erik's bank statements and analyzed them line by line. Anna was horrified to discover that Cortney had stolen nearly $50,000 from Erik's bank accounts in just a few months.

Fearful, Anna suddenly dropped what she was doing and took what she had found to the L.A. County Sheriff's Office. There she filed a report, prompting a detective named David Lingscheit to interview Erik.

Days later, Detective Lingscheit and Erik talked for hours. The detective concluded that Erik was not of sound mind. He was taken aback by how unemotional and disconnected Erik seemed after being told his girlfriend was stealing from him. The detective actually wrote in his report, "It appears Kramer lacks the capacity to make financial decisions based on his own cognitive abilities and thus meets the requirements of a dependent adult."

At this point, Erik's friends and family decided the only thing they could and should do was get Erik into a conservatorship and give his sister and his aunt, both of whom he loved and trusted, complete control of his life and his finances. Several doctors agreed that Erik did not have the mental capacity to conduct his own affairs. Also the thinking was that if Erik's family had full control of Erik's life and finances, they could kick Cortney out of his home and stop her from stealing all his money.

In the meantime, Cortney discovered that Erik had been interviewed by an L.A. County sheriff's detective. She immediately persuaded Erik to call the detective and tell him that it was all a big misunderstanding: Everything was fine and there was no need for any investigation. But Detective Lingscheit, a veteran investigator, suspected Erik was being unduly influenced by Cortney. And he doubled down in his efforts to get to the bottom of things and ferret out the truth.

Months later, Cortney was still living in Erik's home. She went to get his mail one morning, brought it inside, and started opening it all behind Erik's back. (Technically this is a crime in and of itself, though it's minor in comparison to the crime already in progress.) After Cortney ripped open a letter from Wells Fargo to Erik, she was shocked to learn that the criminal investigation against her was still open and was proceeding at a rapid pace. She pieced together that the bank had sent all of Erik's prior statements to the sheriff's office, as per the search warrant that was issued weeks earlier, and that the letter Cortney was reading was the bank's official communication letting Erik know it was all happening.

Then suddenly Detective Lingscheit requested a meeting with Cortney—a formal interview at the sheriff's office. Now, most regular people would be freaking out at this point. But con artists are cut from different cloth. Demonstrating a braggadocio common in most inveterate scammers, Cortney actually drove to the sheriff's office alone, *without a lawyer,* and met with the detective. In that meeting she shockingly confessed to everything they accused her of: stealing what by then was nearly $50,000 of Erik's money, forging his checks, and taking advantage of him. Then she walked right out of the sheriff's office free as a bird.

Cortney Baird was not charged or arrested that day, to the shock of everyone in Erik's life who knew she was fleecing the hell out of him. This completely jibes with my own experience of trying to bring my con artist to justice. Even when confronted with a mountain of evidence and witnesses and probable cause of fraud and theft, authorities often seem loath to do anything about it in a timely manner.

Then, in true con artist fashion, Cortney figured out a jaw-dropping and devious way to use the legal system to avoid prosecution altogether. On December 22, 2016, just three days before Christmas, Cortney legally married Erik in a surprise ceremony that she secretly arranged in Santa Barbara, about an hour north of Los Angeles. None of Erik's family or friends were there. Nor did they have any idea this "wedding" was even taking place.

Cortney knew "the system," as most con artists do. She had figured out that if she was Erik's "wife," *her* spending *his* money would not be considered a crime by anyone, especially the criminal justice system. And she was 100 percent correct, because at that point, the criminal case against her was abandoned. Cortney won the right to continue scamming Erik.

Professional con artists know how to manipulate the legal system to their advantage. Many times this knowledge enables them to escape prosecution. And when it's a situation where a man and a woman are at odds, a concept called "chivalry theory" comes into play.

In 1950, a renowned sociologist named Edmund Pollak surmised that the vast majority of criminal justice actors like judges and police officers are men, so they are all preprogrammed in a sense to act in a "chivalrous way" toward women—all women, regardless of the situation. Consequently, Cortney Baird's plan to marry Erik Kramer so she could continue scamming him worked like a charm—for a while. In the eyes of the law, she was his wife. And there was nothing criminal about her spending his money.

But then something amazing happened. Erik's brain actually started to heal, fast. It had been more than two years since his suicide attempt and since Cortney had taken over his life and his finances. But then, in June of 2018, Erik was attending a Chicago Bears golf outing when suddenly he came to. He said it felt like he'd been in a coma up until that point and now he was wide awake. He instantly realized he'd been "out of it" for a long time and now was completely lucid.

"In that moment, I never wanted to be married to Cortney or to anyone. I felt like I had been forced into it all," Erik said to me. "And I wanted out."

So Erik flew back to Los Angeles and told Cortney he wanted a divorce and he wanted her out of his house. Cortney called the police the next day and invented a story that Erik had assaulted her. The evidence of an "assault" was a tiny scratch on her arm that Erik says was self-inflicted. Regardless, police showed up and arrested Erik based solely on what Cortney told them: that he had attacked her.

That wholly fictious incident made headlines all over the world. "Former NFL Quarterback Erik Kramer Charged with Assaulting Wife," reported CBS News. "Erik Kramer's Wife Says She Is 'Terrified' That He Is Coming to Kill Her," reported the *Daily Mail*. "Ex-NFL QB Erik Kramer Charged with Battery in Domestic Violence Case," was the headline *TMZ* ran with.

While Cortney Baird may have never heard the phrase *chivalry theory* uttered in her entire life, she certainly knew how to put it into practice. In a matter of hours, Erik was in jail and his reputation was in tatters, all because a crafty con artist knew how to "work" the system.

EVENTUALLY ERIK WAS ABLE TO CLEAR HIS NAME AND GET THOSE BOGUS DOMESTIC VIO-lence charges against him dropped completely. But do you think *TMZ* or the *Daily Mail* or CBS News ran stories about that?

Now that Erik was completely of sound mind, he was able to get his marriage to Cortney nullified by the courts too. And he reported Cortney's brazen and calculated theft to authorities. The L.A. County Sheriff's Office actually restarted their criminal investigation. Not long after that, in February of 2020, the Los Angeles County District Attorney's Office stepped in, charging Cortney with a dozen felonies, including identity theft, forgery, and fraud for her years-long sophisticated and sprawling swindle of Erik Kramer.

Later that same month, Erik Kramer reached out to me, asking for advice about navigating the Los Angeles criminal justice system as a victim of a con artist. I met with him and his childhood friend Anna Dergan at a couple of court appearances for Cortney. And I strategized with him and Anna about what to do next.

The problem was, Cortney Baird, like many con artists, knew how to use the criminal justice system to her full advantage. In the same way she'd had the sinister idea to call police and have Erik arrested after he suddenly came to and told her he wanted a divorce and wanted her out of his house, Cortney pulled out all the stops in the criminal proceeding against her.

She calculatedly changed attorneys five times, which created months and months of stops and starts, while kicking the criminal case against her further and further down the court's calendar. Erik and Anna showed up to court month after month hoping for a trial date to be set, and again and again they left disappointed.

At one point, Cortney fooled everyone into thinking she was going to plead guilty and throw herself on the mercy of the court. But the date for that event came and went and she didn't do it. As I watched her that day in court, she looked innocent. By that I mean she had clearly perfected the act of appearing sympathetic. She carried herself as if she was the victim, which is what every con artist does when they're caught.

I was stunned to hear Anna tell me that someone in the DA's office had told Erik something to the effect of "Well, it's good that you have so much money so restitution isn't that important to you." Both Anna and Erik corrected that person immediately, telling them the case wasn't really about restitution or money. It was about justice.

. . .

AT THE END OF THE DAY, ALL PROSECUTORS WANT ALL PERPETRATORS TO TAKE A PLEA. AND it was no different with the deputy district attorney on Erik's case. They kept hoping Cortney would take a plea. Trials are uncertain and expensive. You have to empanel a jury, a trial can go on for weeks or months, and in the end a jury can be hung or can find the defendant not guilty. Also, a conviction at trial can be appealed multiple times, whereas a conviction that comes from a guilty plea cannot.

After another dozen or so court appearances, in August of 2024, Cortney Baird suddenly decided to plead guilty for scamming Erik out of $300,000 and costing him another $400,000 in legal fees for annulling that scam marriage and getting the bogus domestic violence charge against him dropped. Shockingly, the courts refused to acknowledge all the money Cortney stole from Erik while they were married, and put his losses at $170,000. And in a con artist Hail Mary pass, Cortney managed to come up with $170,000 to pay "full" restitution. Because of that, she got off with a light sentence of 180 days in jail. But on account of inmate overcrowding in L.A. County, she served less than half of that time.

While Erik and Anna really wanted a trial, a guilty plea was the next best thing. That guilty plea told the world Cortney Baird knew that what she had done was wrong and that she had been wrong to do it. Now Erik can move on with his life knowing that his four-year pursuit of justice was not in vain.

And remember how this all started? Cortney Baird showed up one day after Erik was recovering from a gunshot wound to the head. And she offered to help.

Red Flag #1.

Erik actually wrote an incredible book about his life, appropriately titled *The Ultimate Comeback*. And as I write these words now, I'm working with Erik and Anna to produce a podcast about his crazy years-long ordeal called, "The Quarterback and the Con Artist," so stay tuned!

Queen of the Con I

On the evening on May 10, 2013, I was sitting on my couch watching TV—like most winners do on a Friday night.

Shark Tank was on. I was one of the TV producers on this particular season of *Shark Tank,* and when an episode I worked on aired, I joyfully watched it. Yup. I'm *that* kind of dork. Still enamored with zeitgeisty television shows, especially ones that I've produced.

Little did I know that working on a show like *Shark Tank* would make me a target for a crafty and conniving con artist who had just moved into an apartment in my building and was now living a couple hundred feet away from me. And in the end, it was *Shark Tank* that would lead to her downfall in the most bizarre and unexpected way.

Producing *Shark Tank* was an amazing experience. It was hands down the biggest show I had ever worked on. They shot on a huge soundstage at Sony Studios, formerly MGM Studios—where the likes of *The Wizard of Oz* and *Singin' in the Rain* were filmed on giant soundstages (that are still there!) scattered across forty-four storied acres in the bustling heart of Culver City, California—ten miles west of downtown Los Angeles.

So I was sitting on my couch at home watching the fruits of my labor. But I couldn't seem to tear myself away from my laptop. An email chain was quickly growing, twenty-eight back-and-forths deep.

Mair Smyth, a new neighbor, had emailed me days earlier offering to help with an issue that had cast a dark and disheartening pall over the quality of life for me and the residents in my apartment building: the loss of our swimming pool.

This wasn't just any swimming pool, mind you. This was a gargantuan, resort-style swimming pool—as large as ten regular pools combined. It had Olympic swimming lanes, huge indented nooks and crannies where you could congregate with friends, and a twenty-person jacuzzi. The surrounding complex featured a clubhouse with ping-pong and pool tables, a BBQ area, and tennis courts. It was indeed the Disney World of apartment amenities: a much-loved and opulent oasis in the nucleated concrete jungle that is downtown Los Angeles. And the residents of our apartment building, myself included, were mad as hell it had been taken away from us.

We lost the pool, through no fault of our own, because of a legal spat that had sprung up out of nowhere and embroiled the giant corporation that was our landlord. A year prior, a major repair had been performed in the pool area—which had necessitated digging up the entire pool and a bunch of tile to fix and replace an aging network of underground leaky and disintegrating pipes. Since we shared the pool with a neighboring building, our landlord was responsible for hundreds of thousands in repairs.

But they didn't want to pay. Our corporate overlord claimed that since a nicer type of tile was used in the re-tile when the work was completed, this repair actually constituted an "upgrade" and not a bona fide "repair," and in their myopic, legal-cheapskate view, they were not contractually obligated to pay for "upgrades" as per the agreement they had signed decades earlier. So they refused. The other building got mad and vengeful and sued to block access to the pool for residents in our building.

And we were pissed.

My anger and annoyance at the situation spurred me into action. I figured if the hundreds of residents in our building banded together, we could leverage our collective power to broker some kind of agreement to get the pool back. We'd have strength in numbers. The challenge would be getting everyone on the same page.

So I took it upon myself to post flyers up at various places in and around our 444-unit apartment building: in the elevators, the parking garage, the courtyard. The flyers basically read, "Miss the pool? Want it back? Let's meet and do something about it!" And it included my email address. I also stuck it under the doors of all 444 apartments in our building. By the end of the day, I could barely walk, my legs were so sore. You ever try bending down (to slide a flyer under a door) and popping back up 444 times in a row? It's brutal.

That flyer ended up inspiring a couple hundred neighbors from all walks of life to email me: engineers, police officers, film editors, registered nurses, car salesmen, graphic designers, and of course, one international con artist on the run from authorities, hiding out in my building and posing as a helpful, friendly, and benevolent Mother Teresa–type neighbor.

I had no idea that my taking it upon myself to post flyers everywhere and spearhead this herculean effort to get our pool back was all this sophisticated scammer would need to craft the perfect con just for me. It was a con I would fall hard for—hook, line, and sinker.

"I think we need to meet," Mair Smyth's twenty-ninth email to me read.

We'd been discussing our pool situation in the twenty-eight preceding email exchanges. And she really wanted to get involved and move the needle—she was by far the most motivated neighbor I had heard from.

Looking back, this was the first red flag. But I was so naïve to the way con artists operate at the time. Remember, at that point in my life, I thought professional con artists were only something you'd see in movies.

My phone suddenly pinged with the arrival of a new text: "You available to meet now?"

It was Mair. I had given her my number.

This was the precise beginning of my inviting her into my life and into my home. Con artists are like vampires that way. They need to be invited in to exert their power. She was a bloodthirsty vampire, to be sure. And I, plump, unwitting prey—without a single clove of garlic or a wooden stake.

As I was leaving my apartment to meet her, she suddenly changed her mind and texted, "Crap. Something came up. Rain check?"

We eventually agreed to meet face-to-face for the first time the next day, a warm Saturday afternoon in mid-May 2013, outside the wrought-iron gates separating our resort-style swimming pool area from the residents in our apartment building. The gates were locked at this point and we were not allowed in. "The scene of the crime," I jokingly texted her. What a painfully profound harbinger that text would turn out to be.

I got to the gates of the pool area ten minutes early. It's the TV producer in me. In the world of television production, if you're on time, you're considered late. It's a thing.

The pool glittered that day in the Los Angeles sunshine. The sky was as blue as I'd ever seen it. The whole scene looked like one of those "Visit Hawaii" commercials you'd see on TV. But I was not allowed in to partake. I could only yearn for it through those giant, forbidding gates. As I gazed at all the glistening bodies of the people swimming and splashing around, I got angrier and angrier.

Suddenly in the distance, I saw a figure slowly approaching. As my eyes focused, I could tell it was a woman—a limping woman, laboring in my direction. "Could that be Mair?" I thought.

"Hello, Johnathan. It's so nice to finally put a face to the name. How are you, dear?" she said as she got closer. It was Mair all right. I was taken aback. Both her legs were completely covered with bandages and white surgical stockings. She was wearing a frilly white sundress nonetheless. She also had a strange accent that I couldn't place. Being married to an Argentinian with an accent, I had learned that people with accents hate it when you ask them where they're from upon first meeting them based on the sound of their voice. So I bit my tongue.

"I'm well. Nice to meet you. Are you okay?" I asked in a tone of concern, referencing all the bandaging on her legs.

"I'm fine," she said confidently. "I just had surgery last week. I have lupus. But I'll be fine."

Of course, four years later, after I had fully unmasked her as a con artist, I learned Mair did not in fact have lupus—a painful autoimmune disease that can cause major swelling all over the body. Those bandages I saw up and down her legs that fateful day were really the result of an expensive visit to a Beverly Hills plastic surgeon's office a week earlier—*for liposuction*.

But the lupus story elicited tremendous sympathy from me almost immediately. And that was certainly her goal. This lupus story was just one of the many dramatic stories Mair told me about her life. In hindsight, it was the first of a hundred different lies I'd fall for, and it poured the foundation for the Tower of Babel of intricate cons she'd construct during the course of our four-year friendship.

When someone you first meet tells you they have lupus . . . you believe them, right?

We chatted for a few minutes. Mair told me she had moved into our building downtown from the valley to be closer to her boyfriend, Andrew (not his real name). He was a partner in a huge, well-known law firm downtown. He was also mayor of one the most affluent cities in the Los Angeles metro area.

And he was married. With kids.

But Mair said that was fine with her. "I'm not looking for a full-time relationship. I'm not looking for a husband. Been there, done that. I just want someone to be with every now and then. And that's Andrew. I see him once a week. And it's enough for me. Really. It is."

Mair said she had actually spoken to her big-time lawyer-mayor boyfriend Andrew about our pool situation and about me in particular, which I found . . . intriguing.

"He's impressed by you," she said matter-of-factly. "The way you put up all those flyers and started organizing all the residents. He wants to meet you. He wants to help you."

As I write these words now, it suddenly occurs to me: The way I bristled at the injustice of our pool being wrongfully taken away. The way I diligently used my own time and resources to plaster flyers everywhere and get the word out. The way I meticulously organized and galvanized the residents of our building to get our pool back. *That* should have been a warning sign to her—not to fuck with me. But it turned out to be more of a road map for her on how she could successfully scam me and weaponize my do-gooder nature against me. As human beings, we tend to give ourselves away in between the lines. That flyer I posted everywhere—and the fact that I took it upon myself to post it in the first place—was all Mair needed to know to craft an effective scam just for me.

Of course, the irony of ironies is: While the possibility of getting scammed by Mair Smyth was the furthest thing from my mind when we met that day, I'm sure the possibility of my putting her in jail had to be the furthest thing from her mind too.

I'd like to think that makes us even. But the idea sickens me.

"The whole reason I moved into this building was because of that pool," Mair said with a tone of regret and anger.

We were standing under the shade of a series of giant jacaranda trees just outside the pool area. And the dapple from the leaves and branches of those trees cast ominous-looking shadows on her face as she spoke. It made her look, well, *evil*.

"Swimming is a great exercise for lupus," Mair said matter-of-factly. "I might sue for injuries or something. Since I can't swim for my recovery, if something goes wrong it's their fault."

"I hadn't thought of that," I said in response, mulling over Mair's potential lawsuit.

The next time I saw Mair Smyth was two weeks later in my apartment's living room, holding court. "We need to form a tenants' association to get the pool back!" she said, Norma Rae–style, to the rapt crowd of two dozen angry neighbors gathered in my living room that Tuesday evening on May 28, 2013.

Her dazzling blue eyes sparkled with hope and optimism as she spoke. She had short, jet-black hair and alabaster skin. The bandages on her legs were gone now. She had a confident swagger in her slick, high-heeled Jimmy Choos.

She introduced herself to everyone as Mair Smyth, a transplant from the Republic of Ireland. "That explains the weird accent," I thought.

I knew so little about Ireland at the time. And apparently the same was true for everyone else there that night.

I mean, when a new neighbor tells you they're from Ireland, you believe them. Right? Face value. To live in constant suspicion is not living. I never thought to question her origin story.

That would become the most expensive mistake I ever made.

Professional con artists like to snow you with details about far-off places, like Ireland. No one sitting in my downtown Los Angeles living room that night knew much about Ireland. After all, it was 5,105 miles away. And it's much easier for people to believe a story based halfway around the world than a story that's local. Add to that, none of us would ever lie about where we were from. So we all just believed that Mair was who she said she was: a woman from Ireland. No one doubted it for a second.

"My boyfriend Andrew is a lawyer and he's sued this building twice already and won *big*. They are so scared of him here. If I can get him to legally organize us as a tenants' association, we'll have the pool back before the summer is over!" Mair confidently declared.

Everyone applauded, including me. When was the last time you got an ovation for anything anywhere? At a parent-teacher conference? Or a city council meeting? Or any kind of meeting at all? Swept up in the enthusiasm, I was clapping too. Mair Smyth embodied the charisma of Eva Perón on the balcony of the Casa Rosada addressing her fervent *descamisados* (shirtless ones) in the streets.

Everyone liked her immediately. And that was most certainly her plan. Her impassioned willingness and dedication to aid our cause was attractive to all of us that night. *She wanted to help.* That's how she gained entry into my life and into the lives of several other soon-to-be victims gathered in my living room.

Mair Smyth was what FBI criminal profilers call a "rescue merchant." She suddenly appeared where there was a problem and offered a solution.

After Mair's impromptu stump speech that night, my neighbors and I started socializing: getting to know one another, drinking wine, eating cheese, hanging out.

I soon met Tina, an out-of-work attorney who lived ten floors above me. She had recently passed the bar exam and was looking to get her foot in the door at a law firm somewhere, anywhere. She was in her late twenties, ambitious, outspoken, well dressed.

"Send me your résumé ASAP. I think my boyfriend's firm is hiring. I'll try and get you an interview," Mair said to Tina.

Mair seemed to be always offering to help people. It pains me to confess: That's one of the things I immediately liked about her.

Another neighbor I met that night was Sherry. She was a no-nonsense woman in her early fifties, a broad's broad in the best sense. And she had the most fascinating job: She managed a strip club.

Being a reality TV producer, I immediately pounced. "Has anyone approached you about doing a show?" I asked.

"No. What do you mean?" Sherry replied.

"It's just, I've never seen a reality show set in a real-life strip club. I think it's a fascinating and provocative world," I said. "I bet those strippers all have compelling personalities and would be great on camera."

"Oh my God!" Sherry exclaimed. "You have no idea. The drama and the craziness my girls get up to would blow your mind."

"Yeah? How so?" I asked curiously.

"They're like children!" she exclaimed. "They throw tantrums every five minutes. And they have so much cash they don't know what to do with it. I tell them to invest it. They don't know how. I tell them to take an exotic vacation somewhere. They don't know where to go or how to get there. They've got more boobs than brains."

I laughed.

"Maybe I can help," Mair interjected.

Are you sensing a pattern here?

Mair explained that she worked for a luxury travel agency in Los Angeles specializing in high-end vacations to far-flung places like Tahiti and Bora Bora. "I can get them a great deal on a vacation package," she offered.

These weren't just any vacations, mind you. They were luxury vacations costing ten to twenty grand per person. So the cash-rich strippers that worked at Sherry's club were in for a real treat.

"They want to go someplace where men won't hit on them all day. They want a break from men!" Sherry explained. "Do you know of a place like that? With a beach?"

"Absolutely," Mair said as she held out her business card. "I can arrange a group vacation for them, so it's just them in a bungalow on the Pacific Ocean. The only men there are the local servants bringing them baked lobster and cocktails all day." We all laughed as Sherry took Mair's card.

If first impressions were money, then Mair Smyth was a zillion-aire. She was raking in adoration and trust like lawnfuls of colored leaves on a fall day.

That night, my living room became a real-life *Shark Tank*. But instead of investors, there were "marks" unknowingly waiting to be shook down. And in place of a bubbly entrepreneur there was an in-veterate con artist, licking her chops at her new prospects.

Mair Smyth would end up scamming all three of us. The lawyer. The strip club manager. And me.

3. RED FLAG #2: TOO KIND, TOO QUICK

The Financial Manager

KINDNESS IS A TRULY BEAUTIFUL THING. IT'S THE ABSOLUTE BEST PART OF BEING HUMAN. In the Venn diagram of noble acts, kindness and helpfulness might have a lot of shaded areas in common—but kindness is, in a way, simpler and cleaner and more independent of helpfulness.

Have you ever had someone "pay it forward" for you at a fast-food drive-through? I have. It's a truly random act of kindness. It's when the stranger waiting in line in front of you pays for your food and then drives away so that by the time you get up to the cashier you're told your meal has been paid for. It's completely anonymous so you can't thank anyone. When that happened to me, I was so moved and full of gratitude and love that I immediately paid for the car behind me. You see, kindness got me to act, quickly. And that's exactly why professional con artists use kindness—so they can disarm you and, when your defenses are down, scam you.

Peggy Fulford is the personification of just how far a professional con artist can get by using kindness to open doors, open hearts, and ultimately open wallets and bank accounts to bleed victims dry. Peggy, with her inordinate kindness, managed to successfully get past a seemingly impenetrable wall of lawyers, managers, and agents to scam sports legends like Dennis Rodman and Ricky Williams out of millions and millions of dollars. She did it in the plain light of day, right in front of everyone around them.

Peggy claimed to be a Harvard-educated financial manager. She had what appeared to be a degree from that prestigious school hanging on her office wall.

I spoke to Peggy's former assistant and asked her how real that Harvard degree looked.

"How would I know what's a Harvard degree or not?" she shot back. "I didn't go to Harvard."

And that's exactly how all con artists operate. They are only too happy to fill in the blanks and the gaps, to fill in the things you do not know (or are not sure about)—with stories, explanations, reasons to believe this or that.

You give a professional con artist a blank canvas, and they'll give you a Rembrandt in no time flat. It'll look real. It'll feel real. It'll fool a lot a people, even experts. But it will be fake.

Peggy Fulford presented herself as a brilliant financial guru, a tough and savvy woman who had made millions of dollars on Wall Street and many millions more in lucrative real estate deals, selling hospitals and properties in the Bahamas. But none of that was true.

Peggy was breathtakingly beautiful too. Born in New Orleans and of Creole descent, she has long, auburn-blond hair, sparkling blue-green eyes, and a billion-dollar smile that could light up a solar system.

Without a doubt, Peggy Fulford waved every single one of the fourteen red flags for being a con artist at her victims. But the red flag that stands out most of all is #2: Too Kind, Too Quick.

Peggy used kindness like a weapon. It gave her entry into all her victims' lives. It made them love her. It made them trust her. And it enabled her to scam them for years before they figured out what was happening. Shockingly, even when some of her victims discovered she had scammed them, they were paralyzed by a mixture of disbelief, lingering affection for her, and an outright refusal to go after her. I've never seen anything quite like it.

In the late 1990s, NFL running back Ricky Williams was living in New Orleans and playing for the New Orleans Saints. He quickly made a name for himself in the world of professional sports, and he had the multi-million-dollar paychecks from the NFL to prove it.

From 1999 to 2001 Ricky Williams reportedly earned more than $9 million playing for the Saints. And what do rich people with millions of dollars do? They buy real estate. So Ricky Williams bought a house in New Orleans, and then a swanky condo in the French Quarter.

But when *MTV Cribs* wanted to film an episode in Ricky's new condo there was a problem: It was still empty. So Ricky scrambled to get it ready for television. He headed to a local furniture store owned by a decorator named Pam Carey whom he had previously hired to decorate his other house. And Pam started helping Ricky design and furnish his new condo.

But the next time Ricky was in Pam's store picking stuff out, an enchanting woman suddenly appeared. Her name was Peggy King, but she was also known as Peggy Barard, Peggy Rivers, Peggy Simpson, and Devon Cole. Sometimes she'd even tell people to call her "Raquel" in public.

Peggy radiated sophistication and class. She dressed to the nines in designer clothes, carried a Louis Vuitton handbag, and smelled like expensive French perfume.

She struck up a friendly conversation with Ricky. She was a very attractive woman in her forties but easily looked ten or even fifteen years younger. Ricky, a wide-eyed twenty-something athlete, was immediately impressed by this new mysterious woman who seemed so nice, so friendly, so giving of her time and attention.

So Ricky started chitchatting, casually explaining his *MTV Cribs* predicament to Peggy, and her eyes lit up. Peggy immediately offered to use her exquisitely sophisticated taste to help him pick out all the right stuff that would be certain to impress *MTV Cribs* producers and their younger-skewing viewers alike.

Peggy Fulford had been a complete stranger to Ricky Williams five minutes before. But in an instant she was in his life. And she wasn't asking for money, or a job, or anything like that. She just came across as a wealthy Good Samaritan with a heart of gold.

She was too kind, too quick.

As it turned out, Peggy was a childhood friend of Pam Carey, the owner of that furniture store. Ricky knew Pam pretty well, so it didn't set off any alarm bells.

But in reality, the whole encounter was planned and flawlessly executed by Peggy. By this point in her career of conning, she was an expert, second to none, at orchestrating events and putting herself in the right place, at the right time, selling just the right story to net her millions of dollars.

Peggy was planting a seed in Ricky Williams's brain that day that would grow and yield her more than $6 million. And he had no idea it was happening. Nor did anyone else, except Peggy.

Pam, the owner of the furniture store, said that Peggy "just showed up, and she made herself available to Ricky. She said, 'Oh, you need sheets, you need this.' She made her way into his life. And at that time, I didn't think anything of it. But I now realize that she was scouting him."

What Pam had no way of knowing at the time was that Peggy had just moved back to New Orleans from Atlanta, after divorcing her third husband. She'd go on to marry and divorce two more times for a total of five ex-husbands in all.

While that's normally not a crime, in Peggy's case it absolutely was because on more than one occasion she'd marry a new husband while legally still being married to her previous one. Bigamy is a crime punishable by years in jail. But Peggy's other crimes were so monumentally huge, her bigamy pales in comparison.

Over the next few days, Peggy helped Ricky decorate his new French Quarter condo. She actually paid for some of the décor herself.

Waaay too kind, waaay too quick.

Peggy had high-end taste. She convinced Ricky to purchase one of George Rodrigue's famous *Blue Dog* paintings for $250,000 to hang in his living room. It was quite a showstopper.

The *MTV Cribs* segment was a huge success, and Ricky was grateful to Peggy for all her help and guidance. But mostly he was grateful for all her kindness and for all the stuff she'd bought him. Peggy seemed to really care about Ricky Williams. She quickly became like a mother figure to him.

Out of the gate, Peggy portrayed herself as a financial manager for professional athletes. Tragically, at the time this was true. Sort of.

You see, during her divorce from husband #3, Peggy was given full control and ownership of her soon-to-be ex-husband's sports management company, King Management. Peggy had one notable client at that time: NBA point guard Travis Best. He'd played for the Indiana Pacers when Peggy first met (targeted) Ricky Williams.

Of course, Ricky Williams had no idea that Peggy was in the process of scamming more than $2 million out of Travis Best. But he'd find out years later, after he realized Peggy had stolen millions from him.

Peggy portrayed herself to Ricky Williams as someone with millions and millions of dollars, someone who'd made a killing on Wall Street and a killing in real estate deals, and who didn't need money anymore.

By the way, Peggy also portrayed herself to Ricky as not having any children of her own. That was a complete and utter lie, because she actually had four kids at that point. One of those kids had been taken from her by the courts, and full custody of that child had been awarded to her second ex-husband.

Oddly enough, Ricky Williams knew one of Peggy's children—a son named Elkin. But he'd been told that Elkin was Peggy's brother, not her son. Elkin, who was in his twenties at this point, played along and pretended to be Peggy's brother for years. He was supposedly helping his "sister" Peggy run King Management.

This wasn't the first time Elkin had concealed his true identity at the behest of his con artist mother. When Peggy met the man who would become her fourth husband, she had induced Elkin to lie and say that he was her nephew.

Peggy was all about appearances. She was perpetually concerned with how things looked. And to Ricky Williams? Peggy looked like the kindest, sweetest person he had ever met. She courted Ricky for five years before reaping any financial benefits from him. *Five years!*

During that entire time, she didn't take a dime from him. Quite the opposite. She actually spent money on Ricky, patiently lying in wait, while showering him and his friends and family with gifts, with kindness, with love and support—or rather with what they all mistook for love and support.

Peggy hosted Ricky's wedding at her waterfront mansion in Fort Lauderdale. At this point Ricky was making millions playing for the Miami Dolphins. Peggy moved right along with him to South Florida from New Orleans after he was traded to Miami in 2002. She even drove Ricky's wife Kristin home from the hospital after Kristin had given birth. Peggy was so deeply involved in every facet of Ricky's life, she was like family. He loved her, and she appeared to love him. But Ricky had no idea that while she was waiting for just the right moment to get her hands on his money, she was keeping herself busy and her bank accounts flush by scamming a bunch of other athletes.

Five years into their relationship, Ricky hadn't given Peggy any money, for any reason at all. But that was all about to change.

In 2004 Ricky failed a series of NFL drug tests because of his marijuana use. He had spoken publicly about struggling with social anxiety and mental health issues for years. He was adamant that his use of marijuana was medicinal and that it helped him cope with the high-stakes pressure of playing professional sports.

But his use of it in the early 2000s caused massive problems in his life and in his career. Seemingly out of spite Ricky shocked the world and "retired" from playing, only to go back to work a year later in 2005. Then he failed even more drug tests and got suspended from the NFL. He was really upset and depressed at this point. Later he would describe having felt as if he was drowning in bad press and controversy.

Then Peggy suddenly entered the fray in true Shakespearian fashion and pulled her best "Iago." She started whispering in Ricky's ear, "If you had let me manage you, none of this would be happening."

And after more than a year of whispering, Peggy's sinister plan finally fell into place. Her long con was about to pay off big. In 2007, Ricky Williams signed over power of attorney to Peggy, instantly giving her full and complete control of all his finances. She was supposed to put Ricky and his wife on a strict budget, pay all his bills, and invest the rest of the millions left over to create "generational wealth"—a buzzy phrase Peggy used often on all her victims to enchant them with the idea that the money they were making now from playing professional sports could support their family and their family's family for generations to come.

The other thing worth highlighting here is that Peggy refused to charge Ricky any kind of fee for her services as his financial manager. Talk about too kind!

Peggy claimed she was not doing it for the money. She said that Ricky was like family to her and that she wanted to protect him from all the financial predators out there looking to take advantage of him.

The irony here is blinding.

From 2007 up until 2013, Peggy appeared to be doing a good job managing Ricky's millions. By that point he had retired from the NFL and was coaching college football in San Antonio, Texas. But in mid-2013, things suddenly started going haywire with his finances. His wife's credit card was declined at the local grocery story. Ricky's Range Rover got mysteriously repossessed. All the bank accounts the couple had in late 2013 were now showing zero or near-zero balances.

At this point Peggy was no longer living in Fort Lauderdale; she was back in New Orleans, and she wasn't returning phone calls, emails, and texts from Ricky and his wife, who were anxiously and frequently inquiring about their finances. So Ricky had a close friend drive him from Texas to Peggy's front door in New Orleans. There he confronted her, demanding to know where all his money was. Peggy swore she had his millions invested in stocks and bonds overseas. She told him not to worry and promised that she'd get it to him soon.

And Ricky Williams believed her, at first.

But as the days turned into weeks, Ricky reluctantly realized the truth: Peggy had scammed him out of millions and millions of dollars. Ricky's wife Kristin started doing some serious digging into Peggy's past and uncovered all her lies. Peggy had never gone to Harvard, nor had she graduated from any college or university whatsoever. She wasn't a financial manager either, and she hadn't made any money on Wall Street or real estate deals in the Bahamas or anywhere else. She was in fact a professional con artist who had married a series of wealthy, successful men, learned the lingo and buzzwords of investing from them, and used the affluent lifestyle those husbands (five in all) provided for her to make it look like she was the one with all the money.

On December 16, 2013, Ricky Williams and his wife filed a civil suit accusing Peggy of fraud and of stealing more than $6 million from them.

In and around this time, one of Peggy's other famous clients was NBA superstar Dennis Rodman. As it turned out, Peggy had used her association with Ricky Williams to trick Dennis Rodman into hiring her back in 2009.

Dennis was attending the opening of Ricky's new restaurant on South Beach. His money manager was in rehab at that time and Dennis was looking for a new one. Just as Peggy had ingratiated herself into Ricky's life by offering to help him decorate his new French Quarter condo for *MTV Cribs,* Peggy offered to help Dennis Rodman by managing his finances since he was in the market for a new money manager.

Dennis knew that Peggy had been managing Ricky Williams's money, so he felt completely confident about bringing her on to manage *his* finances. And Peggy wasn't charging Dennis for her services either! She portrayed herself as being so wealthy that she just wanted to help Dennis and protect his money from financial predators.

Too kind, too quick.

Peggy figured out very quickly that Dennis had a strained relationship with his mother and his sisters. He had been kicked out of the house as a teenager and had been homeless for a few years early on in his life. Peggy used that knowledge to form a nearly unbreakable bond with him. She weaponized her well-practiced "too kind, too quick" routine and worked to become the mother Dennis Rodman never had. Seemingly overnight, she created a relationship dynamic that had Dennis relying on her for everything. Shortly after meeting her that night on South Beach at Ricky Williams's restaurant opening in 2009, Dennis signed over power of attorney to Peggy. It gave her full control of every bank account he had and every piece of real estate he owned or was renting, as well as every paycheck he had coming in from doing lucrative public appearances, television shows, and movies. Peggy's job was to pay all of Dennis's bills, especially his child support, and invest the rest of his money to create—again the catchphrase she loved using to ensnare her victims—"generational wealth."

Dennis admits that he hasn't been the best father. This idea of providing "generational wealth" to his kids and their kids and so on was for him kind of a way to make up for his perceived failings. So he was all in.

Three years later, when Dennis Rodman was making headlines for not paying his child support, the public had no idea that it wasn't *Dennis* who was to blame. It was Peggy. Paying Dennis's child support and all his bills was her job and hers alone. Dennis didn't even have access to his own bank accounts because he didn't trust himself to be a good steward of his own money. So he put all his trust in Peggy.

In late 2013, shortly after Dennis started making headlines for not paying child support, Ricky Williams filed that civil suit against Peggy alleging fraud and theft. It ended up going nowhere fast. Ricky first filed it in Texas, then refiled it in Florida, spending thousands and thousands of dollars in the process. Then suddenly Ricky filed a motion to dismiss the suit entirely.

It seemed that Peggy was about to get away with scamming him. I'm sure she was breathing a huge sigh of relief at this point.

But as fate (or karma) would have it, the civil suit that Ricky had filed in Houston, Texas, got the attention of FBI agent James Hawkins, who happened to be reading about it in the *Houston Chronicle* one morning.

Hawkins was a seasoned investigator who'd been with the FBI for more than thirty years. And from that *Houston Chronicle* article he read, Special Agent Hawkins had a hunch that Ricky Williams's civil suit against Peggy was just the tip of the iceberg. Hawkins suspected a major crime had taken place, and he bet that Ricky wasn't the only victim—so he started looking into the case on his own.

Over the ensuing two years, Agent Hawkins uncovered victim after victim after victim: professional athletes and former professional athletes who all lost millions of dollars to Peggy. And on December 16, 2016, Hawkins, flanked by a posse of FBI agents, showed up at Peggy's apartment in New Orleans and arrested her. Peggy was federally charged with wire fraud, mail fraud, interstate transportation of stolen property, and money laundering. And as the arresting federal agents were standing in Peggy's apartment, they noticed a check on her nightstand for nearly $200,000 from an entirely new victim. Turns out, the FBI had inadvertently busted Peggy in the midst of a whole other scam: tricking a local New Orleans doctor into investing in a fictitious retirement home she claimed to be building.

On February 1, 2018, Peggy pled guilty to one count of "transportation of stolen property" and was sentenced to ten years in federal prison. But she got out in less than five years after filing multiple motions for early release. As I type these words, I hear Peggy is planning a big Anna Delvey–type comeback. She wants to tell her story, in her own words. She wants a book deal. She wants a movie. And she wants Halle Berry to play her.

Queen of the Con II

An act of kindness is truly a powerful thing. And it can present in myriad ways.

Mair Smyth was so kind right off the bat that it immediately disarmed me. Her kindness made me really like her, then love her, then trust her.

And that was her plan.

Even to this day, I get extremely angry thinking about it all. Then I get even angrier at the fact that I'm still angry. It's this crazy mental loop I can't seem to break free from.

Kindness wasn't Mair Smyth's only tactic. She was waving *all* the red flags that she was a con artist right in front of my face. But looking back, her being "too kind, too quick" was one that stood out the most in the beginning.

Days after that fateful meeting I held in our apartment back in May of 2013—the meeting where a couple dozen of my motivated and angry neighbors converged in my living room to come up with a plan to get the pool back—my new neighbor "Mair" seemed to be so moved and so impressed by my spearheading this noble operation that she wanted to thank me.

"I want to take you and your husband out to dinner," she said at the end of that night, as people were leaving. "As a small gesture of my gratitude."

"Sure. That'd be great," I replied, not having a clue what I had just consented to.

I was inviting a con artist into my life. Now, you might disagree with me here and say, "No, no she was inviting you into her life." And semantically speaking, you'd be right. She was.

But her inviting me and my husband to dinner that night was not a real invitation at all. It was a cleverly crafted trick to ensnare me, to rope me in. And my God, did she rope me in.

"Would you like to see the wine list?" the well-dressed waiter asked us.

It was a week after the residents' meeting. Mair, my husband, and I were now sitting in Drago Centro, a Los Angeles fine dining establishment just down the street from our apartment building.

It was a place that specialized in high-end Italian fusion cuisine. The restaurant's ultramodern yet eclectic décor was kind of a cross between *Star Trek* and *Little House on the Prairie,* where rustic wood mingled with modern steel and stone to create an opulent splendor.

I ordered the $30 ravioli and was shocked when the waiter put the plate down in front of me. There on a giant black platter sat six coin-sized ravioli dressed with some marinara sauce and green things shooting out in every direction. I never figured out what those *green things* were. While the presentation was artsy and cool, I'd need to eat at least four or five orders to be anywhere near full.

"A toast!" Mair said as she held up her glass of wine. She'd ordered a $200 bottle of Antinori Tignanello.

"To new friends and to getting our pool back before the summer is over!" Mair gushed.

"I'll drink to that!" I exclaimed.

As our glasses clinked, and the evening wore on, a picture began to emerge of who this woman really was—I mean, who she wanted us all to believe she was: a wealthy, witty, outspoken, kindhearted, brutally honest, funny, lovable, outgoing, life-of-the-party, gregarious woman. Mair was fun to be with, all right. Her laugh was infectious, and her company was endlessly enthralling.

When the check came, it was more than $600. I reached for my wallet to pay our share and Mair snatched the bill out of my hand.

"No. No. No. This is my treat," she protested. "I invited you guys to dinner. Remember?"

Reluctantly I let her pay that more than $600 bill. With a 20 percent tip it was over $700.

"I'm loaded," she said airily as she plunked her credit card on the table. And I believed it.

Mair's kindness and largesse were a constant over the course of our friendship. How can you not immediately fall in like or in love with someone who's perpetually buying you dinners and giving you gifts?

One day, months later, Mair called me up out of the blue.

"I have twenty designer dresses that are all size 6," she excitedly said. "Your sister is a size 6, right?"

Mair was referring to Lily, my husband's sister and my sister-in-law. And yes, she was a size 6.

"These would look great on her!" she exclaimed.

Mair explained that a wealthy client of hers who did wardrobe for movies and TV shows here in Los Angeles had just given her twenty brand-new designer dresses that had never been used in any movie or show and that her wardrobe department was getting rid of them to make room for new stuff. The dresses were all size 6. Mair wanted to give them to our sister. We're talking glamorous Chanel, Tom Ford, and Giorgio Armani dresses worth thousands and thousands of dollars.

"Are you sure?" I asked Mair incredulously. "Like, you don't want them for yourself or for your daughters?"

"No," she replied. "I'm a size 8. They won't fit me. And my daughters wouldn't be caught dead in dresses like these. Not their style."

So Mair brought all the dresses over on a rolling rack and we gave them to Lily. She absolutely loved them. She reacted like a kid on Christmas morning as she modeled each dress for us. They all fit her perfectly. There were tears in Lily's eyes as she thanked Mair and hugged her—tears of gratitude for her kindness. My husband and I were extremely grateful as well.

As you can imagine, kind deeds like these went a long way, very quickly, toward making me love Mair. I was completely taken in and blinded by it all.

Her kindness never ceased to amaze me. A few weeks after the dress giveaway, Mair called me up and said, "I have a one-thousand-dollar gift card for the Melting Pot that a client just gave me as a thank-you for the incredible luxury vacation I planned for him."

Now the Melting Pot is this amazing fondue restaurant where you dip chunks of bread or veggies or meat—or all of the above—into fresh little vats of fondue that the waiters make in front of your eyes at your table. It's a pricey but delightful dining experience, especially when dessert rolls around and you get square chunks of cheesecake to dip in vats of melted dark chocolate. Delicious.

Mair wanted to take me, my husband, and some of my friends to dinner at The Melting Pot. On her. "I want to use up this gift card now, because if I put it down I'll forget I have it and then it'll expire, and then that's a thousand dollars down the drain," she reasoned.

So I grabbed my husband and a couple friends and met up with Mair at the restaurant. There we feasted like kings, and Mair paid the $900-plus bill with her gift card. Everyone thought she was the kindest woman ever. They loved her, and by this point certainly I loved her too.

Her kind gestures just kept building. Months later, she excitedly called me up. "One of my clients invited me to stay at his vacation home in Palm Springs. Wanna come? We'll have the entire house to ourselves."

"Oh my God!" I said. "That would be amazing."

Palm Springs is this sizzling desert oasis five hours outside of Los Angeles. Back in its heyday, icons like Bob Hope, Frank Sinatra, and Bing Crosby built a string of ultramodern vacation homes there and secured that tiny town's reputation as a getaway for the rich and famous. In the 1960s JFK had his notorious fling with Marilyn Monroe in Palm Springs. These days, though, it's just a great vacation spot for city dwellers to escape to, boasting triple-digit temperatures and dozens of fun hotels and restaurants. My husband and I had a blast on that weekend getaway in Palm Springs, compliments of Mair Smyth.

It never occurred to me that every single kind gesture Mair made over the course of our "friendship" was a calculated chess move she was making as part of a bigger game that I had no idea I was even playing—a game at which I was losing horribly.

What Mair did to me is what a lot of professional con artists do to their victims. They bombard them with kindness and generosity to quickly gain their love and, more importantly, their trust.

4. RED FLAG #3: DRAMA, DRAMA, DRAMA

ing this book. Con artists don't outsmart you, they out-feel you. And they are like vampires. They have to be invited into your life, your home, and your heart before they can exert any power or influence over you. And after you invite them in, they'll only leave when they've completely bled you dry or when *you* realize *they're* a con artist. Usually, though, the one precipitates the other.

One of the biggest ways con artists trick you into giving them money is by using invented drama.

The case I'm about to get into here is scary, sad, and infuriating. Out of all the con artist cases I've been investigating over the past seven years, this is the one that keeps me up at night. I've gotten to know the victim really well. And I've busted my ass on this case. But as I write these words, I'm still not 100 percent confident that the con artist in question will ever be brought to justice. She may never be stopped.

Authorities have been investigating her for the past four years. I've uncovered a dozen other victims of this particular con artist and served them up on a silver platter to those same authorities. The case has gotten kicked up to the state attorney's office.

Yet nothing is happening, absolutely nothing, because the con artist in question is well connected to judges, to politicians, to attorneys, to the system in general. I think she's got dirt on all of them, and I think she's using that dirt as leverage to avoid prosecution. It's truly sickening.

This con woman targets only vulnerable people—people she thinks, for various reasons, would never be strong enough or bold enough to report her to the authorities. And for the most part she's been absolutely correct. She worked in the mayor's office for a couple years. She used that association to give herself and her scams the appearance of legitimacy.

And the fact that the sheriff's office in the county and state that this con artist operates in completely eliminated their Economic Crimes Unit at the start of the criminal investigation into this particular con artist is very troubling. Just so you know, the Economic Crimes Unit of any police or sheriff's department is responsible for investigating fraud, identity theft, and . . . *con artists.*

But I'm getting ahead of myself.

Carol Porter first reached out to me on LinkedIn on January 28, 2020, with a message that read simply, "I think I was scammed."

Now, there's a strange paradox I've discovered over the years investigating con artist cases and talking to victims. Whenever I receive a Tolstoy-length email from a victim elaborately detailing how, when, where, and why they were scammed, it's usually a somewhat minor con. The victim lost a couple hundred or a couple thousand dollars. They're mad and they want justice. And I certainly try to help them as much as I can. But whenever I get a cryptic one-sentence message like the one Carol Porter sent me that day, "I think I was scammed," it usually indicates a huge, criminally sophisticated, and painful scam—so huge and painful the victim simply does not have the words to describe it in an email or in a message on LinkedIn.

Over the next few days, I responded to Carol again and again with the question, "Why do you think you were scammed?" And she wouldn't really answer me. She said she was having suspicions about someone in her life and had reached out to me because my name came up when she googled the term *con artist* and serendipitously came across an article I had written for *HuffPost* about Mair, headlined "My Best

Friend Was a Con Artist Who Scammed Me Out of $92,000. Here's How I Got Justice." But in her messages she mainly replied to my question with variations of "It's complicated" and politely refused to divulge exactly how she thought she had gotten scammed.

Finally, I got her on the phone. At that point she was in her sixties and living in South Florida. Even on the call she remained quiet and shy and reluctant to reveal much of anything. But I suspected she was the victim of a huge scam, and it sounded to me as if the scam was still in progress because she was still associating with the woman who she said she suspected was scamming her. It all puzzled the hell out of me.

I told her, "Look, you don't have to tell me how or why you think you're getting scammed. But can you at least just tell me the name of the person who you think is scamming you? That way, I can run a background check on them and see if they have a criminal history of any kind or a history of being accused of scamming other people."

In my experience, con artists are a lot like serial killers. If you catch a serial killer at the scene of one murder, rest assured you'll be able to pin dozens of others on them shortly thereafter.

Carol was extremely reticent. She didn't want to tell me the woman's name. There was a long pause on the phone. I could hear her breathing as she contemplated what to say next.

Carol then issued a long sigh and asked fearfully, "Will this person know that you're doing a background check on them?"

"No," I shot back. "When you run a background check on someone, they are in no way notified. It's like when you google someone. That person doesn't know you're googling them. It's the same with background checks."

Carol thought for a moment and then sheepishly uttered the name "Bina Fink."

"Her last name is Fink?" I queried, thinking I must have heard her wrong.

"Yes," Carol said.

"Fink, huh?" I thought to myself.

According to Merriam-Webster, the meaning of the word *fink* is "one who is disapproved of or is held in contempt." Sometimes people really do live up to their names.

So I plugged "Bina Fink" into my background check databases, and bam, I saw that she had a rap sheet longer than a CVS receipt. She had been charged with grand theft and passing bad checks in the late 1990s. She had a bunch of civil lawsuits filed against her over the previous twenty years too, by people who claimed she had stolen from them or just plain scammed them. I also unearthed a ton of anonymous online complaints calling Bina Fink a "thief" and a "scammer" and urging people not to give her money.

At this point I knew Carol Porter was getting scammed by a fink named Fink. I just didn't know how, or for how much. But over the course of a dozen or so phone calls with Carol, I figured it out.

Long story short, Bina Fink waved the Red Flag of Drama, Drama, Drama and tricked Carol Porter out of approximately $200,000 in less than nine months. It appeared to me that her plan was to completely bleed Carol dry.

Carol and her husband Stuey had first met Bina Fink at a political fundraising event years earlier. And they'd see Bina again and again over the years at various other political fundraising events in and around South Florida. So they knew her and they liked her. She was fun, she was outgoing, she seemed politically connected to a lot of important people, and she was very friendly.

Carol and Stuey lived an upper-middle-class life in Boynton Beach, Florida—an affluent city in Palm Beach County. Stuey was a successful pharmacist and made a good living. Carol worked on and off as a photographer and journalist, though Stuey was the main breadwinner by far. Carol and Stuey never had any kids, but they enjoyed each other's company immensely and they liked attending fancy political fundraising events. That was where they first met Bina Fink.

Now if you think about it, a political fundraising event is a great place for a professional con artist to find new victims to scam. These events tend to attract a wealthier-than-average crowd with a higher-than-usual disposable income. The mere fact that they're attending a political fundraising event means they're passionate—translation: They're receptive to drama. And they like to put their money where their mouth is. All of that is chum in the water for a working con artist.

So Carol and Stuey had a wonderful life together in South Florida—until Stuey suddenly got brain cancer.

Carol was devastated by Stuey's diagnosis. From that point on, he was in and out of hospitals for weeks. And then out of nowhere, Bina Fink suddenly appeared—*wanting to help.*

Remember Red Flag #1? Well, Bina Fink was waving it at Carol like there was no tomorrow.

"Since Stuey was supposedly going to get better, I decided to re-model the house so he could come home to a clean house. Our house unfortunately was a real dump. We had neglected it for years. Both of us worked many hours and did not take care of it."

So Bina helped Carol remodel the house. "I thought this woman was a godsend," Carol said.

Bina would visit Carol frequently while Stuey battled brain cancer. She'd buy groceries for Carol. Run errands for her. She'd take Carol out to dinners and to political fundraising events that Stuey was too sick to attend. She quickly became Carol's best friend. Then, tragically, when Stuey died, Bina Fink was the shoulder Carol cried on. She even helped Carol plan Stuey's funeral. She oversaw the execution of Stuey's will and all his posthumous financial arrangements. "I thought she was looking out for me," Carol said.

And that's when the scamming started. That had been Bina Fink's plan all along.

Carol Porter is a supersmart, loving, and inordinately kind woman. But she's also sort of . . . socially awkward/quirky, or eccentric, as she describes herself.

And here's the thing: Carol is somewhat hyperconscious about just how eccentric she might appear to others. I got the impression she's extremely concerned that people around her might think she is "crazy" or unhinged.

Well, apparently Bina Fink also picked up on that insecure piece of

Carol's psyche. Because she quickly weaponized it against Carol, and unfortunately it worked really well.

When Stuey died, he left Carol nearly a million dollars. Fernando, who had been his and Carol's financial manager for more than twenty years, was tasked with handling all that money for Carol. It was invested in profitable stocks and bonds all over the world. Now that Stuey was gone, Fernando's job was to ensure that Carol received all the interest payments from all those shrewd investments deposited into her checking account each month to live on. So Carol would be well taken care of for the rest of her life.

That was Stuey's plan. But sadly, Stuey could have never foreseen the sudden appearance of a diabolical con artist in Carol's life.

Bina started creating drama for Carol—lots of drama, of a type that uniquely spoke to her. It was a type of drama that an eccentric widow with lots and lots of money, and unsure of a path forward, would be particularly susceptible to.

Bina started telling Carol that her close friends and family thought she was crazy: that they were all talking about her behind her back and saying she was incapable of taking care of herself. Bina claimed to have witnessed many instances of this.

"They don't think you can handle your finances," Bina told Carol just days after her husband's death.

At that point the seed was planted. And then it was watered every day and fertilized generously. And it grew big and fast into a full-fledged alternate reality—one that Carol started living in, by herself, unaware that it was all make-believe. The cast of characters unwittingly participating in this alternate reality were real. But they weren't saying and doing what Bina Fink tricked Carol into believing they were saying and doing.

One by one Bina convinced Carol that all the people in her life were trying to get her declared insane or mentally incompetent so they could take over her finances—for her own good, of course. "They were trying to 'Baker Act' me," Carol said, distilling the essence of Bina Fink's elaborate, months-long con down to a single phrase.

The Baker Act is a Florida law that was passed back in 1971. The long and short of it is, any family member or close friend can call up the authorities (anywhere in Florida) to report that they suspect their loved one has "lost their mind" and can demand that their loved one be picked up, held in a psych ward—against their will—and evaluated by professionals.

And if it's later determined that that loved one did in fact lose their mind? All their rights as a free adult—especially access to their finances—get taken away from them and handed to the state or to that friend or family member who reported them in the first place. They're essentially forced into a conservatorship.

This was Carol Porter's worst fear: that a lifetime of demonstrable eccentricity and being socially awkward around people could land her in a Florida psych ward—stripped of her right to self-determination. And Bina Fink deftly used Carol Porter's worst fears against her. She created one dramatic episode after another: round-the-clock drama, drama, drama.

As the days ticked by, the drama quickly reached a fevered pitch. "They're outside your house now. They're checking on you. Don't answer your door," is what Carol says Bina would tell her time and time again. "I keep hearing about my husband's best friend going up there, or the broker going into the neighborhood to drive by the house, and these people checking the house out to see if I'm there," Carol told me, recalling the insanity that became her life months after her husband died.

The truth of the matter was *no one* was outside Carol's house. It was all a lie. It was all invented drama. But Carol didn't know that because she was crouched in the corner of her bedroom, on the floor, hiding under a blanket, too scared to move. At that point, Carol genuinely believed "they" were coming for her. "They" were going to "Baker Act" her. And "they" were going to take all her money.

But convincing Carol that people were stalking her outside her home day and night was only the beginning of this dramatically insane con.

Remember Fernando? He had been Stuey's broker for more than twenty years and was now handling Carol's finances and sending her the interest every month from her deceased husband's investments. Well, according to Bina, Fernando had hired a lawyer and a private investigator, and he was attempting to gather evidence to prove Carol was "crazy" so he could "Baker Act" her and take over her finances.

But that wasn't true at all. It was just more invented drama from Bina Fink.

The truth of the matter was—Fernando became suspicious of Bina after Bina "helped" Carol renovate her home. It was kind of her first scam. That renovation cost Carol $150,000. And after the dust settled—literally—Fernando realized it wasn't actually a renovation at all. It was more of a cleanup and paint situation. Fernando just couldn't understand how it had cost Carol $150,000 to paint some walls and throw some new carpet down. He admonished Carol for spending so much on so little. And he warned her in no uncertain terms about Bina Fink.

Looking back, that was probably why Bina started inventing crazy dramatic stories about Fernando. She knew he was suspicious of her, and she wanted to turn Carol against him as soon as possible.

And by God she did. "You need to move the money away from Fernando," Bina implored Carol, weeks after she invented all those dramatic stalking stories that Carol took as gospel.

It didn't matter that Carol had known Fernando for more than twenty years, or that her husband Stuey had trusted him implicitly with his finances, or that he'd always done right by them, or that he'd always been an honest, stand-up guy, or that he had no criminal history whatsoever and no accusations of wrongdoing either. Fernando's entire reputation as a good person was destroyed in Carol's eyes in one fell swoop, because Carol now believed Fernando was conspiring—along with everyone else—to get her "Baker Acted" so he could take her money.

Remember when I said earlier that love is the most powerful force in the universe? And that if a con artist can get you to love them, you'll do anything for them?

Well, fear is the second most powerful force there is in the universe. And if a con artist can get you to be *afraid* of something, you'll make decisions based on that fear. And those will only ever be bad decisions.

Carol trusted Bina, so she agreed to move her investments over to

Bina's brokers. They were just a couple of guys with some office space in Pembroke Pines, Florida.

But Carol earnestly believed Bina had her back and was looking out for her. "She was going to protect me from the family and friends who were out to get the money that Stuey left me," Carol recalled.

Once Carol's money was with Bina's brokers, the real, unadulterated scamming started. According to Carol, Bina convinced her that several of her friends and family members were taking legal action against her to get her declared mentally incompetent and take over her finances.

Even her deceased husband's best friend, Richard Kaplan, "wanted to do a Power of Attorney on me to gain access to the money that Stuey left," Carol said. That's what Bina made her believe. But it wasn't true, at all.

So Bina got Carol a meeting with a lawyer who, according to Bina, would "protect" Carol from all these people coming out of the woodwork with legal filings in an attempt to take over Carol's money. Carol signed paperwork to hire this lawyer, and Bina signed as a "witness."

Over the next several months Bina called up Carol repeatedly to say that the lawyer needed additional payments to defend her from another attempt by one of Carol's former friends or family members to steal her money. Bina would ask Carol for $5,000 one time. And then weeks later she'd ask for $7,000. And then weeks later still she'd ask her for another $3,000. This went on for more than nine months.

Bina wanted all these supposed payments to the lawyer to be made in cash. Not checks, not credit cards. Bina convinced Carol that the lawyer would accept only cash as payment for protecting her from all the people trying to "Baker Act" her and take over her finances.

Now that normally would have been a sign for anyone that a scam was in progress, right? The lawyer wants to be paid in cash? How sketchy is that?

But human psychology is a hell of a thing. A lot of the time we all act not by using our intellect but by relying on instincts. And there are times when our instincts will betray us—because of stress, fear, depression, or all of the above.

At that specific point in Carol's life, she became extremely susceptible to something called *Sunk Cost Fallacy,* a cognitive bias that makes people feel as if they should continue spending money, or time, or effort—or all three—on a certain endeavor because they've previously "sunk" so much into it already. This "sunk cost" makes it nearly impossible for them to walk away from a situation because they don't want to feel like their resources were wasted.

We are all susceptible to Sunk Cost Fallacy, especially if we've been working on something for a long time and we've poured our blood, sweat, and tears into it. If you're a gambler at a Vegas craps table losing a fortune, "just a little more" is the false belief you unconsciously employ to keep going.

But Sunk Cost Fallacy can also be at play in even the most stupid and mundane situations. How many times have you been thirty minutes into watching a really bad movie, and yet instead of stopping you say to yourself, "Well, I'm this far in already, I might as well finish it."

Why? Human nature. That's why.

In Carol's case, she had sincerely believed everything Bina Fink had told her for months. So one more lie was easy to accept.

The lawyer wanted to be paid in cash? On its own, that's a preposterous notion. But as the latest in a long trail of believable lies, it made sense to Carol at the time.

So Carol would drive to the bank with Bina. She'd write out checks to herself for "cash" and cash them, then hand that cash to Bina, "to pay the lawyer."

In the beginning, it all went off without a hitch for Bina. Carol—incrementally—forked over tens of thousands of dollars to supposedly "pay the lawyer." And nobody was the wiser. Especially Carol.

But eventually, on one of the many occasions when Carol was cashing these checks, one of the bank tellers at one of the banks suddenly became suspicious. She'd seen Carol there multiple times in the past cashing all these checks on her account made out to "cash," and something just didn't feel right to her. So she pulled Carol aside.

"Are you okay?" the teller asked. "I'm worried you might be getting scammed."

"No. No. I'm fine," Carol stuttered. "Everything is fine."

But everything was not fine. At all.

Over the course of nine months, Bina would tell Carol the lawyer needed another payment for $3,000 here and $7,000 there to fight off one of the many legal actions her friends and/or family members were taking against her. Carol would make a check out to "cash" and then cash it and hand Bina the money. By the time all was said and done, more than $200,000 was depleted from Carol's bank account, "to pay the lawyer."

That's when Carol found the article I had written about my experience and contacted me. And that's when I was able to help Carol put an end to the scam. But what happened next I did not see coming.

5. RED FLAG #4: ISOLATION

WHILE A LOT OF CON ARTIST CASES INVOLVE THE RED FLAG OF ISOLATION TO SOME EX-tent, what Bina Fink did to Carol Porter in terms of isolation was just next level. And incredibly cruel.

Not only did Fink isolate Carol by telling her lies that her friends and family were trying to get her declared insane, that is, to "Baker Act" her, causing her to avoid them, but she convinced Carol to move out of her home and into a small apartment forty miles away. Conveniently though, it was down the street from where Bina Fink herself lived, so that Fink could keep an eye on her and make sure that any friend or family member from Carol's previous life would no longer be anywhere near her.

Carol and her husband Stuey had lived in Boynton Beach, Florida, for thirty years. She loved the community. She knew every neighbor on her block. And that was going to be a real problem for Bina Fink, because any professional con artist trying to take advantage of you needs to be able to lure you away from anyone who might talk you out of going along with what they're trying to get you to do, or poke holes in the stories they're telling you, or become curious and raise questions about this or that.

Keep in mind that by this point Carol already believed that her friends and family were out to get her, that they were spying on her go-ings and comings at all hours of the day and night to supposedly capture evidence of her insanity. So it wasn't much more of a leap to think the only rational thing to do would be to move away—far away. Bina Fink convinced Carol that this was the only way she could truly protect her-self from all those money-grubbing hangers-on.

It was Sunk Cost Fallacy all over again. Carol had already believed one hundred other lies to this point, right? What was one more?

So Carol put her house on the rental market and moved into a small apartment in Weston, Florida, an upscale suburban community forty miles south, where she knew no one. And most important to Bina Fink: No one knew her.

Carol was emotionally—and now physically—isolated from every-one she used to know. And her reliance on Bina Fink only grew.

Remember, at this point Fernando, her old broker, was nowhere in sight. Carol had moved all her money to the brokers Bina Fink recom-mended. This was another step in the isolation process. Fernando would've no doubt raised a warning about why Carol was withdrawing all this money to pay lawyers. But her new brokers just did what she asked. Whenever she asked for more money to be withdrawn, they said, "Sure."

There were times when Carol would ask to see corresponding pa-perwork from "the lawyer" to corroborate what she was being told by Bina Fink, and Bina Fink would just talk in circles and never actually produce any paperwork. And that began to strike Carol as odd.

Add to that, a second bank teller pulled Carol Porter aside during a transaction and also asked her point-blank, "Are you being scammed?"

Shockingly, those two bank tellers refused to cooperate with investi-gators. They flat-out refused to go on record and admit what they saw and did. And it makes my blood boil. The only way things will ever change in this world, or in this con artist case, or in any con artist case, is if people go on record and report what they witnessed.

After Carol realized that Bina Fink would never show her any pa-perwork from "the lawyer," and after two different bank tellers at two different banks asked her if she was being scammed, Carol started to balk at Bina Fink's requests for more money to "pay the lawyer." That just made Bina Fink double down on her requests and on her threats that "they" (Carol's friends and family) were coming for her to have her committed so they could take over her financial affairs.

Then Bina Fink started making her case with more gusto. In a November 2019 text message to Carol, Bina wrote: "You know what the only one that has been there for you is me."

The more Carol hesitated about giving Bina Fink money, the angrier Bina Fink seemed to get. In another text message from Bina to Carol in December of 2019, after Carol had stopped giving her cash to "pay the lawyer" and had rebuffed multiple requests for more money, Bina wrote: "I'm so sick and tired of trying to protect you a[nd] you give them reasons to do more shit. All I've done is help you. If that makes you upset, I will walk away. Just do what you want. I don't care anymore. Let Richard serve you. Let Doug continue to say you're not stable. I've tried to help, but I can't anymore."

Richard was Carol's deceased husband's best friend, and Doug was his brother.

Not long after this, Carol started googling "con artist." She found the article I wrote and contacted me for help.

Our first few conversations were stilted. Carol was terrified and extremely reluctant to explain exactly what was happening. But eventually she opened up. When I saw the full extent of what Bina had been doing to Carol, I convinced Carol that she needed to report her to the police immediately.

But there were no "police" in Weston, Florida. The only arbiter of law in the immediate area where Carol was now living was the local Broward County Sheriff's Office just down the street from her apartment.

The difference between police and sheriffs is that police tend to focus on urban areas within cities and are led by appointed police chiefs, while sheriffs have county-wide jurisdiction, are elected by the public, and oversee law enforcement in a more extensive geographic area.

Jurisdiction is everything to these agencies. In other words, if you want to report a crime that happened, you have to do it in the correct jurisdiction. In my experience, the quickest way to determine the correct jurisdiction is to open up Google Maps, type in the address of where the crime happened, and search nearby for the closest police department or sheriff's office. The one that's closest will be the one that has jurisdiction over the crime—for the most part anyway.

So one morning in early February 2020, Carol went to that Weston branch of the Broward Sheriff's Office to report what had happened to her. And they turned her away. "They said they couldn't do anything," Carol told me, "and that since I gave her the money it was not an actual crime."

Funny. That's exactly what the LAPD told me when I first tried to report my con artist here in Los Angeles back in 2017.

I've since learned after interviewing several police officers and law enforcement officials and prosecutors over the years that this sort of pushback is a knee-jerk response. The sad truth is, law enforcement are up to their eyeballs with serious crimes like murders, rapes, and assaults, so they have a tendency to relegate nonviolent crimes like scams to the bottom of their list, if they even make the list at all. The onus is always on the victim to insist and make their case.

The problem is—nobody tells the victim that.

But I knew full well that the Broward County Sheriff's Office was wrong. And by now I had learned how to effectively push back on that canned response "It's not a crime 'cause you gave her the money." That's what they told me too. But they were incorrect. It actually is a crime.

Sadly, I've learned in nearly every single con artist case I have investigated over the past few years, 99 percent of the time police initially turn victims away. That's just the process. And if you're unfamiliar with that process, it might seem finite and "over" to you. Police have said there's no crime and there's nothing you can do about it. But I assure you, that's just the first step.

If life was fair you wouldn't have to do anything more than report the con artist to the police and they would take over. But if life was fair there wouldn't be con artists out there trying to scam you.

I mentioned this in the Introduction, but it bears repeating here: pitching a criminal case to the police (or to any law enforcement agency) is a lot like pitching a show to a television executive. You have to make it sexy. By *sexy,* I mean compelling, succinct, easy to follow, easy to understand—and, most important, *impossible to ignore.*

It has to have a beginning, middle, and end. And like any good movie or TV show, it has to *suck you in.* And it has to make you care deeply about the protagonist, who is the victim in this case.

So over the next few days, I had Carol gather up all her bank records and all her emails and text messages to and from Bina Fink. With them, I helped her write up a detailed ten-page timeline and affidavit "selling" her case to investigators, replete with hard evidence in the form of bank records, emails, and texts that proved what Carol Porter was asserting was true beyond a reasonable doubt—the actual legal threshold in any criminal case. Then I sent Carol back to that same sheriff's office—except this time I was on speakerphone, and together we recounted to a deputy, Elizabeth Lee, exactly what was written in the sworn affidavit that I had helped Carol flesh out and that she had handed to the deputy, along with all those bank records and printed-out text messages and emails.

The first few lines of that affidavit read:

I, the undersigned, do hereby swear, certify, and affirm that:

1. From March 2019 to February 2020, a woman named "Bina Fink" residing at XXXXXX in Weston, FL 33331 used a series of elaborate confidence tricks to scam me out of close to $200,000. This constitutes Felony Grand Theft by Inducement, and I'd like to press charges.

2. I recently discovered Bina Fink is a con artist with a criminal record of felonies for Grand Theft and Passing Bad Checks.

3. I also recently found out Bina Fink has been sued numerous times in civil court for scamming several other people.

4. When my husband, Stuart Martin Ulrich, died in March 2019, I was devastated. Bina Fink, who was only an acquaintance I'd met at a public event, quickly took an interest in me and my tragedy

and took advantage of my weakened emotional state. She inserted herself into my life and systematically separated me from all my friends and family over the course of a year by telling me incredible lies about them to make me avoid them and to make me scared of them. I acted in reliance on her false statements about my friends and family and I avoided them to my own detriment.

So an affidavit is a crucial legal document that courts, lawyers, and law enforcement agents use to communicate things back and forth to one another. It's essentially a written statement of facts. It's kind of like an essay, but each statement is numbered. It's supposed to be as clear and as concise as possible. And it has be notarized.

Carol and I spoke to Deputy Lee for about twenty minutes. She seemed receptive and even impressed with the legwork Carol had done. And she started taking the case seriously. She wrote up a report. Then she said something that completely blew my mind.

"We've actually received numerous complaints about this woman Bina Fink."

I was stunned. I quickly peppered her with questions like "What kinds of complaints?" and "How many people have come forward?"

"I'm not at liberty to say," she demurred.

A few days later, things took a crazy, crazy turn.

When I started investigating Bina Fink I was still producing television shows. That's how I earn a living. Investigating con artists is a passionate side project. So when I started digging in my free time, I found dozens of online complaints about Bina Fink. The victims said she had scammed them out of thousands of dollars by pretending to be a music executive, or pretending to work with an immigration lawyer to get undocumented people a green card, or pretending to be able to help with adoptions.

One of the online complaints had a phone number attached to it. I figured it was the number of the victim posting the complaint. So I called it and started asking the person on the other end about the complaint. But a couple minutes into the conversation I realized I was actually talking to Bina Fink herself! So I quickly hung up.

The very next day I got a call from the FBI. The freaking FBI!

I let it go to voicemail: "Hey, Johnathan, I'm with the FBI down in Miami, Florida. Wonder if you can give me a call back. Today I received a complaint from a young lady that you, I guess, had called on the phone yesterday. I just wanna see what's going on or to tell you that she wants you to cease and desist calling her."

I immediately ran the name and phone number of that "FBI agent" through my background check databases and found that, yes, he was a real FBI agent.

Oh. My. God.

My mind was swimming. I'm not gonna lie. I was scared—terrified actually.

Was Bina Fink in cahoots with a dirty FBI agent? What the hell had I gotten myself into?

But as I continued poring over the background reports I ran on him, I noticed something. His home address was right down the street from where Bina Fink lived.

So I applied Occam's razor to this whole crazy scenario. I do that for a lot of things in my life now. Occam's razor is a scientific principle that posits: All things being equal, the simplest explanation is usually the most likely explanation.

What was the simplest explanation here? That Bina Fink was working with a dirty FBI agent to scam vulnerable people? Or that Bina Fink had asked her neighbor, who happened to be an FBI agent, to call and frighten me by telling him I was harassing her?

Then I noticed something else. This FBI agent had called me at 6:20 P.M. Los Angeles time, which meant it was 9:20 P.M. in Miami. And he was calling from his cellphone. Huh.

What are the chances that any law enforcement agent calling about a case for the first time would do it at 9:20 P.M. from their cellphone? No chance at all.

Also, on his voicemail, which I still have, and have shared with numerous law enforcement agencies by this point, he says, "I received a complaint from a young lady." Yet according to my background reports on both of them, Bina Fink was nearly ten years older than this guy. Why the hell was he referring to her as a young lady?

The more I thought about it, the more I realized the simplest and most likely explanation was that this guy was her neighbor. She had convinced him that I was bothering her and asked him to call me. He was referring to her as a "young lady" because he thought I didn't know who she was. And he was trying to tell a more convincing story. In other words, he was lying. He knew she was not a "young lady." She was sixty years old, for crying out loud. But he thought that by telling me she was, I would be more compelled to stop "harassing" her.

The fact that this guy was using the official office of the FBI and his capacity as an agent for personal and extremely petty business was troubling.

Anyway, the next day, I called this FBI agent back. And he was stunned. "People usually don't call me back," he stammered.

I thought to myself, "How many people are you calling on behalf of this goddamned con woman?"

He reiterated that a "young lady" had come into his office to file a report that I was harassing her and trying to steal her identity.

"And you made a call about this 'new case' the very next day from your cellphone at 9:20 P.M.?" I asked incredulously. "You work all your new cases with that kind of expediency?"

He chuckled uncomfortably.

"Look, I'm writing up a report," he said briskly.

"Can I get a copy of that report?" I asked.

"No. It's not public record. You can't," he said, his frustration apparent in his voice.

"So let me get this straight," I said. "You're filing a secret report on me based on a 'young lady' walking into your office and telling you that I'm harassing her and trying to steal her identity?"

"Look, just leave her alone is all I'm saying," he replied.

During that ten-minute conversation, I circled back again and again, asking for a copy of the report he was supposedly filing or a case number or anything like that. And he refused.

Huh.

The next day, I called the sheriff's deputy who had taken Carol's initial complaint and written up a report about Bina Fink. I told her what had happened and sent her the voicemail that the FBI agent had left me.

Her response, again, shocked the living hell out of me. "Oh yeah," she said matter-of-factly. "She uses that FBI guy to call people who complain about her all the time."

"And no one is doing anything about that?" I asked as my voice rose an octave.

"Not really. Thanks for letting us know, though," she said curtly and hung up.

I didn't know what to think. And I didn't know what to do next.

At that point Bina Fink worked for the office of the mayor of Broward County. Her job title was "administrative specialist." So she clearly had a lot of connections.

According to her LinkedIn profile (I love LinkedIn), Bina Fink is a "PR, Marketing, Media, Photojournalist." There's even a LinkedIn review of her "work" written by some guy who supposedly had professional dealings with her. It reads: "Bina is hands-down one of the most enjoyable people to be around. People are naturally more comfortable around her and she always creates a fun time no matter where she goes." Ironically, *that review* could apply to any professional con artist working today—especially the one who scammed me. Also, according to Bina Fink's profile on X (formerly Twitter), "Bina Fink Kohl of Weston, Florida is a correspondent for HollywoodTV. Bina is also a publicist to stars, charity and politicians for over 25 years." Regardless of how much she was embellishing about her various occupations, it was obvious to me now that she knew a lot of important people in South Florida.

After work and on the weekends, I started making calls on the Carol Porter case. Very quickly I uncovered a bunch of Bina Fink's other victims.

One guy told me he was undocumented, and Bina Fink had tricked him into believing she worked with a lawyer who could get him a green card for $2,500. So he gave her the money. Then he never saw her again. And as you can imagine, he never went to the police.

Another woman told me that after her son had been arrested Bina

Fink said she knew the judge in his case and could get him off for $8,500. But when the money changed hands, she never heard from Bina Fink again.

I heard from the daughter of a wealthy Fort Lauderdale widow who had hired Bina Fink to be her caregiver. Keep in mind, Bina Fink had no history whatsoever of working as a caregiver. Not only did Bina Fink scam this widow out of close to $15,000 by pretending to need money for her son's emergency heart surgery, but she surreptitiously tried to get the widow to change her power of attorney behind her daughter's back.

Four other victims I found were all musicians. Bina Fink portrayed herself to them as a mover and shaker in the music industry. She cleverly created blogs and websites and posted pictures of herself with famous people so that when these musicians googled her she'd appear to be what she said she was. She ended up scamming tens of thousands from those musicians. One of them posted this complaint about Bina Fink (maiden name Kohl) on the website ripoffreport.com:

> Bina F Kohl is a con artist who posses [*sic*] as an entertainment public relations person, who says has contacts in the music industry and that could get "meetings" with music executives to "help aspiring musicians and artists" to land a deal. I felt [fell] for her multiple lies and name dropping of artists, she always got in many entertainment events always saying she was the friend of so[me] big shot person. She knows the names of many people in the industry and what they do, she has study very well her lies so she can look believable. . . . DONT LET YOURSELF BE FOOLED BY THE PROFESSIONAL THIEF AND DELINQUENT.

I talked to another victim—well, the friend of another victim who did not want to come forward. This person told me that her friend, who worked as a nurse in a Broward County hospital, had given Bina Fink $10,000 to assist with adopting a baby from Haiti after the tragic earthquake there in 2010 that killed more than 222,000 people. Remember Red Flag #1 ("I Just Want to Help")? Well, Bina said she was friends with the president of Haiti and could help secure the adoption. But after the money changed hands, Bina Fink ghosted this nurse.

I also spoke to the son of another victim. This victim had died of a stroke. But his son told me how Bina Fink had gotten hired to work on his father's political campaign for judge in Broward County and had tricked his father out of $10,000 by pretending to be doing a transaction with a Florida congresswoman. Well, the victim also happened to be a smart attorney who sued Bina Fink in civil court and got a $10,000 judgment against her. But then tragically he died before he could collect.

A pattern began to emerge: Bina Fink's modus operandi. She basically would pretend to be whatever she thought people needed. Then, for a fee, she offered to give that to them. But once the money changed hands, she bolted.

So, after I uncovered all this evidence against Bina Fink, over the course of a few weeks, her case got assigned to a detective in the Economic Crimes Unit of the Broward County Sheriff's Office. That detective came out and interviewed Carol Porter in person several times for hours on end. And he issued subpoenas for bank records. But that was where it seemed to end.

I tried to make contact with this detective and he was not responsive. Regardless, though, I forwarded him the names and numbers and stories of all the victims and witnesses I had uncovered: people who were scammed out of tens of thousands of dollars by Bina Fink or people who witnessed her scams. I sent him about a dozen names and numbers in all.

To this day, it is unclear to me if this detective was grossly inept, cripplingly lackadaisical, or just coasting along until retirement. But one of the things that made me think he was grossly inept and bad at his job was the fact that he never subpoenaed any banks for security camera footage. Bank records, yes, security footage, no. There were dozens and dozens of times when Bina Fink accompanied Carol Porter to several

South Florida banks as she cashed checks to supposedly "pay the lawyer." Security camera footage showing Bina Fink standing with Carol at these banks would be extremely incriminating in light of all of the accusations and evidence against her. But here's the thing about banks. They don't keep that security camera footage indefinitely. Some hang on to it for three months or six months or nine months, but then it's deleted.

I'm not a cop, I'm not a lawyer, and I don't work for a bank. But I know that they have security cameras and that they only keep the footage for a few months.

And every police detective I've ever spent time with or interviewed has told me that the first thing they do as part of any investigation is subpoena security camera footage. It can make or break a case. The fact that this detective never did that is telling.

The detective also never subpoenaed the two bank tellers who witnessed Bina Fink scam Carol Porter and who pulled her aside to ask if she was okay on two separate occasions. He only ever called and emailed them. When they didn't respond, he just let it go, and let them go.

Here's the scary thing that happened next. Shortly after the detective started investigating Bina Fink, his entire department, the Economic Crimes Unit, was disbanded. He got reassigned to basically do security for high schools.

All of Bina Fink's victims are convinced that she is so powerful, and so politically connected, that she got the Economic Crimes Unit shut down because she's close enough with or has some dirt on the Broward County sheriff himself. Remember, the sheriff of any county is an elected official and extremely susceptible to public opinion—or blackmail. Or both.

At this point, the detective told Carol Porter that he was still working on her case, but he had to fit it in around his actual work schedule at various schools.

Over the next couple years, I went on to uncover even more victims of Bina Fink and sent them to this detective. I even discovered that Bina Fink's brokers took nearly a million dollars from Carol Porter were not incorporated as a brokerage firm when they took the money! They didn't incorporate until months later. I sent the detective all these documents from the Florida Secretary of State's Office that proved this. And his only answer to me was a two-word "thank-you" email.

Change of plans.

By now I had learned that publicity is like kryptonite to a con artist. The more you expose them, the less ability they have to scam other victims and evade the law.

So I pitched an exposé piece about Bina Fink to the local paper in South Florida, the *Sun Sentinel*. They assigned it to a reporter who did a story. This reporter interviewed both me and Carol at length. He was excited about his first draft of the story. I put him in touch with a bunch of other victims, and they're mentioned in his first draft. But before publication he called to tell me that his story had gotten "lawyered" and a lot of the juice had been taken out. That translated to taking out all the stories of the other victims. So his story came down to Bina Fink versus Carol Porter. I could tell he was upset about it.

"You don't know who you're dealing with," he told me. "She's a very well-connected woman. Be careful."

In a chilling twist, that reporter left the paper shortly after publication of that Bina Fink article. I heard from victims that Bina Fink was telling everyone she had gotten him fired.

Oh. It gets better.

In mid-2023, before the detective investigating Bina Fink actually retired, he submitted the case to the Broward State Attorney's Office. That's similar to the district attorney's office in other states and counties.

I waited a couple months, then reached out to the assistant state attorney assigned to the case. She told me they were still determining whether or not to charge Bina Fink with a crime.

Recently I came across a really disturbing picture on Facebook from around the time the criminal case against Bina Fink was kicked up to the Broward State Attorney's Office. It's a group picture of Bina Fink at a social event with the Broward state attorney himself. He happened to be the boss of the assistant state attorney who had the Bina Fink case on her desk trying to determine whether they should charge her for the crime of scamming Carol Porter.

I mean, public officials take pictures with "strangers" all the time at public events and it's certainly possible that the state attorney did not know who Bina Fink was at that point.

Of course, a more troubling read into that scenario is: You have the "well-connected" target of a criminal investigation and the man responsible for charging her with a crime mugging it up at a social event. I think that reeks of impropriety. Especially considering what happens next . . .

I AM WRITING THIS NOW IN OCTOBER 2024.

And you may not be too surprised to learn that the Broward state attorney has decided *not to prosecute* Bina Fink.

A real head-scratcher, right?

But make no mistake, she's still up to her old tricks. I just heard from three new victims.

This case is far from over. Stay tuned.

Queen of the Con III

Getting scammed out of close to $100,000 trying to help an "Irish heiress" claim her inheritance is still hard for me to admit. Each time I have to admit it, it makes me anxious. To this day, seeing these words on a page fills me with anger and regret. I have to talk myself down from the ledge I feel like jumping off of.

But it's important for you to understand that it took her four years to get that money out of me—four years of lies and manipulations. And while she was scamming me, she was scamming dozens of other people out of hundreds of thousands of dollars as well. This was in fact her full-time profession.

For a con artist like Mair Smyth, who's playing the long game, it takes relationship-building—and lots of it. During these sessions of relationship-building the red flags come out, but if you don't know what they look like you'll miss them. Like I did.

It was mid-June 2013, just past 8 P.M. on a super clear L.A. night with a thumbnail-shaped moon hanging low in the distance. We were sitting outside in the cool night air in our building's BBQ area—a private outdoor space for residents to socialize that was decked out with oversized barbecue grills and a couple dozen cushy chairs and lounges strewn about.

"Try some of this," Mair said, as she handed me a heavy embroidered cloth napkin concealing a piece of fresh-baked Irish soda bread.

We were sipping from giant cups of Irish tea that Mair had brought down from her apartment along with the Irish soda bread from her oven. We had only just met a few weeks earlier, yet I felt as if I had known this woman—this eccentric transplant from the Republic of Ireland—for my entire life.

And that was her plan.

"When I was a young girl, my gran would take me to the top of a bridge outside Belfast and teach me how to throw Molotov cocktails down on British soldiers," she haltingly admitted, while clutching her cup of tea.

This revelation shocked me and enthralled me at the same time. Mair said her family had IRA roots. The freaking Irish Republican Army! She said she'd been raised to hate the British, which kind of made sense to me—looking at it through that lens.

After all, I didn't know that much about Ireland.

Looking back, I can see that Mair's childhood story of throwing Molotov cocktails exemplified the con artist's Red Flag of Drama, Drama, Drama. It was meant to elicit sympathy and awe from me. And it worked.

Mair regaled me that night with stories of growing up on large Irish estates with servants at her family's beck and call.

"My cousins were the worst, though." She grimaced as she took another sip of tea. "When I was five years old, they convinced me that a giant bottle of five hundred Tylenol pills was actually candy. So one afternoon when no one was around, I ate the entire bottle of pills."

My eyes widened with shock.

"I was unconscious in a couple hours. I died that night," Mair insisted, looking off into the distance. "I saw God and the angels. It was so beautiful. They told me it's not my time yet. They said they heard my father's prayers begging them to spare my life. And they sent me back."

"Wow," I said. "I bet your cousins felt bad for tricking you after that."

"Not at all," Mair countered. "They've been terrorizing me for my entire life. Especially my cousin Fintan. And they all give no fucks about it."

This "drama, drama, drama" was just the beginning of the story—of "the con" really. Mair and her cousins in Ireland had an acrimonious relationship, and she was introducing me to that narrative. She would continue to elaborate on it over the years—resplendent with shocking details and dozens of crazy twists and turns.

I'd overhear phone conversations. I'd see pictures, text messages, and emails. I witnessed her family in Ireland do the most horrendous things to her. Or at least, I thought I did. I swore I did. It quickly became obvious to me that her family hated her and would stop at nothing until they destroyed her.

One night, she invited my husband and me up to her place for dinner. She made Irish stew. It smelled divine. The scent wafted into our nostrils as she opened her front door to greet us.

"I made a vegetarian version for you, Johnathan," Mair said and then winked at my husband. "But I made a beef version for the non-vegetarians!"

We all laughed.

It touched me that Mair had gone out of her way to accommodate my vegetarian diet. I felt like she really cared.

I'm not a vegetarian for health reasons or anything like that. I just don't believe in killing animals. I've been that way since I was a kid. My husband eats meat and that's fine. I'm not trying to force my beliefs on anyone. I'm a "live and let live" kinda guy.

As we stepped inside Mair's apartment we were taken aback. It was exquisitely decorated with an eclectic blend of contemporary and classical furniture: a baroque antique coffee table flanked by a couple of ultramodern sofas, a classic mahogany burl-top dining table with funky metal chairs.

"This has been in my family for generations," Mair said, pointing to a giant wrought-iron bar in the corner.

The bar really stood out. It was an opulent anachronism with spires and rails pointing in every direction. It looked like something you'd see on *Game of Thrones*, something fit for royalty. And it was stocked with every kind of booze imaginable.

"Whiskey?" Mair asked as she picked up a bottle of Bushmills thirty-year-old single malt.

"No, thanks. I'll just have a sparkling water," I replied. I don't drink that often. And when I do . . . it's to get hammered. It's a pesky facet of my "all-or-nothing" personality, which has been both a great help and a hindrance my entire life.

But I made a mental note that Bushmills thirty-year-old single malt was the type of whiskey Mair liked to drink. And about a year later when I was trying to figure out what to get her for her birthday, I went on a fool's errand looking for that particular bottle of Bushmills.

I was dumbfounded to learn it cost $2,200. So I decided on a $200 gift certificate for the Four Seasons Spa instead.

Mair clearly had a lot of money and came from even more.

"That's my great-great-uncle's signature right there!" Mair said, pointing to a framed document hanging on the wall in her living room.

It appeared really old. It was made out of parchment paper. The writing on it was antique-looking.

She said it was a copy of *the original* Irish Constitution. She said she was Irish royalty but asked me not to spread that around.

"Don't tell anyone at the Consulate of Ireland here in Los Angeles especially," she implored. "They can't know I'm here."

Again, I didn't know much about Ireland at the time. So this all made sense to me.

Irish royalty? Looking back, I want to punch myself in the face. How could I have been so stupid?

I have since learned that professional con artists quickly assess what your weaknesses are upon first meeting you: where your blind spots live, what your gaps in knowledge are. They use that intel to fashion a con custom-made for you.

The night when I had held that meeting in my living room for all the angry residents in our building to make a game plan for getting our pool back and then Mair had told everyone she was from Ireland, I remember confessing to her, "All I know about Ireland is from that Tom Cruise movie *Far and Away*." Movies have always been somewhat of a cultural touchstone for me, filling the gaps in my brain with "knowledge" that it was lacking from more scholarly sources.

"Wasn't Ireland a part of the UK at some point?" I asked, scratching my head. "I don't know much about Ireland." Mair must have exclaimed to herself with glee, "We got a live one here!" And I bet it only reinforced her decision to target me.

"Oh my God, this is so good!" I said after taking my first bite of

Mair's Irish stew. "What's the veggie meat made out of?" I was curious because it just tasted so . . . real.

"It's textured vegetable protein," Mair replied. "But I seasoned it with a ton of spices, so it tastes like meat."

Looking back, I am 100 percent certain that that putrid excuse for a human being fed me meat that night. I mean, I know what meat tastes like. And I know what textured vegetable protein tastes like. And while I was willing to overlook that glaring disparity and take Mair at her word that night, I now know for certain that nothing Mair ever told me was true.

Nothing.

I bet she got off on watching me, a devout vegetarian, happily and excitedly eating meat. I even asked for seconds! I bet it made her feel powerful that she could effortlessly manipulate me that way, just for fun.

I have since learned she is in fact *that evil.*

Most people think professional con artists are just in it for the money. But that's only partially true. The majority of the reason most con artists do what they do is . . . *power.*

Con artists get a godlike sense of power from manipulating people, the way puppeteers manipulate the strings on marionette dolls. Most times, the con artist's manipulations have nothing to do with financial gain. They just get a thrill from the control of it all. They enjoy creating fictitious scenarios and sketching out parts for their actors (victims) to play. Then they delight in it all unfolding before their eyes exactly the way they planned, like a movie they directed or a picture they painted. They are, in a sense, true artists.

But society is their canvas. And innocent unsuspecting victims like myself—their paint.

Tragically, that fake-meat stunt Mair pulled on me that night turned out to be the tiniest and most insignificant—and certainly the most inexpensive—of all her lies and manipulations she inundated me with during our "friendship."

◊◊◊

"My feet are killing me," Mair complained, as she slipped off her ridiculously high, high-heeled Jimmy Choos and then suddenly threw them across the room to where a row of six or seven other pairs of Jimmy Choos were strategically placed in the hallway.

FYI . . . Jimmy Choos are incredibly expensive designer shoes, costing between $1,000 and $2,000 a pair. Or more! There now appeared to be about $10,000 worth of Jimmy Choos in Mair's hallway alone. It certainly caught my attention.

"How many Jimmy Choos do you have?" I asked in amazement, expecting to hear ten or twelve as the answer.

"Hundreds!" she exclaimed. "It's all I wear."

"No way!" I said, shaking my head in response.

Mair quickly got up from her chair and grabbed me by the arm. She then walked me down the hall, into her bedroom, and into her walk-in closet. My husband followed close behind.

I was taken aback by what I saw. There were in fact hundreds of pairs of what appeared to be Jimmy Choos hanging on walls, on shelves, and on the floor.

Hundreds of pairs.

"There's like $250,000 worth of shoes alone in here," I said in disbelief.

"Oh, it's way more than that, I assure you." Mair cackled.

My husband and I turned to each other, silently exchanging the reaction, "I can't believe how rich this woman is!"

Looking back, I had no idea that we had just fallen for a variation of the classic Pig in a Poke con. Allow me to explain.

As far back as the 1500s, in England, scammers would pose as farmers selling "pigs in pokes"—pokes were what they called "bags" or "sacks" back in those days. Customers thought they were getting actual piglets, which they planned to take home, slaughter, and cook for dinner.

I know. That's why I'm a vegetarian.

The scammers would even have a real piglet in their hands to show prospective buyers what was contained in all the sacks and instill confidence in them. It wasn't until the money changed hands and the customers brought their "pig in a poke" home that they realized it wasn't a pig in a poke at all. It was a cat! Scammers put live cats in all those bags. And no one was the wiser until hours later when the scammers were long gone. At the time, cats were free and roaming everywhere, whereas pigs were considered food and had to be bought from farmers.

This Pig in Poke scam was so popular at the time, it made its way into English literature. "I wyll neuer bye the pyg in the poke / Thers many a foule pyg in a feyre cloke," wrote English writer John Heywood in 1555.

Incidentally, this Pig in a Poke con is also where the popular expression "Let the cat out of the bag" comes from. When customers of the pig in a poke got home, they literally let the cat out of the bag and realized the truth: There was no pig. They'd been scammed.

Mair said that the shoes she had on were Jimmy Choos and that the hundreds of other pairs she had in her giant walk-in closet were Jimmy Choos too. But I never actually checked. I just took her at her word, which I now know is worthless.

Looking back, I'm 100 percent certain I fell for a Pig in a Poke. Because if we apply Occam's razor, what's the most likely explanation? That an international con artist on the run from authorities and hiding out in my building had more than $250,000 worth of shoes in her closet that she'd been schlepping around from city to city and scam to scam? Or that she was using fake Jimmy Choos to help trick me into thinking she was a really wealthy woman—a necessary premise she needed to firmly establish in order to scam me down the line?

You be the judge.

◊◊◊

"He's the most brilliant man I ever met," Mair said, in a tone of adoration.

We were sitting in her living room now, having a heart-to-heart.

"I just can't believe I'm dating a married man with two kids. Teenagers," Mair contemplatively admitted.

The mood changed in that instant. You could feel the regret catch in her throat—as if she was on the verge of tears. I got the impression that she was in love with "Andrew the Politician" and that in a way it was tormenting her.

"I'm a devout Catholic," she explained. "I know sleeping with a married man is wrong. But I just can't help myself."

Mair said she had met Andrew eight years earlier at a glitzy fundraiser for his reelection campaign. The attraction was instant. And *animal*.

"He saw me across the room and made a beeline over to me," Mair said. "We talked all night. He was unhappy in his marriage, and his wife agreed that they could both see other people as long as they kept it secret and they didn't embarrass each other publicly."

Mair explained that Andrew needed to keep his wife "in the picture" and his family intact to win reelection and to continue his career in politics. So, going against her better judgment, she had agreed to be his secret mistress.

"God, how did I ever become the other woman?" Mair sighed rhetorically.

Are you picking up all the drama here?

You might be wondering at this point if Andrew the Politician was real or just one of her many made-up stories—and if he was real, just how much of Mair's eight-year backstory with him was true.

Well, the Politician was absolutely real. So was his extramarital affair with Mair. But 90 percent of everything Mair ever said about Andrew the Politician was just dramatic bullshit.

This is something most professional con artists do when they're scamming you. They'll take a real person or a real scenario that you are at least somewhat familiar with and they'll embellish, augment, make stuff up, and fabulize the hell out of it. It'll all ring true to you because you know the ground-floor facts. But then you unthinkingly extrapolate the rest and erroneously conform it to your cognitive map of that specific situation or person. So at that point, most of what you believe to be true about said person or situation is actually false. And it becomes the ultimate mind trick, because then you unwittingly help the con artist spread their lies and their stories by repeating the stuff they told you—and all of a sudden, other people in your social sphere think it's all true too. I mean, they have two sources for it, right? The con artist and you.

A few months later, I actually met Andrew the Politician.

I met him first at Mair's Christmas party in 2013. He showed up in a hella hideous holiday sweater vest, barely spoke to anyone, and left early. But a few months after that, my husband and I double-dated with Andrew and Mair. And he spoke for hours.

Andrew was in his sixties (Mair was forty-four at the time). He was kind of short, maybe five foot five or six. But he was handsome, with graying hair and kind eyes.

"Remember, Andrew? This was the fish that kept swimming under our bungalow!" Mair said, laughing while showing my husband and me a picture on her phone from her and Andrew's recent vacation in Tahiti. They had stayed in a thatched bungalow suspended over the Pacific Ocean on large wooden stilts. And the same giant fish kept swimming by so many times during the week they were there, Mair snapped a picture of it.

"That fucking fish!" Mair said laughing with Andrew. They were gazing at each other like lovers with a secret.

We were sitting in our building's BBQ area and Mair had made a dinner for us. It was a *feast*. I was taken aback by the grandeur of it all. There was lobster and steak. Salmon. Stuffed mushrooms. Corned beef and cabbage. Vegetable casserole. Mac and cheese. Shepherd's pie. Bread pudding. Cheesecake. Fudge. Mair made *so much* food; it was obvious this double date with Andrew was important to her.

"My gran taught me how to make shepherd's pie when I was seven years old," Mair said with a nostalgic smile on her face.

Mair talked about Ireland a lot that evening. Andrew chimed in every now and then with stories from the time he'd visited Ireland years earlier, before meeting Mair.

And even though at this point I believed Andrew was throwing the weight of his prestigious and powerful law firm behind our efforts to get the pool back, I never once asked him about it at dinner that night. I mean, Mair had already shown me dozens of emails and text messages from Andrew about what he was doing to help our pool situation, so I knew negotiations were going well and in our favor. And since Andrew was helping us—for no charge—I didn't want to bring up "work" talk during a social visit.

So I just made polite conversation. Looking back, that polite conversation was *exactly* what Mair was counting on.

The truth of the matter was, Andrew never had the slightest clue that our pool had been taken away. Nor was he or his firm involved in any way with our efforts to get it back. Nor had he ever sued our building in the past for any reason whatsoever—though that night in my living room when I had gotten all the angry residents together Mair had told us he had. And all those emails and texts Mair had shown me from Andrew were fake. They all came from email and texting accounts she had created online.

It turned out, Andrew was an estate planning attorney. And Mair had led Andrew to believe that she and I had been best friends for the past twenty years. Of course, at any point during dinner I could have said something or Andrew could have said something that completely contradicted the stories Mair had told each of us about the other. But we never did. We just made polite conversation.

Four years later I'd learn that Andrew was one of Mair's biggest victims. Turns out, she was scamming us both.

This "mingling victims" strategy was one Mair would use again and again over the course of our friendship. I met all kinds of people through Mair that way. I had no idea that she was scamming them while she was scamming me. She was using them to validate a part of her story to me while using me to validate a part of her story to them. She'd introduce me to some of them as "that producer I told you about from *Shark Tank*." And then try to scam them by claiming she can get them on the show. Mair was a ballsy risk-taker, to be sure. And she was apparently an expert in human psychology and human behavior, because she was 100 percent correct in her assumption: Strangers who meet one another for the first time in a social setting will only ever make *polite conversation*.

At no point did any of us think to compare the origin stories Mair had given us all about herself—which would have no doubt exposed her lies. Because *that* would have been *rude*.

There were times, though, when Mair would go out of her way to keep certain victims separate from one another.

Remember Sherry the strip club manager? She was one of the outspoken neighbors who came to the meeting I held to get the pool back that night in May 2013. Sherry and I kind of became friends after that meeting. Mair and Sherry became friends as well, and sometimes we'd all hang out together.

But then suddenly Mair started telling me scary stuff about Sherry, who I knew was originally from Canada. Mair said that Sherry and her husband were on the run from police in Canada because they were wanted for murder.

Mair was waving not only the Red Flag of Drama, Drama, Drama but also the Red Flag of Isolation, because after hearing this, I avoided Sherry at all costs. I was convinced she was a murderer on the run. When I'd see her in our building's parking garage, I'd walk the other way.

Yet I had no idea that Sherry was also avoiding me. Unbeknownst to me at the time, Mair was telling Sherry that I was mentally ill and unstable and violent. I came to find out later that Sherry was scared of me too.

So Mair isolated both of us from each other. Then she scammed each of us with different stories, knowing full well we would never hang out again to compare notes about what she was saying.

Mair got $5,000 out of Sherry by telling her she had borrowed it from me and didn't have it at the moment to pay me back. She said I was losing my shit and having psychotic episodes because I needed that money to pay rent. I was so desperate for that money I was flying into rages and breaking things in our apartment.

Drama, Drama, Drama.

So, Sherry loaned Mair the $5,000 to pay me back. Meanwhile, Mair was scamming me out of tens of thousands of dollars in ways you will soon learn about.

Isolation is a trick con artists use a lot. Sadly, it's human nature to believe the worst about other people, especially people we don't know very well. And lies are always interesting and compelling anyway. So they spread fast and wide. And the truth? Not so much.

Hence the expression: A lie can make it halfway around the world before the truth can even get its pants on. And FYI: If you go searching for the origin of that quote, you'll quickly disappear into a labyrinth where the likes of Winston Churchill, Mark Twain, and Confucius are duking it out for the posthumous accolade. It's probably another con. But I digress.

6. RED FLAG #5: "I'M BETTER THAN YOU"

WHEN YOU HIRE A PROFESSIONAL TO DO SOMETHING—ANYTHING—YOU NATURALLY defer to them. Whether it's an accountant or a lawyer or a doctor doesn't matter. You figure they're the "expert." They know way more than you do about this particular thing that you hired them for. So you're going to do what they say to do.

For all intents and purposes, these people are better than you at knowing what deduction you qualify for on your taxes or what legal argument you should use to get a court case dismissed or what bone in your finger is fractured on the basis of the X-ray they're reading. These experts, these professionals, they're better than you—in these instances. So you'll pretty much believe what they say, and you'll trust them implicitly.

Professional con artists know all of this better than most, and they use it against their marks with tremendous success. Good con artists need their victims to believe that they're better than them. They need their victims' trust, admiration, and belief in them to succeed in their scams.

"I just can't get over this. I cannot let go. I cannot move on," sixty-nine-year-old Carmen Hereter haltingly confessed to me on a call from her home in Puerto Rico.

I'd been talking to Carmen for four years at this point. She had gotten scammed out of $850,000 by a man she'd known her whole life, a man she loved, a man she would have sworn was a good and noble person. A husband. A father. A sixty-two-year-old man by the name of Wendell Pfeffer. He was in fact Carmen's cousin—the son of her beloved aunt and uncle. They had grown up together.

But sifting through the wreckage of what had transpired in late 2018, Carmen now realized that her cousin Wendell was not a good and noble person at all. In reality, he was an unscrupulous wolf in sheep's clothing. He scammed or tried to scam everyone he ever knew with a compelling story, a firm handshake, and a trusting smile. And for many years he got away with his blatant theft because his victims weren't going public. They weren't sharing what Wendell did to them with anyone—which ultimately enabled Wendell to scam Carmen and many others.

To successfully steal millions of dollars from dozens of victims all over the world, Wendell convinced everyone in his sphere that when it came to finance and investing he was better than them. He had the Midas touch. He was a baller, a big shot, a rainmaker.

Of course, he was none of those things. But he appeared to be. And we all get taken in by appearances, right? The one thing getting conned has solidified for me and I hope this book solidifies for you is: Seldom is anything ever what it first appears to be.

You need to go deeper than appearances. You need to dig. You need to question everything all the time. You need to check and double-check and triple-check. You need to *pretend* to trust, but then painstakingly verify, even at the risk of appearing rude or untrusting.

As a teenager growing up in South Florida in the 1970s, Wendell was a bright student, excelling in English and math. He went on to attend Tulane University and graduated with a degree in computer engineering—landing a job with IBM straight out of college. He was thought of as a brilliant guy. "I think he speaks four or five languages," Carmen said.

Looking back, though, it's obvious that Wendell Pfeffer was meticulously curating the perception of being thought of as a "brilliant guy." And unbeknownst to everyone, he was weaponizing it.

He'd eventually go on to marry the daughter of a mega-wealthy family from Brazil. You know what language they speak in Brazil? Portuguese—which also happens to be one of the four or five languages Wendell speaks. In no time, Wendell had cozied up to his new father-in-law, who was apparently so impressed with him that he gave Wendell one of his multi-million-dollar beverage companies to run.

Not surprisingly, news of Wendell's meteoric rise—personal and professional—spread fast to family and friends far and wide.

"My brother was that kind of a guy. He always was looking to make money. And that's what I knew him as back then," confessed Wendell's sister Karen, who recounted a time back in the 1980s when Wendell had tried to hoodwink her into buying his leased BMW (that he was in the process of returning) for a premium price.

"So I call the auto broker up and Wendell is in my office and I have her on speakerphone and I tell her the price that my brother wants to give me, and she's like, 'Wendell, you're not trying to make money off your sister, are you?' And I just looked at him and I said, 'Really, Wendell?'"

While occurrences like these were certainly troubling, no one knew the heartless psychopathy they were dealing with until years later.

So once Wendell was running that huge beverage company for his in-laws in Brazil, he lived part-time there and part-time in Miami, where he and his wife bought a $20 million mansion on the water as an opulent pied-à-terre. It was a glittering showpiece, really. That mansion became the physical evidence Wendell used to convince people of his profound wealth and financial acumen. And boy, did it work well.

Wendell's wife, however, had no idea that he was robbing her and her family blind—allegedly stealing millions of dollars from his in-laws and the company they'd put him in charge of. He'd become a real expert at deftly moving money around; robbing Peter to pay Paul, while keeping all his plates spinning in the air flawlessly—all the while giving the impression of being an investing whiz making millions of dollars. To further that end, he invited family members and other "marks" to his ten-thousand-square-foot Miami mansion on the water. And their eyes popped out of their heads.

"It was a beautiful house," Karen said. "It was actually showcased in *Architectural Digest*."

And it was a brilliant prop when it came to making investors feel comfortable enough to fork over millions of dollars to Wendell Pfeffer. I mean, obviously any man who can afford a house like that must know how to make some serious dough, right?

A couple years later, Wendell called up his cousin Carmen who was living in Puerto Rico and told her he was flying in to invest a few million dollars in real estate on the island and he wanted to visit her while he was there—a family visit, just to say hi and catch up. At this point, Carmen earnestly believed Wendell to be a wealthy investing oracle with powerful connections in South America, Miami, and all over the United States.

So Wendell flew to Puerto Rico and hired a real estate agent to show him dozens of multi-million-dollar properties. He invited his cousin Carmen along on some of these mansion-hunting expeditions. And she was inordinately impressed. Who wouldn't be?

The truth of the matter was: Wendell had no intention of buying any real estate in Puerto Rico. I mean, anybody can get a realtor to show them property. It doesn't cost a thing. Wendell's search for high-dollar Puerto Rican real estate to invest in was all just an elaborate ruse he used to impress Carmen. And it worked really well. Carmen was beyond impressed. She'd always known her cousin Wendall was a brilliant man—a mover and shaker, a wealth maker. And here she was witnessing it all unfold in real time. Or so she thought.

At some point, Wendell pretended to take pity on Carmen. She was approaching seventy years old and living on the money she and her husband had saved up their whole lives. Her husband had recently been diagnosed with Parkinson's, and money was tight. So Wendell offered his cousin Carmen a lifeline.

Wendell confided in Carmen, in a top-secret kind of way, that he'd gotten a huge contract with AT&T to expand their footprint in the Caribbean and Central America. They planned to open hundreds of AT&T stores and sell millions of dollars' worth of merchandise. Early investors could double and even triple their money very quickly.

"You'd be able to afford the best doctors," Wendell told her, callously playing on her husband's Parkinson's diagnosis.

It was a potent pitch. And Wendell had elaborate and official-looking documentation to back up everything he was saying: PowerPoint presentations, financial records, permits from various countries corroborating all the new AT&T stores' plans to break ground in the near future. Carmen never suspected for a second that it was all fake—every document, every record, every factoid in Wendell's PowerPoint. Fake. Fake. Fake.

After all, in Carmen's mind, Wendall was a millionaire with a well-known reputation for making people a lot of money. Carmen had seen his $20 million mansion in Miami with her own eyes. She knew the kinds of circles he ran in. And here he was now, offering her the investment opportunity of a lifetime—out of the kindness of his heart. It was abundantly clear to Carmen that Wendell was just *better than her* when it came to finances and investing. He was a moneymaking dynamo. Besides, he was family. So she trusted him.

Carmen gathered up all the money she had and all the money she could get her hands on from friends and neighbors. In all, she gave Wendell $850,000 to invest in this purported AT&T expansion into the Caribbean and Central America. She was excited and hopeful about the future. With the millions she'd be making on this deal, she could easily care for her infirmed husband and herself for the rest of their lives. In that moment, Carmen thought Wendell was a godsend, a true angel from heaven.

And then the Devil revealed himself—slowly at first. But as the months ticked by it began to dawn on Carmen that not only would she not be making millions of dollars on her $850,000 investment, but she'd never see any of that $850,000 ever again.

The first sign that something was wrong came at the ninety-day mark. It was then that Carmen was supposed to receive the first portion of her investment back. That was the deal. That's what was clearly stipulated in the agreement she signed. But ninety days came and went and nothing. So Carmen called Wendell and got his voicemail. She texted him, called his office and his home, emailed him. Wendell eventually replied in a text that he was traveling. He apologized for the inconvenience and promised to make payment in the next few days. When that didn't happen, he said it would be in the next few weeks. And when that didn't happen, Carmen started panicking.

"Could this all have been a trick to take my money?" Carmen thought to herself.

At this point, Carmen started making phone calls. She talked to Wendell's sister Karen, who told her Wendell had just scammed an old girlfriend out of more than $80,000. Carmen called Wendell's now ex-wife in Brazil and learned that Wendell had scammed her and her entire family out of millions of dollars. That was the reason she had divorced him—she had figured out her husband, Wendell, was a con artist and left him then and there. Carmen also learned that Wendell had scammed his own children, who later insisted on changing their last name because they wanted nothing to do with their father anymore.

So this is the teachable moment I want to point out here. Yes, hindsight is 20/20. I know. But if Carmen had made those phone calls to Wendell's sister and his ex-wife *before* she invested, she never would have given him a single dime. And the same applies to my own experience. If I had started calling around to people, especially people Mair told me to stay away from, I would have immediately figured out that she was telling different stories to different people, and I would have ended our friendship before ever giving her any money either.

The only reason Carmen and I—and every victim of every con artist—never made those kinds of phone calls before any money changed hands is: We didn't want to appear rude or disrespectful. And *that* is a deceptively powerful motivator if you think about it.

I remember watching *The Oprah Winfrey Show* years ago when Oprah was interviewing a rape victim who had been assaulted on an elevator. This woman revealed that when the elevator doors opened and she saw the guy, who would turn out to be her rapist, standing inside, she immediately felt uneasy and had the impulse to not get on that elevator. She wanted to turn around and walk away. Actually, she wanted to run. But she never acted on those feelings because "I didn't want to appear rude," she said.

If you want to avoid being the victim of a con artist, you need to banish that fear completely. You can always apologize later for appearing rude. It's an easy trespass to forgive. But you can never get your money or peace of mind back if you fall hook, line, and sinker for a sophisticated scammer's con.

As the months passed, Karen and Carmen started researching con artists to try and figure out what the hell they were dealing with. And they reached out to me for advice.

"What should we do?" they asked. "Now that we know he's a con artist, how can we get him?"

I prefaced my response by saying, "I'm not a lawyer. I don't work in law enforcement. I'm just a guy who managed to put his con artist in jail even after police turned me away. And I'm happy to share my experience with you. But I'm not telling you what to do. I'm not advising you in any way, shape, or form."

They understood.

I went on to tell them that the greatest weapon I had used against Mair, and the reason she was ultimately convicted by a jury of her peers and sentenced to five years behind bars for scamming me, was a blog I started. I posted the Irish heiress's picture there. Under that picture, I posted the complicated and sprawling story of how she had scammed me. And I warned people not to give her money for any reason whatsoever. I asked anyone reading that blog that if they had been scammed by Mair to give me a call.

As the weeks rolled by, I started getting contacted by a bunch of victims who had found my blog while googling her legal name: Marianne Smyth. I heard from people she had scammed in California, New York, Maine, Michigan, Florida, and Tennessee, and all the way across the Atlantic in Northern Ireland! That blog enabled me to build a compelling criminal case against the Irish heiress that the police, as hard as they tried (and it felt like they tried *really* hard), could not ignore.

"We'll start a blog!" Carmen exclaimed, without hesitation.

But I warned her. When I started my blog, I was contacted by a well-meaning big-time Los Angeles attorney who was trying to help me, and he advised me to take the blog down immediately.

"You can't call Mair a liar and a con artist on your blog," this big-time attorney admonished. "She'll sue you for libel and slander."

"Sue me?" I said quizzically. "I would welcome the opportunity to flesh all this out in a courtroom."

The only defense for libel and slander is truth. For Mair to success-fully win a libel or slander case against me, she would have to prove that I was lying, that I was making everything up. And I most certainly was not. So I thanked that attorney for his advice but replied, "I'm not tak-ing the blog down. Ever." And it is still up to this day. Just google "Marianne Smyth" and see for yourself.

So Carmen started a blog of her own with pictures of Wendell and the story of how he had scammed her. And in no time, she began to hear from other victims of Wendell from all over the world.

Carmen also went to the police and the FBI. She started building a compelling criminal case against Wendell. As the years passed she'd check in with me from time to time and we'd strategize about what to do next.

Without revealing anything that might compromise the case, I can tell you that Wendell fled to Spain to avoid prosecution and was able to trick his way into obtaining Spanish citizenship under a new name. Sadly, extradition arrangements between Spain and the United States are not great.

But on the upside, Wendell's accomplice in that AT&T scam, a woman named Luz Elvira Escobar de Salcedo, who helped Wendell scam Carmen and many others, was recently arrested in Florida and charged with fraud. A trial date is still pending.

This case is not over.

Queen of the Con IV

In life I have learned that you can't really know what something will feel like until you're actually feeling it. You can't know what something will be like until you're actually being it. You can't know what the red flags are for anything, especially a sophisticated con artist in your midst, until you have missed them all when they first presented themselves—and now you're looking back at your life scratching your head wondering, "How the hell did I fall for that?"

Welcome to my world.

Mair Smyth waved the "I'm Better Than You" flag at me many times in many ways, large and small, though I hesitate to use the word *small* because it's a misleading word. *Small* connotes tiny, insignificant, unimportant. And in the world of cons, *small things* that you're inclined to instinctually overlook can cost you your life savings. Con artists use a lot of small things to build a very big thing, aka the scam, to successfully separate you from your money. So in reality there's no such thing as a *small thing* because all the small things are connected and artfully combined to create the big thing that you will never see coming until it's too late.

If you want to avoid getting scammed, you need to pay close attention to all the *small things*.

This chapter is about all the small things that Mair said and did that made me truly believe she was better than me. Better than everyone really, in every way: more thoughtful, more kind, more caring, more loving, more giving, more talented.

"I'm flying out tomorrow, first class," Mair said to me in July of 2013. We were sitting outside in our building's plaza area that night sipping the Irish tea Mair had brought down from her apartment, as was her wont. I had known Mair for a couple months by then, and I was, if I'm being totally honest, dazzled by her.

Mair said she was flying out to the Pacific Islands to do surprise inspections on all their five-star hotels to make sure they were up to snuff. She said the president of French Polynesia himself, Gaston Flosse, personally flew her out first-class every couple of months and put her up in these fancy hotels because Mair was the number-one seller of luxury vacations to the Pacific Islands in the United States and she was personally responsible for infusing their economy with millions of dollars every year. The president was eternally grateful to her. He relied on her ability and her instincts, and he figured she could better sell even more luxury vacations to the Pacific Islands if she experienced them herself.

Now that is a detailed story, right? But *none* of it was true.

The only reason Mair told me that story was to impress me. She wanted me to think that she was better than me and that I should look up to her and admire her. And it worked. I did.

The truth of the matter was so far from the stories Mair was telling me that it's almost comical. Yes, Mair worked for a high-end travel agency selling luxury vacations to the Pacific Islands. That part was true. But she was not the number-one seller of vacations to the Pacific Islands at all. And the president of French Polynesia was not flying her out every couple months to do surprise inspections on their five-star hotels. He didn't even know who she was.

The truth of the matter was that between 2014 and 2016 Mair was arrested, charged, and convicted of stealing more than $200,000 from that very travel agency. The way she stole the money was by creating a PayPal account using the name of the travel agency and then taking every seventh or eighth client's payment into her own account for a couple years straight. Then she'd forge all the paperwork internally to cover her tracks. And no one noticed. No one!

The *only* reason she got caught was because Mair herself went on vacation! She was not in the office when a repeat client of hers called to book another vacation with her. So one of her co-workers took the call. And when the client asked, "Can I pay with PayPal like last time?" Mair's co-worker responded, "I'm sorry but we don't take PayPal." And the jig was up.

The company quickly called the police. They set up a sting operation and caught Mair red-handed. But sadly, she got off light—serving only thirty days in jail. Welcome to the criminal justice system, where nonviolent crimes are almost treated like a parking ticket. Or an expired tag. Or really—no crime at all.

Do you want to know how Mair explained her sudden thirty-day absence—because she went to jail—to the guy she was dating at the time?

You just can't make this stuff up. Correction: Only a professional con artist can make this stuff up.

Mair told the guy she was dating/scamming, a Newport Beach engineer named Bob (after she had moved on from scamming the Politician), that her uncle in Ireland, a high-placed bishop in the Catholic Church over there, had suddenly died. She was flying over for the funeral—*that the Pope himself would be officiating*—and she was going to observe a month-long period of silence and mourning. So she'd be turning off her cellphone and would be unreachable for a month.

Incredible!

As much as what Mair did to me disgusts and angers me, I can't help but be impressed by—and even morbidly envious of—her inexhaustible creativity. As a TV producer, a writer, and a podcaster, I wish I had that level of creative fecundity.

It was around this time when she was dating that Newport Beach engineer named Bob that I figured out she was scamming me and I started gathering evidence. I met with Bob after he found my blog, and I saved him from adding her name to the titles of his homes. And he became one of the star witnesses in my criminal case against her.

More on that in a later chapter. Back to the red flag at hand.

Mair was constantly showing me that she was better than me by using the time-honored craft of storytelling. The stories she'd tell were not at all true, but they advanced the "I'm better than you" narrative effectively.

For instance, Mair was always raising money for charity: for underprivileged kids, for ALS, for cancer. Mair truly appeared to be a tireless supporter of the less fortunate and of anyone in need. A couple years into our friendship she created a GoFundMe page and raised nearly $17,000 for cystic fibrosis in the name of her daughter, Courtney, who had died of that disease years earlier.

All of these stories served to reinforce my belief that Mair was better than me. After all, I was working long hours trying to pay rent and keep my head above water living in Los Angeles. *It's really expensive to live here.* And I didn't have the bandwidth or the resources or the time to plunge myself into charitable pursuits. But I profoundly admired Mair for seeming to do what I could not.

I had no idea that all this money she was raising, she was actually stealing. She wasn't donating anything to anyone.

And while Courtney had died of cystic fibrosis years earlier, Courtney wasn't really Mair's daughter. I mean she was—biologically. But courts took Courtney from Mair shortly after she was born and declared Mair an unfit mother. So Courtney was not in Mair's life. But that didn't stop Mair from using the tragic death of a daughter she never raised to scam nearly $17,000 out of well-intentioned people in Los Angeles—while giving Mair the appearance of *being better than me.*

And FYI, once I figured out this GoFundMe scam, I contacted them and got Mair's GoFundMe page taken down. Then I contacted the police and the Cystic Fibrosis Foundation. And I was taken aback by how unfazed they all seemed to be by this blatant fraud. That was my take anyway. The police told me that since I was not the victim in this case, the Cystic Fibrosis Foundation and/or GoFundMe would need to contact them. GoFundMe assured me they'd "look into it." And the Cystic Fibrosis Foundation told me they were not going to file a police report because they felt they could not prove Mair was raising money for them specifically—though they admitted to me that Mair did copy and paste language from their website onto her bogus GoFundMe page *verbatim.* And for the record, *not a single dollar from that scam was returned to any of the victims who donated.* And I personally escorted two of those victims to the LAPD to file their own police reports. And not a single officer/detective/agent from the LAPD ever called them in for questioning to pursue the case.

This is how and why sophisticated con artists can get so far for so long. The system just doesn't seem to care. Shame on them.

Anyway, Mair had another daughter, Chelsea, whom she actually did raise. Well, not so much "raise" as horrendously abuse and use in her scams.

Early in our friendship Mair told me that when she was pregnant with Chelsea, doctors told her that she needed to get an abortion because giving birth to Chelsea would kill her.

"But I just refused!" Mair said to me that day with tears in her eyes.

God, she was so good at tearing up at a moment's notice.

"I'm a devout Catholic, and I will never get an abortion for any reason." Those tears were streaming down her face at this point.

"If I'm meant to die giving life to my baby, then so bloody be it." Mair issued with a tiny hint of an Irish lilt.

And the Oscar goes to . . .

Again. None of what she was *tearfully* saying was true. But I have to admit, the tears really sold it.

Never for a second did I think she was making it all up. And it certainly reinforced the "I'm better than you" narrative. I mean, how can you not admire a woman who was willing to give her life so that her daughter could be born?

About a year into our friendship, I learned that Mair had become close friends with the secretary of the married politician she was dating—well, *scamming* really. It appeared to me that she really loved this politician and he loved her—as much as any married man with kids could love a mistress.

But unbeknownst to the Politician, Mair was forging a close friendship with his secretary. We'll call her Cindy (not her real name).

Mair would meet Cindy for secret brunches behind the Politician's back. They'd go to baseball games and concerts together. Cindy felt honored that a wealthy Irish heiress like Mair, such an important person of nobility, wanted to be friends with her.

In fact, in an email that I was able to get my hands on, an email from the Politician's secretary to Mair, the secretary gushes: "You're quite the amazing person. . . . And do all you do flawlessly and still have enough time for someone like me? It truly is a privilege and an honor."

What the secretary did not realize at the time was that Mair was using her, drilling her for information about the Politician that Mair would then use to scam the Politician out of hundreds of thousands of dollars in myriad ways.

And do you think for a second the Politician reported Mair to the police?

But I'm getting ahead of myself.

I'm bringing up Cindy the secretary here to explain that when Cindy's husband suddenly died of a heart attack, Mair became Cindy's right hand, and her left hand.

Mair and I were best friends at the time, but I did not see her for a couple months. She sort of just moved into Cindy's house to help with her grief. Every time I'd call her she'd tell me she was at Cindy's house assisting with funeral arrangements. Or she was at Cindy's house helping her settle her deceased husband's affairs. Or she was staying with Cindy until her house sold. Yes! Mair helped Cindy put her five-bedroom house on the market and actually got it sold.

I was so impressed by Mair's apparent selflessness in Cindy's time of need. What a truly beautiful human being she appeared to be. It moved me, and it really made me feel that yes, Mair was better than me. By a lot.

I have since learned that Mair wasn't actually helping Cindy at all. She was scamming her—robbing her blind by taking cruel advantage of her husband's sudden death.

You know how easy it is to take advantage of a grieving widow if she thinks you're her best friend? Ask Mair. She does.

The Politician and I have discussed this whole situation at length. And while he does not know exactly how much money Mair tricked out of Cindy, he figures it must be a lot because "she refuses to talk about it."

7. RED FLAG #6: TECHNOLOGY

IN THIS DAY AND AGE, IT SHOULD COME AS NO SURPRISE THAT PROFESSIONAL CON ART-ists rely heavily on technology. I mean, we all do if you think about it. So that's not a red flag in and of itself. That's just a fact of life.

But where technology becomes a red flag is when you've already witnessed some or all of the five previous red flags in action with a new person in your life:

Red Flag #1—Out of the blue, they just really want to help you.

Red Flag #2—They are too kind, too quick.

Red Flag #3—There's suddenly a lot of drama surrounding them.

Red Flag #4—They're trying to isolate you from other people.

Red Flag #5—They want you to believe they're better than you.

If any of these five red flags are present in a person you recently met, *and* they're demonstrating a heavy reliance on technology to "sell" their stories to you—well, then, you just spotted Red Flag #6: Technology.

And what do I mean by a heavy reliance on technology to "sell" their stories to you? I mean, they are constantly showing you emails and texts to demonstrate what someone said or did; the story they're laying out is often happening over the phone; or they're frequently pointing you to documents or websites on their computer (which can all be easily and convincingly photoshopped or otherwise faked) to back up the narrative they're unpacking for you.

Every now and then I come across a con artist who takes the Red Flag of Technology to the next level. One such con artist is Lizzie Mulder.

How Lizzie Mulder used technology to scam her circle of friends and associates out of close to $2 million may seem unbelievable. But it happened, and it's happening every day because the world is full of Lizzie Mulders. So pay close attention now to how people like this can scam you.

Lizzie Mulder grew up in Orange County, California, in the 1980s and '90s. "She was, I don't want to say the ugly duckling, but she always tried to fit in, and she just never did," said a woman I spoke to who graduated from Dana Hills High with Lizzie in 2001 but does not want to be identified.

It's entirely possible that Lizzie's many unsuccessful attempts "to fit in" with the other kids at school when she was a teenager are one of the reasons she became a con artist later in life. All of her friends from that era were much wealthier than she was, lived in nicer homes than she did, and wore designer clothes and drove flashy cars. They all possessed the kinds of accoutrements that Lizzie's family could not afford.

So when Lizzie became an adult, she started lying to attain all the things she had never had as a kid. Then she calculatedly circled back to the classmates she'd known in high school so she could show off to them. Then she conned them all out of millions of dollars using technology.

In 2013 Lizzie Mulder flew to Italy to attend the wedding of a high school friend. She knew that a bunch of people she'd grown up with would be there, people she hadn't seen since high school. Lizzie saw this wedding, held on the gorgeous Amalfi Coast, as an opportunity to recast herself from downtrodden ugly duckling to radiant and uber successful swan. She had had plastic surgery and lost weight. And when she arrived at the reception, her hair, makeup, and wardrobe were red-carpet ready. As Lizzie circulated and mingled that night, she dazzled the crowd with her glamour and sophistication. When asked by her former classmates, most of whom she hadn't seen for more than a decade, what she did for a living, she looked them dead in the eyes, smiled, and said, "I'm a CPA. I have my own accounting business now."

Lizzie did in fact have her own accounting business, Mulder Financial. She had an office overlooking the ocean in opulent Laguna Beach, with an accounting degree from prestigious Pepperdine University hanging on her wall.

But that degree was fake. As was her career. Lizzie was not a CPA, and she had never gone to Pepperdine. In fact, she had never even graduated from college—any college. But she pretended to be all those things very convincingly—she was in her early thirties and already quite the sophisticated con woman, with a roster of clients she'd been robbing blind for years. And they had no idea. When it came to stealing money and then hiding her theft in plain sight, Lizzie was a master.

"Lizzie bragged about her education, where she did her undergrad and where she did her master's program. She told us often about how she passed the CPA test on the very first try. But as you know, Lizzie didn't graduate from college. She has zero credentials. She's a self-taught con artist," said Lauren Scaccia, one of Lizzie's many victims.

Lauren hadn't seen Lizzie Mulder since high school when she bumped into her at that wedding in Italy. She was impressed by what she saw. Lizzie had seemingly morphed into an entirely new person. She was outgoing, fun, and extremely gregarious. After that wedding, Lauren and Lizzie quickly became good friends—best friends really. And as fate would have it, Lauren and her business partner Geneva Mendosa were planning to open a high-end hair salon in tony Newport Beach, a stone's throw from where Lizzie lived and worked in Laguna Beach. Suddenly Lizzie offered to be their CPA for free. Well, in exchange for doing Lizzie's hair.

"You need somebody you can trust. You can't afford me, but that's okay. I'll take care of you guys," Lizzie said, as Lauren recalls.

Now that's Red Flag #1 right there: "I Just Want to Help."

She wasn't exactly a stranger, but she hadn't been in Lauren's life before except as a distant acquaintance in high school. Then suddenly she'd appeared at that wedding in Italy and she'd become a best friend in no time flat. Lizzie just wanted to help Lauren and her business partner—seemingly out of the kindness of her heart.

"She always let you know how great she was, how much money she made," recalled Lauren's business partner Geneva Mendosa when we spoke about Lizzie back in 2022. And that's Red Flag #5 right there ("I'm Better Than You"). "Lizzie made sure that we knew how lucky we were to have her in our lives. And we felt it," Geneva added.

So Lizzie took over the finances for Lauren and Geneva's new salon. She became their de facto CFO. She did their taxes, handled their payroll, paid their rent, electricity, and water. In fact, every dollar coming into the salon went into a bank account controlled by Lizzie Mulder.

And as the weeks passed, the drama began. Crazy, crazy drama. All of a sudden, the electricity in the salon went out while the place was packed with clients getting their hair done. It appeared the light bill had not been paid. But a little later, in a bizarre twist, the power company called Geneva and said actually that was a mistake—the light bill had been paid.

Then more drama. Every two weeks, all of the employees who had signed up for direct deposit never got their paychecks. Lizzie blamed a technical glitch with the direct deposit company. She showed Lauren and Geneva emails corroborating what she was telling them.

"It was so chaotic every two weeks. It gave me so much anxiety even going to work," Geneva told me.

And this is Red Flag #3: Drama, Drama, Drama.

At one point, Lauren and Geneva found out that they hadn't paid rent or their vendors or their suppliers in months—which did not make any sense at all because that was entirely Lizzie's job. But then strangely, one by one, all these people the salon owed money to would call up Lauren and Geneva and say everything was actually paid in full and not to worry about it.

The truth of what Lizzie Mulder was actually up to would go on to blow everyone's mind—especially mine. It turned out that Lizzie had downloaded a bunch of voice-changing apps on her phone, a relatively easy thing to do. Then she'd call up Lauren and Geneva using different voices to trick them into believing this or that. She'd just open the app and talk into her phone, and the app would change the sound of her voice in real time to make Lizzie sound like a cast of different characters of her own choosing.

Lizzie had a voice she used for the power company, a different voice for the payroll company, other voices for the bank, the landlord, suppliers, vendors. She even had a voice she'd use to impersonate an IRS agent.

You can't believe what you hear over the phone anymore. So it's a good idea, when there's chaos around things like rent or the light bill *or whatever,* to call up the landlord or power company *or whoever,* even though they may have called you first. You need to double-check and confirm it was really them and not some scammer like Lizzie pretending to be them.

Now with AI, scammers can sound exactly like your mother or father or son or daughter or anyone you know and love—over the phone. It's a real threat.

The only way to protect yourself is to have a talk with your friends and family and come up with a verbal password. Let's say for argument's sake the password you all agree upon is *wildebeest.* So from now on, if you or anyone in your sphere gets a call from a loved one giving you a dramatic story like they've been arrested or they had an accident or they're in the hospital and need money wired to them to save their lives—keep in mind they will sound exactly like your loved one—ask them, "What's our verbal password?" And if they draw a blank or don't know it's *wildebeest,* hang up and call the number you have for that person and get them on the phone and clear everything up.

Remember, scammers can spoof any phone number. They can be calling you from Nigeria, and the technology they use will make that call pop up on your phone and appear as if it's your mother calling. But they aren't calling from your mother's actual phone. So if you hang up and call the number you have for your mother, you can quickly figure out if it's a scam or not.

As for Lizzie Mulder, by the time all was said and done, she had stolen close to half a million dollars from Lauren and Geneva's salon in less than two years, while stealing hundreds of thousands more from a dozen other clients with the same voice-changing app techniques. And the way Lizzie was surreptitiously moving all that money out of her clients' bank accounts without notice is meticulously duplicitous and a stinging indictment of our banking system.

"The coup de grâce was the checking account with the name 'Income Tax Payments,'" Mike Cochrane, one of Lizzie's other victims, told me back in 2022. Mike had been running a print shop in Orange County for decades when Lizzie Mulder started doing his books back in 2009. But unbeknownst to Mike, Lizzie had created a bank account at Bank of America called "Income Tax Payments." She'd make out checks on behalf of all her clients, including Mike, payable to "Income Tax Payments" and have them sign those checks under the guise of paying their taxes year after year. FYI, any payments to the IRS need to be made out to "the U.S. Treasury," but most people, especially harried business owners, aren't paying close attention to those kinds of details—especially when they've hired a CPA whiz like Lizzie Mulder to do their books.

So all those checks never made it to the IRS. Instead, they went straight into Lizzie's Bank of America account called "Income Tax Payments." And no one suspected a thing.

Sadly, the nearly $2 million Lizzie stole from her friends and clients pales in comparison to the millions they all owe now to the IRS in back taxes and penalties because of all the years Lizzie was pretending to file and pay their taxes when in reality she wasn't. Mike Cochrane's Orange County print shop went out of business. "We have thirty-seven levies on us from the IRS. They sent out 420 letters to all my top clients, instructing them that they were no longer able to pay me directly and that they had to pay the IRS, which killed my customer base. The IRS shut us down," Mike said.

The other thing I want to point out here is how absolutely meaningless a signature on a check is. Hundreds of checks that Lizzie made out to Income Tax Payments and deposited into her own account either were not signed or had a squiggly line that Lizzie drew in over the signature line that looked nothing like the actual signature linked to the clients' bank accounts.

I sat down with forensic accountant Jen Rodriguez, one of the people who helped investigators ferret out all of Lizzie's financial scams, and she explained to me why a signature on a check is worthless. "For all of us consumers and people that want to get their money fast—check deposits are automated. And so they go through. So, unless something is flagged then, it's not caught. There were so many checks that didn't have signatures but they never got caught. And the bank cashed them. And banks aren't responsible for protecting you from fraud. Only credit cards are. So that's one thing where you have to do due diligence as an account holder to really check all of your statements."

Sadly, Rodriguez is correct. Even though the banks cashed all those checks that Lizzie fraudulently deposited with no signatures or clearly forged signatures, the banks never returned a single dime to any of the victims. In fact, one of Lizzie's other victims, the owner of a travel agency, whom Lizzie scammed out of close to $800,000, sued Bank of America in 2020 in an attempt to hold them responsible for that theft for allowing Lizzie to open a bank account named "Income Tax Payments."

The travel agency owner lost. She appealed and then lost again. The court actually ruled *twice* that Bank of America had no duty to monitor customer accounts for fraud. "And that's the way it is," as Walter Cronkite used to say.

Here's something else you're going to find unbelievable. After police in Laguna Beach investigated Lizzie Mulder for nearly two years and uncovered a dozen other victims she'd scammed, the Orange County District Attorney's Office refused to file charges! They refused to prosecute. And they told the detective who was investigating to *drop the case!* "The district attorney told me, 'I don't think this is a winnable case. It doesn't really have any jury appeal and quite honestly, it's too convoluted. And I don't think you have enough to win in court,'" Laguna Beach fraud detective Jordan Mirakian told me back in 2022.

I just couldn't believe it.

But Mirakian, who is now a police sergeant in Seal Beach, a small seaside city about thirty miles north of Laguna, flat-out refused to drop the case. And he ingeniously figured out a way to go over the Orange County DA's head.

"So I started thinking about it, and I was like, well, you know, I bet she's falsified her income taxes. So I called a criminal investigator from the IRS, and the minute he got attached to it, it became a federal case," Mirakian said.

This guy is my hero. We've become close over the years since meeting on the Lizzie Mulder case. And I consult with him a lot about the various con artist cases I'm investigating. Once, when I needed a bulletproof vest to borrow in an emergency because I feared that some armed and unhinged lunatic that Mair had turned against me was going to shoot at me outside court, Mirakian loaned me his vest.

Anyway, the IRS started investigating the Lizzie Mulder case in late 2016. They eventually got the Department of Justice involved. And before long Lizzie Mulder was federally charged with wire fraud and falsifying tax returns in May of 2017.

"When we get involved in a case, it shakes people up, it shakes up defendants. This is a federal case now," said former assistant U.S. attorney Scott Tenley, who prosecuted Lizzie Mulder for the Department of Justice. Backed into a corner, Lizzie ultimately pled guilty to both charges and was sentenced to five years in federal prison.

Scott Tenley is a criminal defense attorney now at Tenley Law. We were sitting in his shiny marbled conference room overlooking picturesque Newport Beach when he explained to me that, had Lizzie Mulder not pled guilty, she'd have been looking at a bunch of other charges and potentially decades behind bars.

"We would have charged her with multiple counts of wire fraud, multiple counts of filing false tax returns. We would have probably considered charging her with something called aggravated identity theft, because she was impersonating people that she knew were obviously real people, so by coming in and resolving the case early, she helped kind of control her exposure." That's because when criminals plead guilty, especially in a federal case, they spare the government from potentially spending millions of dollars on an actual trial: empaneling a jury, paying experts like forensic accountants, and taking up an entire courtroom and staff for weeks or months. In return, the government tends to go easier on them with fewer charges and generally a lighter sentence.

Keep in mind here that if Detective Jordan Mirakian had dropped the case like the Orange County DA had instructed him to, Lizzie Mulder would have walked away scot-free. "And I'll share with you, the DA was pissed. Because we kind of made them look bad. . . . But I was like, well, if you're not going to do your job, then I'm going to find somebody that will," Mirakian said.

Queen of the Con V

Looking back over our four-year friendship, it's mind-boggling to real-ize how the Irish heiress, Mair Smyth, proved to me that everything she was saying was true simply by using her iPhone. A lot. I never once doubted the veracity of what she was telling me, even though her entire origin story was an utter fabrication.

I mean, how many times has someone held up their cellphone to you and said, "Look what so-and-so just texted me"? Did you ever once suspect that that text was not from so-and-so but actually from a Google account that the person holding up the phone had created to impersonate so-and-so to sell you a story about so-and-so?

Me neither. But this was a technique Mair used to create vibrant, living and breathing characters who I believed were 100 percent real. I would've bet my life that they were real. But alas they were not.

Early on in our friendship, I was introduced, in a manner of speak-ing, to Mair's cousins who lived in Ireland. They had Irish-sounding names too: Fintan, Diarmuid, and Tristan.

Mair would frequently show me her phone, pointing me to emails and texts from these cousins. In the beginning, these emails and texts consisted of her cousins teasing and taunting her about a guy she was dating or about how much weight she had gained since they last saw her. Or they'd send her Gaelic proverbs that she would translate for me, like *Níl bua gan dua* (There's no victory without hardship), *Is maith an scáthán súil charad* (A friend's eye is a good mirror), and *Is fearr lúbadh ná briseadh* (It's better to bend than to break).

These specific details painted an elaborate and realistic picture for me. At the time there was no doubt in my mind that I was witness-ing a relationship between Mair and her cousins back in Ireland.

Of course, the only problem for me was, her family didn't actu-ally exist. Well, not the family she told me about anyway. Her real family had in fact disowned her decades ago for being a pathological liar and a scammer, and for causing them incredible shame and embarrassment—a cold, hard fact that I didn't know until much too late.

Looking back, all those texts and emails she was frequently showing me from her Irish cousins correspond to the Red Flag of Technology.

Mair had a penchant for creating email accounts and texting accounts online in the names of dozens of other people (some impersonated, others outright invented—like her Irish cousins). She'd email and text herself as those people and then show me those emails and texts in order to bring all her made-up stories to life.

And it worked amazingly well. I genuinely believed all those people were real, and I believed what they were all saying was true. But none of it was.

So the next time a new person in your life holds up their phone, saying, "Look what so-and-so just texted me," make a note of it. Again, on its own, it doesn't mean they're necessarily trying to trick you. But if there are other red flags present, be suspicious.

As the weeks passed, Mair and I would spend many evenings in our building's BBQ area. She'd text me, "Wanna grab a cuppa?" and I'd usually reply, "Sure." And I'd head down.

"My uncle is not doing well," Mair said as tears filled her eyes.

It was a cool evening in late April 2014. I had known Mair for nearly a year at this point. Or at least I *thought* I knew her.

We were sitting in our regular meeting spot, and Mair was showing me text after text from her cousin Fintan, explaining how cancer had taken over most of her uncle Partridge Clarke's body. Doctors in Ireland said he didn't have long to live—days, maybe weeks.

Mair was overcome with grief and regret. I put my arms around her and comforted her.

"He was like a father to me," Mair sobbed. Tears streamed down her face as she cried and dampened my shirt. She was a wreck. I instinctively rocked her back and forth, like a baby, as she wept.

There was no way you could have convinced me those tears

weren't real, or that her uncle Partridge Clarke didn't exist, or that I was in the midst of falling for an elaborate confidence trick. But they weren't, and he didn't, and I most certainly was.

"I should never have left Ireland," Mair sobbed. "I should have known that this would happen."

Over the course of our friendship, Mair had painstakingly unpacked her Irish origin story to me in living, breathing color. She'd convinced me she'd left Ireland a decade earlier because she wanted to experience life free from the strictures and obligations of her noble family. She'd fallen in love with America and American culture as a child, watching shows like *Wonder Woman* and *Dukes of Hazzard* on TV. Mair explained that in the early 1980s her wealthy family had installed multiple satellite dishes—back when satellite dishes were a new consumer technology and very expensive—at their various estates around Ireland so that they were able to watch American television shows and movies whenever they wanted.

"We saw the pornos too!" Mair laughed as she explained this all to me. "There was the Playboy channel and another one called American XXXtasy. My cousins and I would watch with our jaws dropped."

Mair made it sound like being born into a wealthy family in Ireland was a blessing and a curse, but more of a curse. For every satellite dish-type of advantage, there were a dozen painful disadvantages, like perpetual family infighting and tragic loss.

Mair told me her father had been killed—assassinated—by an MI6 agent from the British Secret Intelligence Service. Her father was, as she told it, one of the leaders of the IRA and a major target.

You see, the IRA was an Irish paramilitary force fighting to end British rule in Northern Ireland. They hated the British, and during the four years I knew Mair she hated the British too. I mean, she pretended to anyway. One time, she threw this ritzy party with expensive catering and an open bar. About a hundred people came. It was one of those parties where people who were invited brought people who were not. And Mair actually asked a man (someone an invited guest had brought) to leave her party because he was British.

"I'm not feeding a fucking Brit in my house," she said to me after he left. I was shocked. But again, stuff like this reinforced that Mair was who she said she was.

If I haven't made it clear enough, everything Mair said was a lie. She was not from Ireland. All of that was made up. She was an American, born in Bangor, Maine.

Mair told me that when she was a little girl, she'd frequently run away from home and live in the forest surrounding her family's estate for days and days before she'd return. She said fairies and angels bathed in orbs of glowing white light would appear to her at night and give her messages of hope and nudge her to go back home. And she always did find her way back home eventually.

Even as I'm writing out these details for you, I have to remind myself that none of it was real. Intellectually, I know none of it was real, but part of me still feels it was. That is the power of details. Con artists use details to convince you that what they're saying is true. They *snow you* with details.

About thirteen months into our friendship, in June of 2014, Mair got word that her uncle Partridge Clarke had passed away. She was devastated. She flew to Ireland for a week to attend the funeral—or so she said. In any event, I didn't see her for seven days and I believed she was in Ireland.

I now know for a fact she never went to Ireland. So she probably just laid low and avoided me that week.

When she "returned from Ireland," she started unpacking the particulars of her inheritance to me using technology again—showing me countless texts and emails from this person and that person.

Mair said her uncle Patridge's 25-million-euro estate was being divided up among her and her cousins Fintan, Diarmuid, and Tristan. Remember—I *knew* all these "people." Mair was supposed to get 5 million euros cash, which given the exchange rate at the time was close to 7 million U.S. dollars. She'd constantly show me text messages and emails from her cousins and from her "barristers" in Ireland. I had to google what "barristers" were because I had no idea. Come to find out, it's what they call lawyers over there. Little details like that made her story seem true.

As the weeks passed, Mair and her cousins were at one another's throats. She'd show me the cruelest text messages from her cousin Fintan, calling her a "cunt" and telling her she'd never get a "bloody farthing," aka an Irish penny, of her inheritance.

Nice touch, right? Colorful and specific details. They make everything ring true.

Fintan had considered Mair a deserter when she left Ireland ten years prior. In his mind she was not entitled to any of her uncle's money because she had abandoned the family.

"I have no family now," Mair sobbed to me one night. This bonded me to her profoundly because I was going through a similar "I have no family now" situation of my own.

Years earlier I had come out to my family as gay. And it hadn't gone so well. Very quickly thereafter I was told to "keep that away" from them, and I was no longer welcomed home for holidays and family events. In fact, by the time Mair was crying to me that her family had essentially disowned her, it had been nearly eight years since I'd been home for Christmas to see my own family.

And the truth of the matter was . . . Mair *knew all those details* of my life at this point in our relationship. And she painstakingly used them to craft the perfect scenario to create a powerful bond with me.

I felt extremely sorry for Mair. My heart broke for her as she told me more and more about her life in Ireland and her family. She seemed to be in a lot of emotional pain and turmoil, and I completely related. And I got sucked into it all really deeply.

I know now that I felt exactly how Mair Smyth wanted me to feel and planned for me to feel. As I said before, **con artists don't outsmart you, they out-feel you.** They use your emotions to scam you. And that's exactly what my con artist was doing to me, because when you're making decisions with your heart and not your head, you're as good as sunk.

It's impossible to adequately express to you now how angry I am as I write these words. For four years straight, I was emotionally assaulted by this woman—this perverse caricature of a human being. I cried with her, and I cried for her—again and again and again. Come to find out, everything I was crying over was completely made up, by her. *Nothing was true.*

I even had knock-down, drag-out fights with my husband over her. "You don't understand!" I yelled at him one night in our kitchen, my nostrils flared and my pupils fully dilated by rage. "They're trying to destroy her!"

My husband had gotten a bad feeling about Mair a few weeks before I started catching her in lies myself, but at this point the money had already changed hands and I was still 100 percent on Mair's side. And when my husband tried to imply that Mair was not being truthful, I fiercely defended her and screamed at him. How a straight woman could come between two gay men madly in love with each other speaks to her unparalleled skill of manipulation.

Of course, I have since apologized to my husband, many times. But that I had *ever* raised my voice at him at all and took her side over his makes me incredibly angry, even to this day. I will never forgive myself for treating him that way. Shame on me.

Con artists like Mair don't just take your money, they take a piece of your soul. And you can never get that back. I can never undo what I did in her name and at her behest because I made the grave mistake of believing all her lies. I can only use what happened to me to help other people avoid getting scammed by the crazy Irish heiress archetypes in their lives.

8. RED FLAG #7: SCARCITY

THE IDEA OF SCARCITY IS A POWERFUL MOTIVATOR. IF YOU THINK SOMETHING IS IN LIMited supply, all of a sudden you are naturally going to focus on getting as much of it as you can before it runs out. Also, the way the human psyche works, scarcity can create a desire for something you previously had not even thought about until you heard it was unavailable or about to become unavailable—and now you want it more than ever.

This applies to anything and everything. It could be a romantic interest or a new car. It could be a store or a donut shop that's going out of business: Even though you've never shopped there or eaten there before, the idea that it will no longer exist kind of makes you want to check it out before it disappears.

In economics, this pattern of behavior is known as the Scarcity Principle: The less available something is (or appears to be), the more intrinsic value it has in the world, and the more desire people have for it. So things like diamonds or classic works of art or vintage sports cars from the 1950s are all ridiculously expensive because they're rare—or *considered* rare. (The idea that diamonds are "rare" is really just a myth created to jack the price up and increase their perceived value. But that's a whole other book.)

Regardless, scarcity has a uniquely powerful effect on human behavior. It's an effective tool professional con artists use to manipulate people into giving them lots of money.

So if you meet someone new and they're waving one or two or more of the previous chapters' red flags at you, and suddenly there's an element of scarcity to what they're saying—make no mistake, you are in the midst of a scam in progress.

Enter con artist David Bloom.

Here is a guy who is the living embodiment of the principle that scammers never change. It doesn't matter how much time passes or how many victims they've stolen from or how many times they've been in jail—scammers will always scam.

As I write these words, David Bloom is sixty years old and sitting in a Los Angeles County jail cell awaiting trial for scamming dozens of people in and around Southern California out of hundreds of thousands of dollars. But this ain't his first slammer-jammer. For the past forty-five years, he has scammed hundreds and hundreds of other victims out of millions and millions of dollars. He's served time behind bars multiple times for elaborate cons he pulled in the 1980s, the 1990s, and the early 2000s.

David Bloom will never change. And he is the master of using scarcity to trick people into parting with their money. I first started investigating him a couple years ago when I was hired to investigate, write, and produce a new podcast called *Once upon a Con* with reality TV star Caroline D'Amore, who was David's latest—and most vocal—victim.

She did what I did after she got scammed. She yelled it from the highest rooftops and made it a media spectacle. And that helped put the noose around David Bloom's neck because remember—publicity is like kryptonite to con artists.

You might know Caroline from that MTV show *The Hills* or that Fox show *Gordon Ramsay's Food Stars*. She's also acted in a few films and modeled for some big-name designers, but for the past few years her passion has been a marinara sauce line that she created called "Pizza Girl"—a moniker she was given as a child delivering pizzas while working for her father, who owned a pizzeria in Malibu. And it was actually her desire to make her "Pizza Girl" sauce a success that led her to getting scammed by David Bloom.

"He walks over to me; he had heard that I had this company called Pizza Girl, and he had gone and bought my sauce at the supermarket next door and was so impressed with my company," Caroline told me. That was the first time she laid eyes on David, a short, pudgy man in his late fifties with thick gray hair and charismatic eyes. Caroline, in her late thirties, was myopically focused on the goal of making her new company a huge success.

That well-known expression "Flattery will get you everywhere" is a well-known expression because it's true. How do you not immediately like a stranger when you first meet them, if they are flattering you or flattering something you wholeheartedly care about?

It was April 2021 and Caroline had gone through a divorce a couple years earlier and was living with her young daughter at the exclusive Villa Carlotta, an uber-luxury apartment building in the shadow of the Hollywood Hills, where a two-bedroom goes for $10,000 a month or more. So the assumption was, if you're living at the Villa Carlotta, then your neighbors must be pretty wealthy—or at least of some renown—to be able to afford that hefty rent payment every month, right? And certainly, by and large, residents of the Villa Carlotta were wealthy and prestigious movers and shakers in Los Angeles. I mean, at one point, Julia Roberts and Sean Penn were staying there while shooting their latest project.

"I remember looking terrible very early in the morning with sweatpants on, all disheveled and walking my dog, and Sean Penn was just walking right by me and he is like, 'Hi,'" recalls Caroline.

Make no mistake, in the high-end circles of Hollywood, the Villa Carlotta was well known for housing the crème de la crème. So when David Bloom walked up to Caroline D'Amore in the building that day and complimented her company, she immediately assumed he was one those wealthy, important people too.

Only he wasn't. He was actually fresh on the heels of using the thousands of dollars he had just scammed from another victim to move into the Villa Carlotta, because he knew a place like that would be prime hunting ground for wealthy and trusting marks. And oh boy was he right.

Caroline had no idea, nor did anyone else at the Villa Carlotta, that David Bloom was a convicted con artist who had run a multi-million-dollar Ponzi scheme in New York back in the 1980s and a fraudulent investment scheme there in the 1990s. But in 2021, if you were to google the name "David Bloom"—as Caroline did—the only search result that would have come up was the television news reporter David Bloom who had tragically died in 2003 covering the Iraq War. That explains why con artist David Bloom never felt the need to change his name while he was pulling his new scams; he knew that when you googled "David Bloom" the only results that came up had nothing to do with him or his many criminal exploits. Thanks, Google.

To Caroline and her neighbors, David Bloom presented himself as a gregarious billionaire, an investing oracle, someone who was good friends with Warren Buffett and frequently golfed with Netflix CEO Ted Sarandos. He actually showed Caroline texts from Ted Sarandos, which obviously were fake (Red Flag #6: Technology), to help breathe life into the papier-mâché world he was constructing.

"He had this story that he was staying at the Villa Carlotta because he was going to buy it," said Caroline. "He just had a big presence, and everybody seemed to know him and like him. So I had no reason to think anything, you know?" No one else at the Villa Carlotta did either.

To get in deep with Caroline, David Bloom pretended he was going through a divorce too. He actually teared up talking about it with her. (God, I think I should go back to the drawing board and add another Red Flag about a con artist's innate ability to cry on cue! Because it really seems to be "a thing" they all do.)

Anyway.

David and Caroline bonded closely over their recent divorces. It's identical to what Mair did to me over family estrangement: that bonded us closely as well.

Caroline saw David as this sensitive, yet super successful financial wheeler-dealer with a heart of gold. She looked up to him, and he appeared to relish that fact because he offered to mentor her. So before long, Caroline and David were meeting regularly at the pool area or the clubhouse or the lobby of the Villa Carlotta to discuss business. At that point, Caroline's Pizza Girl marinara sauce was available in just a few supermarkets. But her dream was to get it on the shelves of Whole Foods nationwide. And that was all the inducement David needed to proceed with his multifaceted scarcity scam.

David used a two-prong approach to scam Caroline and a bunch of other people at the Villa Carlotta. There was one scam he created solely for the purpose of distracting Caroline from the other scam, the real scam, the scam designed to take her money. Here's how it worked.

When David heard that Caroline desperately wanted to get her Pizza Girl marinara sauce on the shelves of Whole Foods stores across the country, he told her that as luck would have it, he was good friends with the CEO of Whole Foods, and he showed her the requisite texts between them to back it up.

David even went so far as to draft an accomplice, an actor, who pretended to be the CEO of Whole Foods on a phone call with Caroline. So there was no doubt in Caroline's mind not only that David knew the CEO of Whole Foods but that the CEO was now interested in meeting with Caroline to talk about getting her Pizza Girl marinara sauce on their store shelves.

Caroline was so excited at this prospect, she literally jumped for joy. She started working feverishly with David to prepare for this supposed meeting with Whole Foods.

Now, this Whole Foods scam was only meant to distract Caroline and prime her for the next confidence trick David had up his sleeve. At this point, Caroline was low on cash, and she worried that if Whole Foods were to order a bunch of Pizza Girl marinara sauce, she might not have enough money to fulfill that large order.

"You need some fast cash," David told her. "I'm a really good investor and I have this IPO for Soho House going public. Just round up as much money as you can. It's going to be worth twenty-nine or twenty-eight times whatever you put in, in a couple months."

Soho House is this private club for rich people, with locations all over the world. If you'd googled around at that point in 2021, you would have seen real news reports that Soho House was preparing to go public. So what David was telling Caroline here made sense. It was completely believable and verifiable. But in reality, that Soho House IPO was just a dangling carrot. David was not involved with any kind of investment whatsoever.

And here's where David masterfully used scarcity to get Caroline to act fast. This IPO was supposedly days away from happening. So Caroline didn't have a lot of time to think about it because she was worried she'd miss out on this investment opportunity of a lifetime.

And that was David Bloom's plan. He knew human nature better than anyone. And he knew that if Caroline thought she'd miss out on this opportunity by not forking over money fast enough, it would make her do it that much faster.

And he was right. Caroline was already in the midst of—and inordinately preoccupied by—preparing for her big meeting with that Whole Foods CEO, aka the distracting scam. So she scrambled fast, borrowed money from friends and family and even from her boyfriend at the time, and managed to get her hands on $35,000 cash—which David assured her would be worth more than $1 million in just a few months.

After the money changed hands, David sent Caroline on a wild-goose chase to Whole Foods headquarters in Austin, Texas. She boarded a plane and flew out there. She checked into a hotel in downtown Austin, on her own dime, and prepared for her life-changing meeting with that Whole Foods CEO, scheduled the very next morning.

Only David called to tell her it was postponed to the next day. And then the next day. And then the next day. And then the next.

Caroline spent a total of five days in Austin before realizing that the meeting with Whole Foods was never going to happen. She was able to get an associate of that CEO, the real CEO, on the phone, and he confirmed that he had never heard of Pizza Girl marinara sauce and there was no meeting. It was all an elaborate hoax orchestrated and perpetuated by David Bloom.

Caroline was devastated. She had what appeared to be a nervous breakdown. For days, she was inconsolable and borderline catatonic.

But then she courageously picked herself up and put herself back together. And she fought back.

Caroline started telling other neighbors about what happened. She discovered that David Bloom had scammed a bunch of them too with similar IPO stories. She organized all the evidence she had—emails and text messages and bank statements—and submitted everything to the police.

Oh, and she actually confronted David Bloom and recorded it all on her phone. That insane confrontation, featured in the *Once upon a Con* podcast, is one of the most compelling things I've ever heard.

At this point there was just one problem: Despite all the evidence authorities had on all the new scams and all the new victims of David Bloom, the Los Angeles District Attorney's Office was not filing charges. And they were not explaining why. Caroline was upset by their lack of action and asked me what she should do.

"Let's stage a rowdy protest outside the DA's office!" I rallied.

I went out and bought poster boards and giant markers and made signs. Caroline put the word out on her socials to get people involved. And days later a dozen of us converged.

"Charge David Bloom!" we shouted in a frenzied loop, holding up signs while walking in circles for hours on the sidewalk outside the Los Angeles District Attorney's Office downtown as cars drove by honking their support. Lawyers from all walks of life came by inquiring what we were up to and why we were there. There were even people poking their heads out from the DA's office wondering what the heck we were doing. The *L.A.* freaking *Times* came by and shot some pictures of us protesting and conducted some interviews. And Caroline D'Amore spectacularly gave that *L.A. Times* reporter a string of billion-dollar sound bites for his article.

"We have nothing to be ashamed of. It's David Bloom who should be ashamed. Charge David Bloom with a crime already!" Caroline defiantly issued.

And that protest seemed to pay off, because not long after, on August 27, 2023, David Bloom was arrested and charged with scamming Caroline and a bunch of other victims in and around Los Angeles. He's sitting in jail now awaiting a trial that could be another year away because the case against him is so complicated and sprawling, with so many victims and so many moving parts.

David Bloom was waving a bunch of red flags that he was a con artist at Caroline and everyone else. But no one spotted them. I mean, I hadn't written this book yet so who even knew they were a thing? But looking back now it's obvious:

Red Flag #1—He offered to help Caroline out of the blue.

Red Flag #2—He was too kind, too quick.

Red Flag #5—He led Caroline to believe he was better than her at investing.

Red Flag #6—He relied on technology to sell his stories—fake emails and texts.

Red Flag #8—He used the element of scarcity to get Caroline and others to give him money on a sped-up timetable.

Red Flag #9—He had a good day job. Or at least he appeared to.

Red Flag #12—He told *a lot* of stories from faraway places.

Red Flag #13—He used the TMI technique to get close to Caroline FAST.

Red Flag #14—He used all the Dale Carnegie techniques to "*win friends and influence*" his victims.

9. RED FLAG #8: BEAK WETTING

BEAK WETTING IS A TERM OF ART IN THE WORLD OF CONFIDENCE TRICKS THAT ENCOMpasses a powerful manipulation technique professional con artists use frequently. They will let you "wet your beak," meaning, they will give *you* money. And that money will dazzle you and distract you and convince you that what they're saying is true. And it will motivate you to give *them* money.

That's the whole point.

You'll mostly see beak wetting in investment scams. But it's also present in love scams and even inheritance scams like the one I fell for. My con artist skillfully used beak wetting to trick me—as I'll explain in the next chapter.

But tragically, the most powerful example of beak wetting I can share with you happened to my own family. They do not want to talk about it, and they certainly don't want me talking about it, or worse, writing about it. So out of respect I won't name names. But I will say that more than a dozen members of my family lost millions of dollars to a truly monstrous con artist by the name of David Smith—who managed to trick a total of six thousand other victims out of $220 million. The sickening irony here is that this scammer shares a last name with

Mair Smyth, and though they are spelled differently, they are pronounced the same: Smith.

David Smith was a renowned foreign exchange trader on the Caribbean island of Jamaica back in the early 2000s.

It might surprise you to learn that I am actually Jamaican. I was born there and lived there for twelve years of my childhood—from ages five to seventeen.

Whenever I tell people I'm Jamaican, they immediately do a double take and say suspiciously, "You don't look Jamaican." I mean, ethnically, I'm a white Middle Eastern–looking guy. That's because back in the early 1900s my great-grandparents, who were in Lebanon, along with hundreds of other Lebanese families, all hopped on boats and set sail for a better life. By some accounts, they were heading for America. But it was a perilous six-month journey, and my grandfather's mother actually died giving birth on that voyage. So when they got to dry land in Jamaica—which was one of the ports they stopped at on the way—my great-grandparents were thrilled. And they decided to stay. That's how my Lebanese family got started in Jamaica.

Cut to 2001 and con artist David Smith, the ambitious middle-class son of two high school science teachers. He was twenty-four years old when he landed a job at a well-known Jamaican investment firm. While working there he earned a BS in business from Nova Southeastern University's Jamaica campus.

I know. I wasn't aware they had a campus in Jamaica either. And I grew up there.

Anyway, David Smith worked for that investment firm for two years. Then he was suddenly let go in 2003. Fired. The reason for his termination was not clear, but a high-placed source at the company told a news reporter from Bloomberg that Smith had violated the firm's core values. They would not elaborate on what that meant exactly, but it does give me the impression that he was up to some shady stuff, which is further evidenced by what he went on to do after he was fired from that investing company.

From 2003 to late 2004, David Smith started dabbling in foreign exchange trading—the buying and selling of global currencies. It's kind of like the stock market, but for cash. Forex traders, as they are called, speculate on fluctuating exchange rates, converting large amounts of money from currency to currency. They try to buy low and sell high. And David Smith was horrible at it.

Most people are. And he lost money. Most people do.

So in early 2005, David Smith did what we all do. He took to Google, researching how to learn foreign exchange trading like a boss. And he found a Forex trading school in Orlando, Florida, where $7,000 would buy him a four-day course and make him a professional foreign exchange trader.

Four days. Nothing scammy going on there, right?

So David flew to Orlando and completed that course and started his official foreign exchange trading business in Jamaica called OLINT— short for Overseas Locket International. While that four-day course didn't teach him how to make money with foreign exchange trading, it did teach him the lingo, what paperwork to use, which banks and institutions to affiliate with—essentially it taught him how to "appear" to be a foreign exchange trader. And David Smith quickly figured out how to capitalize on that appearance to scam my family and *many* others.

He started small with only a handful of investors. And those investors shockingly made 10 percent interest on their money every month— consistently.

That would seem to equate to 120 percent interest a year. But we're actually talking about compound interest here. So, by the end of the year investors stood to make more than 200 percent on their initial investment because it was compounding every month.

Not surprisingly, word spread fast. Those initial investors told their friends and family, who told their friends and family, who told their friends and family. And before long, David Smith had hundreds and hundreds of investors who were all making 10 percent interest on their money every month. Or so it appeared.

That's how more than a dozen members of my family got sucked into it. At the time I was working as a television reporter for the CBS station in Houston, Texas, KHOU-TV. When I'd go home to Jamaica for the holidays, my family would regale me with compelling and dramatic stories about the magical, mythical David Smith, the investing oracle and foreign exchange trading dynamo. He was being compared to Moses, leading his flock to the Promised Land. The backstory that I got from my family was that David Smith knew too much and was too good at foreign exchange trading and that's why that Jamaican investment firm had fired him. They were jealous of his talent and were angry that he wouldn't do what they wanted him to do. They were mad that they could not control him. That's why he had gone out on his own and started OLINT. He had figured out the foreign exchange trading game and was using what he had learned to help his investors make money— massive amounts of money.

It was one hell of a conspiracy theory that thousands of people believed. And not a lick of it was true.

The truth of the matter was, David Smith was running an elaborate Ponzi scheme. He wasn't investing anyone's money in anything. Keep in mind, this was three years before Bernie Madoff got busted for running his gigantic Ponzi scheme. If you recall, before Bernie Madoff was arrested in December 2008, Ponzi schemes weren't really "a thing" in the public consciousness. And while Bernie Madoff pretended to be delivering his clients 10 to 12 percent on their money per year, David Smith was much bolder, pretending to give his clients 10 percent per month.

"Everybody was talking about it," said Marcos Dabdoub Jr., a childhood friend of mine who witnessed the David Smith craze as it was happening and as everyone around him was fervently investing.

"If somebody you know and trust is supposedly making all this money and they're telling you, 'You need to do this,' it's a lot easier for you to jump in. Because whether or not you trust David Smith, you trust the person that's telling you that, right?" Marcos pointed out.

But Marcos Dabdoub Jr. had a bad feeling about David Smith from the get-go. He never invested any money, nor did anyone in his family. But a lot of his friends and associates did, even though he urged them not to.

"To me, alarm bells would go off. Because I know, from experience, that's not how money is made. It's really hard to make money. It doesn't just come to you like that. This isn't normal. You don't make 10 percent a month on any investment consistently. It ebbs and flows. If it goes up, you have to have months that it comes down. And from what I was told, David Smith was offering a consistent return of 10 percent a month. So immediately, it just didn't feel right."

David Smith skillfully used beak wetting to manipulate and grow his investment roster from a handful of victims to more than six thousand people. Here's how he did it.

He created an interactive bank-type website. This was an enormous undertaking because this website looked really legitimate. It enabled thousands of his clients to create individual logins and passwords and use those logins to access their individual accounts. So they could see, with their own eyes, their money growing every month, by 10 percent consistently, like clockwork. And it thrilled them.

It also did something else. Paying that kind of monthly dividend made clients reluctant to withdraw money, because the more money they would withdraw the less money they would make. Let's say they had $1,000 invested. They'd be making $100 every month on that $1,000. But if they withdrew $500, then they'd be making only $50 on their investment every month instead of $100. So this was a cruel yet ingenious way to incentivize his investors not only to refrain from withdrawing money but to keep adding more money to the pot, so they could take full advantage of that massive compound interest.

David Smith calculatedly used his clients' own greed against them. That greed blinded them, and it enabled him to bleed them all dry.

Again, con artists don't outsmart you, they out-feel you. And make no mistake, greed is a powerful "feeling." Once it gets ahold of you, your intellect takes a backseat.

When some of his clients wanted to withdraw money, he'd let them. He used the money he was taking in from new clients to pay for the withdrawals made by existing clients—in classic Ponzi scheme fashion. So when people got cash out of David Smith's system, it confirmed to them that everything was on the up-and-up and everything was real. They doubled and tripled down on their investments and their belief that he was who he said he was: a foreign exchange trading whiz.

David Smith quickly became a celebrity in Jamaica, the Caribbean facsimile of a Warren Buffett or an Elon Musk. He was interviewed on TV talk shows and radio shows and he was quoted regularly in magazines and newspapers.

His six thousand investors came from every walk of life: poor people, rich people, government officials, local celebrities. But reportedly the largest group of his investors were uber-religious Christians.

Not only was David Smith waving Red Flag #8 (Beak Wetting) at his victims, he was waving Red Flag #6 (Technology) by creating that bogus website to trick his victims into thinking they were making money. He was also waving Red Flag #5 ("I'm Better Than You") by painstakingly curating the image that he was a foreign exchange trading genius.

But the two red flags that especially attracted all the churchgoing Christians were Red Flag #1 ("I Just Want to Help") and Red Flag #2 (Too Kind, Too Quick), because David Smith appeared to everyone to be a good man, a great man, a godly man, as kind as he was generous. His only stated desire in life was to help people make money.

Like Jesus, he performed miracles. But instead of turning water into wine, David Smith was turning poor people into rich people. "He was the savior of the poor," wrote Jonathan Chambers, a former classmate of David Smith, who published a lengthy online essay about his experience with him.

David Smith's clients had 100 percent trust and belief in him. They knew him to be "a good Christian" who frequently attended church and donated money to charity. He and his wife even created the OLINT Foundation to help Jamaican children with special needs.

David Smith was loved by everyone. And that love blinded them all and caused them to do some really dumb things.

As I said before, love is the most powerful force there is in the universe. And if a con artist can get you to love them, you will overlook a lot.

Case in point, when authorities started investigating David Smith after receiving a tip that he was running a Ponzi scheme in March of 2006—just one year after he started his company—they tried to shut him down. And there was a tremendous backlash, a revolt really, from every stratum of Jamaican society. Poor people who invested with David Smith were incensed—accusing "the authorities" of trying to keep them down and prevent them from getting rich. David's wealthy investors were equally angry, claiming that any investigation into David Smith would destroy the Jamaican economy. And David Smith nakedly donated millions of dollars to Jamaican politicians and lawmakers of every political stripe. So, shockingly, that investigation ended up going nowhere. David Smith's Ponzi scheme continued, and even more people invested with him than before.

Two years later, however, it all came crashing down.

In July 2008, David Smith was arrested and charged with running a $220 million Ponzi scheme. Authorities identified at least six thousand victims. A dozen or so of those victims were members of my own family—who lost a couple million dollars combined. David Smith was later convicted and sentenced to thirty years in prison.

I realize that it's easy to get swept up in a craze that everyone seems to be swept up in and celebrating and praising. But whenever this happens in life—and there's money involved—take a step back and see if there are any of the red flags waving that I lay out in this book.

If there are—do not part with your money.

Queen of the Con VI

It was July 8, 2014. I was producing a History Channel documentary series called *10 Things You Don't Know,* hosted by Henry Rollins.

Yes, *that* Henry Rollins, of Black Flag fame. Great guy. Amazing show.

Anyway, I was sitting at my desk at 11 A.M. when I got a desperate phone call from Mair telling me she'd just been arrested. It shocked the hell out of me. Yet it was exactly what I had known would happen.

Let me explain.

Weeks earlier, when Mair was showing me text after text message from her angry cousins and from her barristers in Ireland about the inheritance, one of those barristers outlined a clause in her uncle's will that denied the inheritance money to any heir ever convicted of a felony or any other kind of criminal act. Reading that text terrified me.

Looking back, I responded exactly as she knew I would. I mean, I knew that her family in Ireland hated her and that her cousins were telling her she didn't deserve any inheritance money. I knew that Fintan was good friends with the owner of the company she worked for. And now I'd found out that there was a clause in the inheritance where anyone convicted of a crime would forfeit their inheritance money. So I naturally put it all together. And I warned her. Weeks before she was actually arrested, I said, "You'd better be careful. Fintan—who is best friends with your boss—may try to set you up to make it look like you stole money or something from that company to get you disinherited."

I mean, stories of husbands knocking off their wives for million-dollar insurance policies are in the news every other day. And here Mair stood to inherit the equivalent of $7 million (US) and her cousins hated her, so why wouldn't they try to set her up and take her money?

God, the details she snowed me with about this scam were epic.

But again, it's human nature to believe a story is true if there are many colorful details, and con artists love to use human nature to their advantage. Still, I am amazed at the intricate way Mair laid out all the breadcrumbs for me to pick up.

"Don't be silly, Johnathan." Mair laughed off my concerns. "My family would never do that." Then suddenly, weeks later, I was fielding a jailhouse phone call where Mair was sobbing and telling me the police were charging her for stealing $200,000 from that very travel agency.

"I told you this would happen!" I yelled indignantly into the phone.

"You were right," she sobbed.

I have to point out here how powerful a manipulation this was. Again, nothing Mair was telling me was true. But I had sincerely believed that I was right when I warned her that her evil cousins would set her up to make it look like she'd committed a crime in order to get her disinherited.

And again, she was using human nature against me. Everyone loves to be right, and I am certainly no different. So I *knew* that this was real and that I was right about it.

My buddy, fellow reality TV producer Evan Goldstein, was sitting in the cubicle beside me, overhearing everything, mouth agape.

"What's going on?" Evan asked after I hung up.

"I need to find a bail bondsman," I said aloud to myself. And I started frantically making phone calls to try and bail my best friend, my de facto sister, out of jail.

How Mair got arrested in the first place is a truly bizarre story.

One day in early July of 2014 Mair got a call from a detective at the Los Angeles Police Department. This detective told her that her car (a black Audi A5) had been involved in a crime, or had been used in a crime, or had showed up on surveillance video somewhere near a crime scene. And they needed to inspect her car ASAP. They assured her she was not in any trouble; they just wanted to take a close look at her car.

As Mair was telling me this I didn't know what to think. I mean, we did live in Los Angeles, and there were plenty of surveillance cameras (and crimes) everywhere. And Mair said she had loaned Sherry, the strip club manager, her car for a few days while Sherry's was in the shop and Mair was out of town.

So Mair suggested that maybe Sherry had committed a crime or had been near a crime scene in her car. That sounded reasonable to me, because remember how I thought Sherry was a murderer on the run from police? Add to that, she was the manager of a strip club located near Skid Row—a blighted part of downtown Los Angeles where the crime rate is much higher than most other places in the city.

Sherry Cooper was not in fact a murderer. That was just a lie Mair made up. But the LAPD did call Mair and tell her that her car had been involved in a crime. And Mair had loaned Sherry her Audi A5 a few weeks prior.

Those two things really happened. So Mair legitimately thought Sherry might have had something to do with the LAPD wanting to inspect her car.

Shockingly, Mair agreed to meet with those detectives *without a lawyer* to show them her car, explain to them that she had loaned the car to strip club manager Sherry Cooper a couple weeks prior, and suggest that maybe Sherry was the one they should be talking to.

Mair met up with those LAPD detectives in a downtown Los Angeles parking lot at 10 A.M. on July 8, 2014. She drove right up to them. And after she waved "Hello" and got out of her car . . . they grabbed her. "You're under arrest," they said as they handcuffed her and threw her up against the car in question.

The detectives had completely made up the car story to trick Mair into meeting them so they could make an easy, hassle-free arrest for a different crime entirely: stealing $200,000 from her employer. The cops had essentially conned the con artist. And it was totally legal. Law enforcement agencies are allowed to invent pretexts to arrest accused perpetrators because the ends can usually justify the means.

"If there's a choice between mobilizing a SWAT team to storm a house where a violent criminal might start shooting at the first sight of police or setting off the alarm on a criminal's car at 6 A.M. so he runs out in his underwear, what do you think a law enforcement agent is going to choose?" asked Scott Tenley, a former federal prosecutor with the U.S. Department of Justice and current criminal defense attorney at Tenley Law in Southern California. "So police could have stormed Mair's apartment to arrest her, but they got her in cuffs without risking their safety. There's nothing illegal about tricking an accused criminal into coming out in public. Where problems might develop is using trickery to obtain consent to search a suspect's home, because you typically need a warrant to do that."

You might be thinking that Mair was pretty naïve for agreeing to meet with police in the first place, and without a lawyer to boot. But after investigating hundreds of con artist cases over the past seven years I have learned that even though they're masters of deception themselves, the strange irony is, con artists are the easiest to fool—because at the end of the day, a professional con artist is a narcissist. They have an ego the size of their grandiose delusional aspirations, so they always think they're the smartest people in the room. Never for a second do they suspect anyone would *ever* have the smarts or the chutzpah to try and trick *them*.

They're the only scammers—in their minds. They're the ones fooling everyone else. They're the lions; the rest of us are just defenseless lambs waiting to be pounced on. So surprisingly con artists are very trusting people.

Here's more proof of that fact. At one point during our four-year friendship, Mair trusted me with her email password!

She was stuck in rush-hour traffic on the 405. And she couldn't access her email account from her phone, so she called me in a panic thinking she had been hacked. I was at work. And she asked me to log in to her email account from my computer to check if I could get in. So she actually gave me her email password over the phone. I paused what I was doing at work and logged in to her email account. And it was fine. I told her to just restart her phone and maybe that would fix things. And it did. And I completely forgot about that fleeting exchange until much later—when I ended up using her email password against her, in myriad spectacular ways that ultimately took her down—hard.

But before all that, we were best friends and Mair was in an L.A. County jail cell begging me for help on July 8, 2014. And I was at work calling around trying to find a bail bondsman who could get her out. Her bail was set at $70,000, and every bail bondsman I called wanted $7,000 from me, 10 percent of the $70,000, to secure her bail.

The way bail works is, I give the bail bond company 10 percent of the bail—which in Mair's case was $7,000—and they agree to take the risk of securing $70,000 for the actual bail. In this case, if Mair skipped town or didn't show up to court, the bail bondsman would have to give the court $70,000. And then they would come after me for that money.

Keep in mind that when Mair got arrested, she was like a sister to me. I loved her like family. So I desperately wanted to bail her out of jail.

And this is the Red Flag of Scarcity. I felt overwhelmed by the immense pressure to bail her out of jail as soon as humanly possible. If I didn't, who would? All of a sudden I felt as if there was a ticking clock and I had to act fast before it was too late. Every minute that passed felt like hours, and every hour felt like days.

As I was frantically googling around trying to find a bail bondsman who could spring Mair for less than the $7,000 I kept getting quoted, suddenly my phone rang. It was the married politician Mair had been dating—urging me to do something.

"You gotta get her out of there," he begged, intensifying the time pressure that I felt.

"I'm trying!" I exclaimed. "You're a lawyer, can't you do anything?"

"I can't," he said. "If I get involved and it becomes public record in all the court documents I could lose a lot. And I just can't risk that. But I know someone who can help get her out for much less than $7,000." And with that, the Politician texted me a number to call of a bail bondsman he knew who agreed to get Mair out of jail for $4,200. So I let that guy charge my debit card, and $4,200 cash got taken out of my checking account.

It was during this process of filling out all the bail paperwork that I learned that "Mair Smyth" was not her real name. "Marianne Elizabeth Smyth" was. But I thought nothing of it. I surmised "Mair" was short for "Marianne" and I let it go.

Big mistake. There was in fact a nefarious and calculated reason "Marianne" went by the name "Mair" once she'd moved to Los Angeles years earlier: Because if anyone were to run a criminal background check on "Mair Smyth" *nothing* would have come up, whereas if someone were to run a criminal background check on Marianne Smyth, a rap sheet longer than a line at Disneyland would have come up, resplendent with felony charges in multiple states for fraud, grand theft, passing bad checks, shoplifting, and forging documents.

But have you ever thought to run a criminal background check on your best friend? I sure as hell wish I had. Our friendship would have ended right then and there.

But it never occurred to me. And now it's actually the first thing I do when someone new comes into my life. And I *highly* recommend you do it too.

There are consumer websites like BeenVerified.com and Intelius .com that can run the most basic background checks, which a lot of times include criminal records, for around $30. But if you hire a licensed private investigator, they can do a deep dive for a couple hundred dollars that will 100 percent bring up any criminal record attached to the person in question.

Or you can search local courthouse websites in the counties you know this person has lived in—for free or in some cases for a dollar or two per search—and that can bring up any criminal or civil cases attached to the name in question. You can also go to the website Pacer .UScourts.gov, sign up for an account, and search for federal criminal cases in the person's name—though there is a ten-cent-per-page charge if you want to review any documents in any of the criminal or civil cases that may come up in search results.

This is all stuff I know now but didn't know back in 2014—stuff I had to learn the hard way.

As for Mair, even after I paid her bail, it would be awhile before she was released from jail. And as the day turned into evening, Mair was calling me collect from jail multiple times. All. Night. Long.

"Why aren't they releasing me yet?" Mair cried over the phone.

"The bail bondsman said the jail is on lockdown and all inmate releases have been paused," I replied.

"That's not true!" Mair shrieked. "I see inmates getting out every hour. I know my family is behind this. They set me up. And now they're making sure I stay in jail no matter what."

Of course, Mair was lying. And the bail bondsman was telling the truth.

The jail was actually on lockdown. Jails go on lockdowns for various reasons: inmates fighting, security breaches, guards getting attacked. When a jail is on lockdown no one gets released. Period. All inmates are forced to stay in their cells and wait for the lockdown to be lifted.

But even from the confines of a jail cell, Mair figured out a way to stoke my resolve to help her by using the time-tested Red Flag of Drama, Drama, Drama. She strengthened the detailed illusion that her wealthy family back in Ireland (who did not exist) had so much clout and so much insider influence in Los Angeles that they were tweaking the criminal justice system to keep her behind bars, even after I had posted bail to get her out.

Her story worked really well. I bought it, and I kept buying it for years to come.

"The woman I'm sharing a cell with just got released. And she murdered her husband!" Mair bawled to me at two o'clock in the morning. "My fucking family! They've got their thumb on me. They won't let me out of here."

I truly believed that Mair's tyrannical family was doing anything and everything to keep her $7 million for themselves. I just knew they had set her up for stealing so they could get her convicted of a felony and force her to forfeit her inheritance. I knew this like I knew that my name was Johnathan, and that the sky was blue, and that water was wet.

At around 7 A.M. on July 9, 2014, I got another call from Mair, this time from her cellphone and not from the jail's collect-calling system. "They just let me out. Can you come pick up?" Mair asked. So I hopped in my car, picked Mair up, and took her out to breakfast.

"I'm going to get you the $4,200 in bail money tomorrow," Mair assured me. "Don't worry."

"I'm not worried," I said.

True to her word, the very next day there was a knock on my door. And standing there in a dark blue suit was the Politician.

"This is from Mair," he said as he handed me $4,200 stuffed in an envelope in crisp hundred-dollar bills.

Cash has its own allure, doesn't it? Cold, hard cash. When you write a check for that amount it's pretty ho-hum, but when you hold a stack of bills that thick, it feels pretty cool.

Oh, and the other thing about cash? It's untraceable.

Now it might be hard to discern here, and certainly I was clueless while it was happening. But what had just transpired was textbook beak wetting.

Mair paying me back the $4,200 in bail money I loaned her—the next day—made me believe she was a woman of her word. That gave me complete and utter confidence to loan her even more money, *way* more money, down the line. And that was her plan all along. That's how she extracted tens of thousands of dollars out of me.

While the Politician did in fact hand me an envelope with $4,200 in it that day, telling me it was from Mair, it actually wasn't from Mair at all. It was from the Politician's own bank account. I had no way of knowing this at the time, but the Politician was getting scammed by Mair in a dozen different ways that I couldn't have imagined in a million years.

And as close to the bone as her confidence tricks cut with me, the scams that the Politician fell for cut much, much closer and much, much deeper. I'm going to unpack them all for you in vivid detail in another chapter, so keep reading.

Mair and I weren't neighbors anymore at that point, because in May of 2014, at the one-year mark of my meeting Mair for the first time in my building, she moved to another building a few blocks away.

It was a glitzier, more expensive address. Her building had its own rooftop swimming pool, an art deco-style clubhouse, and an amazing game room with pool tables and video games.

Then after she got arrested, she moved *again* because some of her neighbors in that building had seen her getting handcuffed that day. And Mair was really bothered by that. She said she was too embarrassed to stay at that place. So she ended up moving to an even more expensive building across from L.A. LIVE—the entertainment complex near what was then called the Staples Center and is now the Crypto.com Arena.

Her rent at that new fancy place was nearly $6,000 per month in late 2015. It had valet parking, an observation deck with a sky lounge, and a freaking movie theater. Remember the film *Fifty Shades of Grey*? I saw it with Mair in her building's movie theater.

But at this point in July of 2014 Mair was out of jail and determined to clear her name. She hired a lawyer. And she was talking to me about going to the news media to try to get some coverage to publicly expose what her family had done to her.

You see, from 1997 to 2007 I had worked in the news business for various TV stations around the country. I was a news producer at WAMI-TV and WSVN-TV in Miami and a news reporter at KABB-TV in San Antonio and KHOU-TV in Houston. And I knew that what had happened to Mair, or rather, what I believed had happened to Mair, would make a sensational story that no news reporter in their right mind could resist. Headlines like "Evil Family Frames Cousin to Steal Inheritance" and "Irish Heiress Being Cheated Out of Family Fortune" immediately came to mind.

But wouldn't you know, every time I offered to help Mair write up a press release and pitch her story to the local news media here in Los Angeles, she would put me off. "I need to focus on my court case now. Let's not do this today," she'd say. Obviously, looking back, she was a professional con artist, and the last thing in the world she wanted was to be on the news—for any reason.

Early on in the process of Mair's criminal case, the one where her family supposedly framed her to make it look as if she had stolen

$200,000 from her employer to get her disinherited, I went to several court hearings with her, and I met her lawyer. But at no point did I ask her lawyer, "So do you think you can prove Mair's evil family is trying to set her up?"

We just made polite conversation, like most people do.

And if you have ever been a part of any criminal case, whether as a witness or as a victim or even as the accused, you know firsthand that nothing much happens at those court hearings. There were dozens and dozens of them, and nothing revealing was ever said out loud at any of them. All they ever seemed to do was unanimously agree to meet again in thirty days so they could repeat the whole process another time. They'd make motions for this and motions for that and ask for continuances. Then they'd agree to meet again in thirty days, and then another thirty days, and then another.

The criminal justice system moves like molasses—coagulated molasses. So, at the few court hearings I attended with Mair, I never saw or heard anything that made me think she was lying to me. And the entire time her case was moving through the court system she was showing me emails from her attorney making it look like he was close to getting the bogus case against her—that her family was behind—dismissed.

This harkens back to the Red Flag of Technology. Con artists revel in using cellphones, computers, dating apps, voice-changing apps, and nowadays AI to trick you. I had no way of knowing that all the emails Mair was showing me from her attorney were really from online email accounts she had created in her attorney's name (a crime in and of itself: identity theft) and had emailed herself so that she could show me those emails to convince me that what she was saying was true.

So I was 100 percent hooked on all of Mair's stories in 2014. I really did believe them. But little did I know, things were about to take a wild, wild turn.

10. RED FLAG #9: A GOOD DAY JOB

NOW, THIS RED FLAG IS KIND OF TRICKY. IT'S NOT SO MUCH A RED FLAG AS IT IS A CUE TO not ignore other glaring red flags that might be presenting themselves. Because the truth of the matter is, professional con artists all have great day jobs or careers or other impressive avocations. And it's easy to dismiss or overlook the other red flags when they present because you might be thinking, "This couldn't be a con; this person has an amazing career." And that's the point.

So the lesson with this red flag is to be aware: Just because someone has an impressive career doesn't mean they're not a con artist. Maybe they have a prestigious job in the mayor's office. Maybe they run a huge charity that does a lot of good in the community. Maybe they have their own accounting firm. Maybe they're an on-demand investment broker. Those are all extraordinary careers. But for a working con artist, a job like that is just a "cover career"—it's not the moneymaker for them.

The moneymaker is the scam. But their job or career gives them the appearance of legitimacy.

Take Jen Shah, for instance. You may have heard that name before. Jen Shah shot to international fame in late 2020 when she became one of those cantankerous, drink-throwing, expletive-slurring housewives on the hit Bravo reality series *Real Housewives of Salt Lake City.* She was a larger-than-life character, Hollywood glamour on steroids. And of all the housewives featured that season, she stood out from the pack. She wore over-the-top designer gowns, lived in an opulent mansion, drove flashy cars. And her temper tantrums were theatrical spectacles.

Out of the gate, when the other housewives asked Jen what she did for a living, she proudly responded, "I own three different marketing companies. And we do lead generation and data monetization."

Impressive, right? But no one knew what that meant exactly.

Lead generation? Data monetization? Those are magical details that are ironically as specific as they are vague.

So Jen elaborated for her fellow housewives on one of those Bravo TV specials. "When ads are popping to you guys and they're like, how the hell do they know I'm shopping at Neiman Marcus? That's me. Do you know how much traffic is on the internet every second? All the people clicking? I'm making money on every click. Every time you click on anything I'm getting some money."

Then Jen said something else on television that lines up with what a lot of criminals inadvertently tend to do. They tend to reveal themselves—unintentionally, of course. But make no mistake, Jen Shah outed herself as a con artist for the millions of people watching all over the world when she famously elaborated on her moneymaking empire: "The best way to describe it is, I'm the Wizard of Oz basically. I'm like the one behind the curtain that nobody knows exists, but I'm the one making everything happen."

Now, if you've seen that 1939 classic movie *The Wizard of Oz,* then you know that the Wizard isn't actually a wizard at all. He is a con artist—a mere mortal, literally using smoke and mirrors to fool everyone up until the end of the film, when he gets found out. "Pay no attention to the man behind the curtain," he pleads, trying to deflect from what Dorothy, the Scarecrow, the Tin Man, and the Cowardly Lion all see with their own eyes: a desperate old man pushing buttons and throwing levers to blow smoke and fire in an attempt to portray himself as something he is not.

Jen Shah portrayed herself to the world as a brilliant self-made mogul. In reality, she was a duplicitous con woman who built a scammy multi-million-dollar empire on the backs of thousands and thousands of victims, most of them elderly. No one suspected a thing because she had such an amazing day job. She was a Real Housewife, for crying out loud. She was the star of a television show.

But that was all just a cover. Because that's not where she made her millions.

"Jen Shah stole money by lying. The types of lies and the way that the lies worked are a little more complex, but she lied and stole people's money based on those lies," said former Los Angeles prosecutor Emily D. Baker, who now hosts a popular podcast called *The Emily Show,* compellingly (and hilariously) analyzing celebrity legal troubles on the daily.

I've spent hours talking to Emily for my podcast *Queen of the Con* and she has an amazing knack for summing up the elaborate con Jen Shah successfully executed for years under everyone's noses:

> If I was explaining it to a nine-year-old, I'd be like, "Look, it's as if she was going to sell you a skin for Roblox [a popular video game]. And you paid money for the skin, but then the Roblox skin never worked. And she's like, 'Oh no, you just need this other program to make it work.' And then she sold you that program to make it work. And then that didn't work. And you were like, 'But this isn't working.' And she's like, 'Oh no, but you need this other thing, so pay me for this other thing and then it will work.' And then you end up down this chain of all these things you tried to do to make the one thing you wanted work that was never, ever intended to work. It was intended to milk you out of all your money."

That's the best and most easily understandable description of Jen Shah's scam I've ever heard, because her con was extremely complicated. And that was by design.

All con artists like to make their scams complicated—very complicated—because the more complicated the scam is, the harder it is for a victim to explain it to the police, and the harder it is for a prosecutor to explain it to a jury. Reasonable doubt is a hell of a thing. It's the legal threshold for guilt in our justice system. All any juror needs is reasonable doubt to choose "not guilty" when they're deliberating. And if a jury can't understand the scam because it's too complicated, that leaves a gaping hole of reasonable doubt that you can drive a truck through, which can ultimately enable the con artist to walk away scot-free.

Jen Shah grew up outside Salt Lake City, Utah, and in her twenties began working for a telemarketing company. She excelled at telemarketing and rose up the ranks quickly, becoming a manager in record time and soon after that a co-owner of one of these telemarketing companies.

Jen Shah was a huge fan of loopholes and a much bigger fan of money and closing sales and getting rich quick. She astutely figured out that it's much more profitable to hook a customer for years with monthly payments for things than it is to just close one sale and move on to the next customer. So Jen Shah devised a way to trick thousands and thousands of customers to pay monthly for something that did not actually exist and was not real in any way. And she ruthlessly targeted the most vulnerable people—the elderly, the unemployed, and the desperate.

"It's essentially a high-pressure sales floor," said Joseph L. Flatley, a journalist who investigated one of the companies Jen Shah was affiliated with early on, called Prosper, Inc., for *The Verge,* an online tech magazine. I've spent hours talking to Joseph, and he unraveled exactly what Jen Shah and Prosper, Inc. were up to.

> They say that they sell distance learning. So it's kind of like modern-day versions of correspondence courses where if you want to work on anything, from professional development to more like New Age, the Secret, Course in Miracles–type stuff, you enlist in one of their programs and you get information in the mail or you get coaching over the phone. But what we've found out about Prosper's products is that they're basically worthless. It's basically like any other scam where you're

buying something that promises the world and then you get it and it's practically useless, if not totally useless.

As Jen Shah progressed in her career in telemarketing, she created a way of generating "lead lists"—directories of names and phone numbers and email addresses of people who had inquired online about starting a second career or starting a business or learning a new skill. She then created an armada of bogus websites with headlines like "Wanna double your income from home?" or "Learn how to do drop ship and make $10,000 a month," or "We'll build a website that'll make you $20,000 a month." When elderly people or unemployed people or otherwise desperate people googling to find work online clicked on these websites and filled out their forms to "request more information," giving the website their names and phone numbers and email addresses, Jen Shah not only marketed to those people with her scammy telemarketing company but also sold their contact info to other scammy telemarketing companies who would do the same thing.

This goes back to that bedrock phrase I coined in chapter 1 that I will keep repeating until it's drilled into all of you: Con artists don't outsmart you, they out-feel you. If you're unemployed and desperate for money, if you're one month away from getting kicked out of your apartment because of your inability to pay rent, if you're seventy years old and you feel like technology and the internet have passed you by and you want to try and get a grasp of it and make some quick money because your Social Security check isn't cutting it anymore and homelessness is looking like a real possibility—then your emotional needs have completely hijacked your intellect, and these various Jen Shah work-from-home websites are irresistible to you. So you click.

"We probably will never be able to be retired. We'll have to work until we can't work anymore," sixty-five-year-old Penny Pucket soberly confessed to me when we spoke back in 2023. She had gotten scammed out of more than $30,000 by one of Jen Shah's telemarketing companies, who called her up after Penny clicked on one of those bogus websites promising her tens of thousands of dollars working from home.

Penny was a farmer in Kansas, but she had a real talent for sewing baby car seat blankets. And once she revealed that to one of Jen Shah's telemarketers, he pounced and silver-tongued Penny into enrolling in her first (of many) courses, guaranteeing her thousands of dollars a month in sales if she completed the course successfully.

"It was a course that was designed to teach you how to market your stuff on social media," said Penny, who at the time did not know much about social media.

So Penny completed that $3,000 course successfully, and yet did not make any money. Then Jen Shah's minions pounced on Penny again.

"They started telling me, well, maybe you need to do a website, you know, if you do a website you can make a thousand dollars a week. Well, if it costs $8,000 to do a website in a couple months, if a thousand dollars a week is what you brought in, it wouldn't take much to get a return on your investment."

So Penny forked over $8,000 and signed a bunch of contracts and paperwork, and the telemarketing company appeared to build her a website. But in reality, it was just a fake website slapped together for appearances. It was not functional at all. Penny never made any money from it. So they offered to fix her website for a few thousand dollars more. And Penny paid them a few thousand dollars more.

All those telemarketing calls and the fact that some of the documents Penny signed included a money-back guarantee made Penny feel like she had nothing to lose. But the money-back guarantee was not real. Neither was anything else. And Penny lost more than $30,000.

According to court records, federal prosecutors say Jen Shah was the one who wrote all the scripts for the hundreds and hundreds of telemarketers she had employed to do her bidding. Jen Shah was the mastermind, instructing all these telemarketing operators on exactly what to say and how to push back on victims who said they didn't have any more money to spend.

"The operators, they pump you for information," said journalist Joseph L. Flatley. "They find out you have $5,000 available on your Visa card and the first tier of their program just happens to be $5,000. But if you really want to improve your life and you really want to benefit, you've got to spend $15,000. So now you're going out of your way to get more credit or to get loans or whatever to mortgage your house. And there's never an end to the products, or I should say the products don't end until you're bankrupt."

And a lot of Jen Shah's victims went bankrupt. Thousands of them. And they started filing complaints with law enforcement agencies across the country. Eventually the Department of Homeland Security started investigating, and in March of 2021, Jen Shah was arrested while shooting an episode of *Real Housewives.* She was charged with masterminding a sweeping telemarking fraud scheme.

So naturally, like all con artists do when they're caught at first, Jen Shah pleaded not guilty and said publicly, "I'm fighting this. I am innocent. And I will fight for every person out there that can't fight for themselves because they don't have the resources and the means. I will fight. Because, number one, I'm innocent. And number two, I'm going to represent every person out there that can't fight and hasn't been able to."

As I watched her deliver these lines in a televised interview with tears welling up in her eyes (remember all professional con artists can cry at the drop of a hat—or a felony charge) she seemed so believable and so innocent. And if I didn't know what I know about this case, and if I hadn't spoken to her victims and to investigators, I would think that maybe the federal government had gotten it wrong.

Jen Shah went so far as to accuse authorities of targeting her because she was a "woman of color," as she was of Tongan and Hawaiian descent. But in the end, once her lawyers got ahold of the government's discovery—all the evidence they had against her, all the incriminating text messages she sent, all the telemarketing scripts she wrote herself, all her cellphones (she had about a dozen cellphones when they arrested her)—Jen Shah changed her tune and pled guilty. She was sentenced to more than six years in federal prison.

Finally, her decade-long telemarketing fraud scheme was over. But make no mistake, right now there are a thousand Jen Shah–type scammers picking up right where she left off.

Queen of the Con VII

Mair Smyth's day job when I first met her was selling luxury vacations to the Pacific Islands. She had convinced me that she didn't actually need to work, that she had more than enough money to live on for the rest of her life. But she said there were only so many Rodeo Drive shopping sprees she could tolerate before a sense of uselessness enveloped her and depressed her. "I didn't feel like I was contributing anything to this world," Mair said to me at the time.

So her cousin Fintan, who was best friends with the owner of that luxury travel agency in Los Angeles, had gotten her a job there years earlier, back when she and Fintan were on good terms. And she loved it. And she was really good at it, or so she said.

The truth of the situation was that, yes, Mair did work for this luxury travel agency, but she had gotten the job on her own after getting fired from another travel agency. There was no Fintan and no family in Ireland. That was all just part of her elaborate con.

But Mair told a Newport Beach engineer named Bob an entirely different story about what she did for a living. And in the end, it almost cost him the two multi-million-dollar homes he owned. He was getting ready to sign them over to her, or rather, to add her name to the homes' titles.

Then fate (aka, me) intervened.

Bob met Mair on Tinder back in late 2016. And as Bob was told, Mair worked for the city of Los Angeles County as a child custody investigator. A 730 expert—that's what they're called. That's what she told him she did for a living on their first date together.

Looking back, it's obvious to me that Mair told Bob she was a 730 expert because Bob had told her earlier that he had recently gone through a divorce and was not happy with the custody arrangement in regard to his kids. So Mair offered to help him (Red Flag #1) by convincing him that she had the power to change things because she worked with Los Angeles County, investigating child custody cases for the courts. And Bob was thrilled to get the help—or what he took for "help."

So Mair appeared to have a meaningful and important day job (Red Flag #9): she was a child custody investigator! Obviously, that was a total lie. But Mair knew how the child custody system worked from her personal experience years earlier—when a "730 expert" declared her an unfit mother and the courts took her daughter, Courtney, away from her. So she knew how to convincingly portray a 730 expert to Bob.

After a few dates, Mair and Bob grew pretty close, and Mair confided in Bob that she trusted him enough now to reveal that she was an Irish heiress with a $25 million inheritance coming to her over the next few months. And of course, she showed him the requisite texts from her family back in Ireland and the emails from her barristers that corroborated what she was saying (Red Flag #6: Technology).

Of course, if Mair was so wealthy and about to be even wealthier, she didn't need to work. But she told Bob she was working as a child custody investigator for the same reason she'd told me she was a luxury travel agent—there were only so many crazy shopping sprees a woman of means could indulge herself in before she started feeling useless and depressed. And helping abused children gave her a tremendous sense of purpose (Red Flag #5: "I'm Better Than You").

So Mair started orchestrating two extremely elaborate scams for Bob at the same time. One scam was to distract him so she could execute the other scam to take co-ownership of his two Newport Beach homes.

Now, Newport Beach is an extremely affluent seaside city in Southern California, about an hour and a half south of Los Angeles. The median household income is $150,000, but I'm guessing Bob made way more than that because he was a big-time engineer for a huge tech company.

SCAM #1—DISTRACT

During the course of their relationship, Mair convinced Bob that she was using her private investigator to investigate his ex-wife so she could make the case to the courts to get Bob a better custody arrangement. She started showing Bob texts and emails from the private investigator communicating what she'd uncovered about his ex-wife, so there was no doubt in Bob's mind that this was all real.

At the same time, Bob started getting texts from other characters Mair was impersonating too. Early on Bob told Mair he was a huge hockey fan, and as luck would have it, Mair said she was best friends with the manager of Bob's favorite hockey team. Small world, right? Mair started showing Bob texts from this hockey team manager, and eventually the hockey team manager started texting Bob too. A lot of that texting conversation had to do with what an amazing woman Mair was and how protective the hockey team manager was of her and her $25 million inheritance. But he told Bob that he seemed like a good guy, so he was going to trust Bob to take care of Mair and all those millions coming to her.

Oh, it gets better.

Bob had an amazing nanny named Sarah who helped with his kids, and Mair became good friends with her. At one point, Mair took Sarah to a hockey game where the team manager whom she'd been impersonating over text—to both Bob and Sarah—was working. And while Sarah and Mair were watching the hockey game, Mair locked eyes with the manager of the hockey team, who was on the sidelines, and Mair waved at him. And he waved back at her, so there was no doubt in Sarah's mind that the two knew each other.

Only they didn't. At all.

It's human instinct, when someone looks at you and waves, you look back and wave in response. It doesn't mean anything at all. But in this case, accompanied by a detailed backstory from an inveterate con woman like Mair, it appeared to be proof that Mair and the team manager knew each other. So when Sarah the nanny got home to Bob's house, she told Bob she'd seen the manager of this hockey team at the game and Mair knew him for sure.

Shortly after that, Mair's "private investigator" began texting Mair and Bob some disturbing things she'd uncovered about Bob's ex-wife. Again, this private investigator did not really exist. It was just a character Mair had created over text to sell her stories to Bob. The investigator texted Mair and Bob that she had tapped Bob's ex-wife's phone and had learned that Bob's ex-wife was running a BDSM sex club out of her home—while she had Bob's kids sleeping upstairs (Red Flag #3: Drama, Drama, Drama). In reality, there was no sex club and no private investigator—it was all made up by Mair.

But Bob was incensed at the thought of his ex-wife running a sex club out of the home where his children slept. And Mair calmed him down by telling him this was all great evidence they could use to get Bob sole custody of his kids. Remember, Bob believed wholeheartedly that Mair was a child custody investigator who worked for the courts. And he was so grateful at this point that Mair and her private investigator had discovered all this BDSM sex club stuff and were going to help him get through it and get full custody of his kids.

Again, con artists don't outsmart you, they out-feel you. They use your emotions against you. And that was exactly what was happening to Bob here. He was thinking with his heart and not his head. He was worried about the safety of his children and blindingly angry that his ex-wife was running a BDSM sex club out of their home.

Obviously, none of that was true.

SCAM #2—THE PAYOFF

At the same time all this private investigator BDSM sex club stuff was going down, Mair had convincingly established a whole other storyline that she'd been carefully unpacking for Bob: Her $25 million inheritance was coming any day. At this point, Bob knew it to be true. Mair had shown him all the text messages and emails from the American lawyers and the Irish barristers. It seemed like it was really happening.

Of course it wasn't. But when Mair hired a Newport Beach realtor and started touring $12 million mansions—one of which she planned to buy with her inheritance—there was no doubt in Bob's mind that this was all going down.

Mair and Bob looked at a dozen or so different homes together with that clueless realtor before Mair zeroed in on the mansion she was going to buy. Then she ordered a home inspection and put in a written offer on the home for more than $12 million. It was just outside Newport Beach in the tony beachside community of Corona Del Mar.

"I'm going to add your name to the title," Mair lovingly told Bob, because she saw a real future together and she wanted to own this home with him.

"I can't let you do that," Bob replied. "If our relationship goes south, I'll own $6 million worth of your home. And that's just not fair."

Mair knew Bob would say that. She was literally banking on it. "Okay," she replied, not missing a beat. "If you want to make it fair, just add my name to the titles of your two homes and we'll be even." And she started drawing up all the paperwork for Bob to do just that.

Bob actually brought his kids to that mansion to pick out their bedrooms. And Mair told Bob that when his son turned sixteen, she was going to buy him a Lamborghini. After all, with that $25 million inheritance, she'd have millions left over after she bought the house for cash.

So it appeared Bob was getting ready to add Mair's name to the title of his two Newport Beach homes, making her a co-owner.

Then fate intervened.

Around the time that Mair started dating Bob, I started loaning her money to live on. Mair had tricked me by showing me texts and emails from her lawyers indicating that the courts had frozen her bank accounts after she was arrested for stealing $200,000 from that luxury travel agency—or rather, after she was framed by her evil Irish family who were trying to get her disinherited.

Remember, I had paid $4,200 to bail her out of jail and she had paid me back the next day (Red Flag #8: Beak Wetting). So I was confident loaning her more money after they froze her bank accounts.

But after she got more than $20,000 from me over the course of a few months, she told me she needed $55,000 more to pay court fees and to get the bogus case against her dismissed so she could get her inheritance. That's when I let her charge my credit cards $55,000.

Again, she was like a sister to me at this point. I truly loved her and cared about her. And I wholeheartedly believed that her evil family back in Ireland was not only trying to disinherit her but trying to destroy her. I rallied to her defense, out of love.

There were numerous times when I'd held her as she wept, convulsing, and I'd cried along with her. This was all 100 percent real to me. The dampness on my shirt collar from her tears—it was real. I felt it.

I just had no idea that I was falling for an elaborate con.

After I paid the $55,000 court costs—I mean, that's where I thought the $55,000 went—Mair was jubilant. She was going to get her inheritance any day now. We went out and celebrated with champagne.

Clink. Clink.

But days later, when I went to pick Mair up for brunch, I found her doubled over crying. And I embraced her once again.

"What's wrong?" I asked as I took her in my arms.

"The judge in my case is angry at me for using your credit cards to pay my court fees." Mair's voice cracked through tears. "He considers it money laundering and he's going to punish me for it."

"Money laundering?" I asked incredulously.

At that point I knew nothing about the criminal justice system. The last time I had been involved with a court case was twenty years earlier when I fought a traffic ticket. So I accepted what she was telling me at face value.

Again, Sunk Cost Fallacy was at play here. I had believed so many lies over the four years of our friendship—one more lie was that much easier to swallow.

Mair told me that the judge was punishing her with a thirty-day jail sentence. Not a felony conviction—merely a slap on the wrist to teach her a lesson. When she got out of jail, she'd get her inheritance and all would be well.

So Mair went to jail for thirty days. During the first two weeks, she called me collect every day.

I insisted on coming down there to visit her. "No!" she screamed over the phone at me. "I don't want you to see me like this. I am so ashamed and embarrassed."

But I ignored her, because she was like my sister at this point. I scheduled a visit to the jail by logging on to the sheriff's website and creating a profile—which is a requirement to visit anyone in L.A. County Jail. I then clicked on the inmate I wanted to schedule a visit with: Marianne Elizabeth Smyth. And I was blown away by what popped up.

Right there on my computer screen in black and white I discovered the first of ten thousand lies. Mair was not in jail for a "slap on the wrist" for money laundering. According to what I was reading, she was in jail for felony grand theft after pleading guilty for stealing $200,000 from that travel agency.

The reason she was serving only thirty days and not five years was that she had scammed me out of $55,000 to pay partial restitution to the travel agency! The judge interpreted her payment of partial restitution as a good sign that she was going to pay the rest back. So he gave her only thirty days in jail.

From there I finally figured out that Mair was not even Irish. She had actually been born in Bangor, Maine. There was no family back in Ireland. There was no inheritance. I then uncovered her rap sheet for fraud, grand theft, and forging documents in multiple states.

At that point I had loaned her more than $70,000. The interest rates on my credit cards were piling up fast, especially after I called up the credit card companies to tell them I'd been scammed. Instead of helping me, they raised my interest rate to 24.99 percent. I was paying thousands of dollars every month in credit card interest alone.

But then—I did what the vast majority of victims never do.

I went public.

I started a blog with Mair's picture, warning people not to give her money and informing the world that she was a con artist. And I told the story of how she had scammed me.

It was around this time that Bob, the Newport Beach engineer, whom Mair was deep in the process of tricking into adding her name to the titles of his two homes, called me up.

"Your blog saved me from her. Thank you," Bob gushed.

Apparently, Bob's ex-wife was getting curious about Mair. She wondered who the new woman in Bob's life was and why she was now spending so much time around her children. So she googled "Mair Smyth" and found my blog and sent it to Bob.

When Bob confronted Mair with my blog (she was staying in his home for a few weeks at the time post jail), Mair didn't say a word in response. She just turned around, ran out of his house, and drove away. Bob never heard from Mair again.

This is why it's crucial for victims to speak up and share their experience. Silence only helps the con artist scam more people. I feel such a tremendous sense of purpose and relief that my blog saved Bob from getting conned.

Who knew that it was only step one and that I was about to out Mair on national television?

11. RED FLAG #10: WIRES

THE TECHNOLOGY TO WIRE MONEY WAS INVENTED BACK IN THE 1870S WHEN PEOPLE would send cash to one another using the telegraph. Western Union was the first company to do it in 1872 using its existing telegraph network made up of thousands and thousands of miles of cable running from sea to shining sea.

Wires have certainly come a long way since then. These days when you wire money, it can be nearly instant. Or it can take a few minutes or a few hours or a few days to reach the recipient depending on the country they're in and the banks that are involved in the transaction.

But make no mistake about it, once you wire your money to someone, that money belongs to them. The reason you wired it is completely irrelevant to the bank. And once you wire your money to someone, unless you catch it very quickly and alert the bank that there's a problem, that money is gone forever.

And just in case you didn't know this fact, I'm here to spell it out for you: *Con artists love wires* because the transactions are quick and permanent. Once you wire money to a con artist, they immediately take that money out of the account you wired it to and put it someplace else. So even if you complain to the bank that it was a scam or fraud, that money is gone, never to be seen again.

There are, however, exceptions to this rule *if* you act fast shortly after sending the wire. There was a case I investigated recently where the victim, who frequently bought supplies for his company from someone in India, wired $25,000 to a con artist who had hacked into that supplier's email account, studied all the past communications between the victim and supplier, and boldly sent the victim a new invoice for $25,000. The victim was actually expecting a $25,000 invoice at some point, but the new invoice had a different bank routing number for the wire.

The victim wired the money and seconds later realized that the routing number was different from the one he always used for that particular supplier. So he called the supplier up on the phone to make sure everything was okay and the supplier said, "What are you talking about? I never sent you an invoice for $25,000."

The victim immediately called the bank. Keep in mind, this was within five minutes of the transaction. The bank was able to expeditiously open an investigation that ultimately led to the victim getting their $25,000 back. I mean, it took a few weeks for the money to be returned to his account. But because the victim acted so quickly, that $25,000 never actually made it the con artist's bank account and the con artist could not take possession of it and move it out.

But my earnest and sincere advice to all who are reading this is: Never. Send. Wires. If someone is asking you to wire them money for business purposes or personal purposes or any other reason under the sun—pause and take a step back and examine the situation.

By now, you know what most of the red flags are:

Red Flag #1—"I Just Want to Help"

Red Flag #2—Too Kind, Too Quick

Red Flag #3—Drama, Drama, Drama

Red Flag #4—Isolation

Red Flag #5—"I'm Better Than You"

Red Flag #6—Technology

Red Flag #7—Scarcity

Red Flag #8—Beak Wetting

Red Flag #9—A Good Day Job

So, if any of those red flags are present in the situation you find your-self in, and *now* the person or entity in question is asking you to wire them money?

Stop. Just stop. Do not send that wire.

In this day and age, there are dozens of ways to pay for things. You don't need to send a bank wire. When a professional con artist is trying to scam you out of a large sum of money in one fell swoop? They're usu-ally going to ask you to send a bank wire.

"The justice system failed, the banking system failed, and no one gives a crap!" wrote Mark (not his real name) in an email to me back in November of 2020.

Mark had gotten scammed out of $365,000 by a man he had known his entire life. He didn't know this man was a con artist though—until Mark himself got scammed by him. And the entirety of the $365,000 that Mark gave his con artist was sent through bank wires.

We all have this tragic and mistaken perception that con artists are "out there" somewhere. They're not people we know. And they are certainly not people we love and trust.

But that's the thing—they absolutely are! You won't know a profes-sional con artist is a con artist until they scam *you*. Up until that point, they're just someone you know or someone you love or someone that's been in your life for years or even decades. And because most victims don't say a word after they get scammed, you won't know the con artist in your life is scamming other people because no one's talking about it.

Mark is a supersmart fifty-six-year-old guy who works in IT in New York. He'd met the con artist who scammed him, a man by the name of Vincent Leli, back in high school. They were good friends, and their respective girlfriends were best friends. They spent a lot of time to-gether doing fun stuff, going to the movies, playing mini golf, going bowling, and hanging out at the mall—as high school kids did back then.

But when Mark graduated high school in 1986, he lost touch with Vincent. The two went their separate ways. Nothing unusual there.

Then, twenty-eight years later in 2014, Mark was still living and working in New York when he suddenly got a Facebook message from Vincent, who was now living in Naples, Florida, wanting to reconnect. The two men exchanged lengthy Facebook messages reminiscing about the good old days. Mark told Vincent he worked in IT now. And Vincent started unpacking what he did—which turned out to be a lot of Red Flag #5 ("I'm Better Than You").

Vincent portrayed himself as a super successful businessman, a home builder, a contractor, a bleeding-heart philanthropist, and a church-going family man. He said he owned a successful car wash and detailing product line that he had developed and sold for a national auto store chain. He also said he'd made a killing as a day trader, buying and selling tons of stocks on razor-thin margins.

Now, none of that was true. But the granular details that Vincent used, that *every* con artist uses, convinced Mark beyond any doubt that Vincent Leli had a Midas touch in life: that he made oodles of cash doing all kinds of things and was very successful and very wealthy.

Weeks later, Vincent happened to be in New York on business. At least that's what he told Mark. He was really in New York to lay the groundwork for his next scam. Vincent picked Mark up in a luxury car and wined and dined Mark at fancy New York restaurants (Red Flag #2: Too Kind, Too Quick).

And Vincent seemed to take pity on Mark because he had not done as well in life financially as Vincent had. So then Vincent suddenly pulled out Red Flag #1 ("I Just Want to Help").

Remember, Vincent, among many things, was a contractor. He said he had an "in" on a bunch of homes in South Florida that he was getting ready to flip for huge profits. And he offered to cut Mark in. He told Mark to get his hands on as much money as he could because he was about to make him a very rich man.

"I asked him why he was offering this opportunity to me. He said that he was very happy old friends reconnected, and he wanted to share his success and that's the kind of guy he is," Mark recalled.

And Mark was grateful—so grateful. Nothing seemed wrong or out of the ordinary. After all, he had known Vincent for decades. He was a good friend from high school.

I want to point out here that at this precise moment in this particular con, Mark was at the same crossroads that I was at with Mair. We were both about to give them money because we had known and trusted these people for years. We'd never seen any red flags waving because we didn't know what those were. (This book was not out yet.)

Also, neither of us had ever tried to independently verify what we were being told. The truth of the matter is, if Mark or I would have run Mair or Vincent through a basic $30 internet background check using BeenVerified.com or Intelius.com or any of the other dozen or so online consumer background check services out there, we would have immediately pulled up their past criminal records for fraud. And we would not have given them a single dime.

But Mark was in the exact same spot I was in—he believed everything Vincent was saying. He a had a years-long relationship with the man and he trusted him implicitly. All of those factors completely blinded him to what really was going on.

In 2015, Mark sent Vincent a series of bank wires totaling $365,000 (Red Flag #10: Wires). Vincent at that point was in Florida, supposedly in the process of flipping all the investment homes he had convinced Mark existed. In reality, they didn't. But that didn't stop Vincent from texting Mark pictures and videos of some of these supposed homes under construction (Red Flag #6: Technology). Vincent even had the audacity to text Mark messages like "Hope you are looking to retire real soon brother," along with the pictures and videos of the houses he claimed they were flipping.

Keep in mind, anyone can walk up to any home under construction and take a picture or video and say it's *their* home. And that's exactly what Vincent was doing again and again to Mark.

Months after Mark sent the bank wires, he began asking more pointed questions about his investment. Vincent always had an answer.

"He played me like an expert chess player. He anticipated my questions. Not only did he have reasonable answers or excuses but also made me feel silly or stupid for asking," Mark recalled.

Months after that, Mark started getting concerned that he hadn't seen any return on his investment yet. So he decided to fly down to South Florida to take a look at some of the homes that Vincent was supposedly flipping. Vincent picked Mark up at the airport in a brand-new $60,000 luxury pickup truck.

That shiny new pickup truck made Mark's stomach sink. It gave him a very bad feeling. Reason being—if Vincent had actually been working on flipping homes these past few months, driving from construction site to construction site, wouldn't his pickup truck be worn and battered by the elements at this point?

Vincent proceeded to drive Mark around all day, showing him all the homes they were flipping. He even walked Mark through an $800,000 property that was for sale that he told Mark they owned and that they'd be getting the profits from real soon.

But it was all smoke and mirrors and sleight of hand. It would have been like me standing outside the Empire State Building telling someone that it was mine and that I was close to securing its sale for $80,000,000,000. Vincent and Mark didn't actually own any of those homes.

After that trip, Mark feared the worst and asked Vincent for his money back ASAP. Vincent said he would get it back to him no problem. But then there was a delay. And then another delay. And then another delay. Then one day Mark received a Facebook message from Vincent's ex-wife: "I know you are in business with Vincent, did he steal all your money?"

At that point Mark's worst fears were confirmed. He was absolutely devastated.

"I fell to the floor," Mark recalls. "His ex-wife and I spoke on the phone for hours. She said Vincent is a low-life con man, and this is what he's been doing for a very long time."

Mark immediately reported Vincent to the police. He was shocked to discover that the entire time Vincent was scamming money from him, he was out on bail for an entirely different scam he was getting prosecuted for that he'd been conducting years earlier. Mark discovered that Vincent was a lifelong scammer with a history of stealing millions of dollars from dozens of victims employing very similar investment scams.

In 2018 Vincent Leli was charged and convicted for what he'd done to Mark and was sentenced to nine years behind bars. Since then, he's also been charged and convicted in several other similar cases and gotten handed years-long prison sentences for those crimes too. But Mark feels like the system failed him. And sadly, I agree. I mean, how can a convicted financial scammer be allowed to open bank accounts and create investment LLCs and get their hands on people's money without these institutions raising a single concern?

Shouldn't banks know exactly who is opening accounts with them? Especially if said people have a documented and easily verified record of financial crimes?

Shouldn't people who have been charged and/or convicted of financial crimes be shut out from opening bank accounts or starting investment LLCs? Or at least be put on the authorities' radar in some way?

"I'm not saying he shouldn't be able to open a bank account, but there should be a system of tracking and monitoring those who have been arrested and convicted of bank or wire fraud," Mark says. "I feel in this day and age this is a reasonable and simple fix."

And I agree. It totally is.

Queen of the Con VIII

Mair Smyth used bank wires to defraud at least one of her victims. She is truly a con artist chameleon, perpetually embodying multiple personas to scam dozens of people from all walks of life. For me, she was an Irish heiress—a damsel in distress. For others she was a child custody investigator. At one point she was even working as a psychologist—with a photoshopped degree hanging on her wall and everything—and she had a dozen or so clients in and around Los Angeles paying her by the hour for therapy. But she wasn't really giving them therapy. She was probing the depths of their psyches and weaponizing their fears and their deepest, darkest secrets to scam them.

And in 2014, Mair Smyth was working as a psychic. That's how she scammed a couple of savvy real estate investors in New York City out of $60,000. They wired that money right to her, and they never saw it again.

Mair didn't use her "psychic abilities" to scam these real estate investors. She just pulled on their heartstrings and appealed to their sympathies. Remember con artists don't outsmart you, they out-feel you.

"I have to use my gift. I have no other choice," Mair said to me as we were sitting in a downtown Los Angeles Starbucks sipping iced coffee one hot sunny day in early August 2014.

She had just been fired from her job, arrested, and charged with stealing $200,000 (at the time I believed her family was setting her up) and her life was otherwise in shambles. You'd think she would be stressed or worried or both. But Mair appeared remarkably calm and nonchalant. That kind of surprised me.

"I just got a job!" She gushed with childlike glee. "I'm working as a psychic now."

I was taken aback and perplexed. It was as if she was telling me she suddenly had X-ray vision or could leap tall buildings in a single bound. "Working as a psychic?" I thought to myself. "Like, what the hell does that mean?" Then I started remembering all the stuff she had told me about her family—all the fantastical and flowery details.

A year or so earlier, Mair had told me that her great-great-grandmother was a world-renowned psychic in Ireland and that world leaders would frequently consult her for guidance. Mair also had said that her sister was working with police in Germany as a psychic to locate missing children. She said the gift of clairvoyance ran in her family. So now her working as a psychic was suddenly making at least some kind of sense in my mind.

Looking back, becoming a psychic was a brilliant con artist move for Mair. It provided her with a revolving door of people to scam— desperate people who were obviously going through some kind of painful issue in their lives and were searching for some direction and advice. I mean, why else would anyone be seeking out a psychic?

I wasn't sure at that point if Mair was psychic. But I'd had some experiences with psychics in the past that led me to conclude that some people really are plugged into a kind of ethereal knowledge that eludes the rest of us. These people seem to be able to see things or know things that the rest of us don't.

Still, in my experience, 99.9 percent of the people who claim they're psychic are not. They're just scammers.

"I took a test over the phone and passed with flying colors," Mair bragged to me that day at Starbucks, her eyes sparkling.

She said she had called one of those psychic 1-800 numbers and asked how to apply for a job with them. They had quickly transferred her to someone who supposedly tested her psychic abilities over the phone by asking her to "read" them. And Mair was able to spit out some pretty detailed and personal things about their life and current situation. So they hired her on the spot.

This of course was all according to Mair. I had no way of verifying any of it. But I can definitely tell you that soon after our coffee in Starbucks that day, Mair had a slew of clients that she was on the phone with at all hours of the day and night, one after another for hours and hours on end. I witnessed this over and over again, because she'd put some of these people on speakerphone sometimes while I was there. I could listen to her "read" them.

And I was impressed. I suddenly started thinking that Mair might well have some clairvoyant abilities after all. The people on the phone with her all sounded so grateful and relieved to be talking to her. And the few phone calls I heard made it seem as if she was helping them through some dark times in their lives. That all jibed with my impression of the person I knew Mair to be back in 2014: an infinitely kind, loving, and helpful person.

"This is bullshit," Mair complained to me one day, just weeks into her new job as a phone psychic. "I'm getting pennies on the dollar talking to these people all damn day. The company is making most of the money. It's not fair."

Shortly after that conversation, Mair appeared to get so frustrated by the perceived pay disparity with that 1-800 psychic hotline that she quit and started her own psychic business called Orchid Psychics. And she was an overnight sensation. In no time flat, dozens and dozens of people in Los Angeles started booking her for readings, in person and over the phone. She seemed to be doing really well.

And then suddenly she had her own Yelp page up with a growing collection of raving five-star reviews:

> I had a phone reading with Mair today and all I have to say is WOW! I was totally blown away by everything she said to me. She is truly gifted. I will never go to another psychic now that I found her. I highly recommend her. Trust me it doesn't get better than her!—Janet O.

> I recently had Mair at an event, where she did a series of one-on-one readings for close friends of mine. She was spot on with everyone, and she made the event a notable success—one my friends are still talking about. I could not rave more highly about her skill, or her personality—sweet, kind, endearing, and a wonderful empathic psychic that I will call on again and again.—Craig G.

I had a reading today by Mair, and immediately felt welcome, and just very calm, we sat down and of course she cut to it and mentioned the first of three things I wanted to know about, she gave me that validation that I needed, if there's anyone gifted that you're trying to seek answers from, don't waste time on anyone else . . . go to her, you won't be disappointed. Mair I thank you for today, you're the sweetest, and I'll definitely keep you updated. Love, Rae:)—Rae Y.

On December 31, 2014, Mair invited my husband and me to a swanky Great Gatsby–themed New Year's Eve party on the beach. The people who were throwing the party hired Mair as a psychic and paid her a few thousand dollars to attend the celebration and read random party guests as an attraction and we tagged along.

Each guest was paying $500 to attend. That price included all the food and drink—and all the Mair—they could stomach.

Everyone dressed up in Gatsby-inspired garb reminiscent of the Roaring Twenties. My husband and I wore tuxedos, and Mair showcased a shimmery green cocktail dress that really dazzled.

It was a memorable night because it was the first time I saw Mair in action as a working psychic when she was meeting with people face-to-face. She sat down at a table where the party planner had constructed a wooden sign that read "Fortunes Told," festooned with a purple-eyelashed eyeball drawn in with iridescent marker.

Mair started her readings. And in about twenty minutes, a line began to develop.

I was shocked. People dressed in Gatsby attire, cocktails in hand, were waiting in line to spend five minutes with Mair on New Year's Eve because apparently word had quickly spread that she was stunningly accurate with her readings. Mair was actually bringing people to tears with what she was "seeing." It was *insane.*

When one woman sat down, dressed like a 1920s flapper, the first words out of Mair's mouth were "You're dating a guy in New York and a guy in Los Angeles. You have to make a decision or you're going to lose them both."

The woman immediately burst into tears. "I don't know who to choose!" she cried as Mair consoled her.

I saw this scene unfold with my own eyes. How on earth could Mair have pulled that titillating fact out of thin air for that woman—a complete stranger? And the bicoastal dater wasn't alone. I watched in amazement as Mair brought party guest after party guest after party guest to tears with her razor-sharp and specific pronouncements and predictions. So, as far as I could see, Mair clearly was psychic.

Years later, after I interviewed several dozen of her psychic clients, a lot of whom went on to become victims Mair scammed, I figured out what her deal was. Mair indeed had a gift for reading complete strangers with stunning accuracy. That's how she won them over initially. That's how they all became regular clients of hers. And that's why they all left her those five-star Yelp reviews. That all checked out.

But here's the tragic twist when it came to Mair's psychic ability: As Mair got to know these people she read—these "clients"—and as they returned to her for readings again and again, her ability to read them quickly disappeared. I came to discover that Mair's gift of clairvoyance applied only to people she did not know. It was only viable for her with complete strangers. Once she got to know someone, she couldn't read them—at all.

It turns out, *familiarity* was Mair's *psychic kryptonite*.

Case in point, she was never able to read me. Not that I ever asked her for a reading. But I was the one who ultimately put her in jail. So if she could read people she knew, I imagine she would've discerned that and stayed the hell away from me.

But apparently she couldn't. So she didn't. So I did.

Anyway, after interviewing dozens of her psychic clients I figured out the process she had used to scam all of them. It went like this.

First, she would suck them all into her world with a great, accurate reading that blew them all away and hooked them and brought them to tears. Mair could read a stranger like I could read a Cheesecake Factory menu, with open-eyed precision and depth—salivating the entire time.

When these clients returned for a second reading, and a third reading, they noticed—and Mair noticed—that these readings were not as accurate as before, or not accurate at all. But the clients in question were still so enthralled by that first reading that had blown them away, they would give Mair a second chance and even a third chance.

During this time Mair would intentionally let slip that she was actually a psychologist. She would say she had worked as a psychologist in Ireland, and she'd point to her psychology degree hanging on the wall.

At this point Mair knew enough about their lives to convince them that they didn't need psychic readings anymore—what they needed was therapy. They needed "life coaching" to take them to the next level in their lives and solve all their problems. And they were in luck because Mair said she specialized in life coaching. She was certified in that too, wouldn't you know. And she showed them the requisite documentation to prove it.

But keep in mind that with today's technology a crafty con artist can produce a legitimate-looking degree from Harvard or medical certification from Johns Hopkins or an accounting degree from Pepperdine with ease. All they need is a good printer.

So one by one Mair would trick her "psychic clients" into becoming "life coaching clients." She'd have them sign a bunch of papers that made the whole process look extremely legitimate and aboveboard. But what she was really doing was protecting herself from criminal prosecution.

I've been investigating hundreds of con artist cases over the past few years, and this is a trick I've seen again and again. But I first noticed it with what Mair was pulling, so it's worth noting and pointing out here.

When you get scammed and you go to the police to tell them about the scam and try to get them to file a police report and start an official investigation, the minute you pull out any kind of contract or agreement or any type of document the con artist tricked you into signing, police immediately lose all interest. That's because in their minds you've just proved to them that the case you're talking about is a civil case and not a criminal case. They'll think you need to hire a lawyer and sue the person who allegedly scammed you—in civil court. The police want nothing to do with it.

When you hand over documents that a con artist tricked you into signing, you're unintentionally telling the police that this is a "business deal gone wrong." For them, and especially for personnel whose job it is to take police reports, this is not a crime. So they immediately turn you away.

The truth of the matter is, they don't want to write up a police report and start an investigation. In their world, people are being robbed and raped and murdered. People are lying in pools of blood calling for help. Those are the cases that need their full attention. So your coming in with signed documents and crying fraud will only make them refer you to the civil courts and pass the buck. That's just the way the system is set up.

The police in this instance are actually wrong: A lot of criminal fraud cases involve forged or signed documents such as contracts or agreements. But the police on the front lines who take reports are not state attorneys or district attorneys or any kind of attorney who might recognize this fact. So they are likely to dismiss your concerns. Next!

The onus is on the victim to push back and prove their criminal case: to cajole or compel or otherwise inspire that police officer at the front desk to take their case seriously and file a police report. It's just that no one tells the victim the burden is on them—except me.

A seasoned con artist knows all this stuff already. This was hardly Mair's first charade parade. So all the scams she pulled as a psychic involved plenty of signed documents and agreements, and plenty of other paperwork too.

Mair was 100 percent correct in her assumption that having all those documents in place and creating a kind of circuitous paper trail would protect her from criminal prosecution. I witnessed this happen one day when I accompanied one of Mair's psychic victims to a Los

Angeles police station to file a police report against her. As soon as this victim pulled out the "agreement" she had signed with Mair for life coaching classes, the officer turned her away. "This is a civil matter," he said. And he refused to take a police report.

In the end, he couldn't have been more wrong. But in the meantime, the victim walked out of that police station crestfallen and defeated. And I walked out with her. Back then I was still naïve. I was still struggling to bring Mair to justice. I didn't know how the system worked (against scam victims), and I didn't know how to push back.

Back in her psychic scamming heyday, as Mair's five-star Yelp reviews kept multiplying, she got a call one day from a couple of real estate developers in New York. They had actually built their real estate empire using psychics to buy and sell buildings, and they were interested in hiring Mair as a consultant. But first she would have to pass their psychic test.

I don't know what the test was exactly. I just know the investor told Mair that he had three questions for her and that if she answered each question correctly, she was hired. Mair answered each question correctly. To this day, the investor has refused to tell me what those questions were.

So they hired Mair and paid her $20,000 per month, and they'd call her for consultation frequently. I overheard some of these phone calls because she would put them on speakerphone.

At one point they flew her out to New York and drove her around to pick buildings to buy. Every single building she picked for them on that trip they said they made money on, and they were thrilled.

But remember Mair's psychic kryptonite? Familiarity. After that trip to New York there were a couple more trips, but on those trips all of Mair's predictions lost them money. The subsequent buildings she picked for them to invest in were not winners. At all. And they told her they no longer needed her services.

Mair, sensing her $20,000 a month salary was about to go byebye, sucked both of them in with a compelling scam. "I'm sorry I've been off lately," she told them. "It's just that my daughter is in the hospital. She's suffering from stage 4 cancer, and she needs this experimental treatment that insurance will not cover. And I don't have the cash for it."

Of course, none of that was true. But Mair convinced those real estate investors that she needed $60,000 fast to save her daughter's life (Red Flag #7 Scarcity), and they agreed to give her the money. They were going to let her charge their credit card $60,000. But Mair told them it would be better and more effective if they just sent her a bank wire.

So they did. They wired her $60,000. Mair made them believe that the money actually saved her daughter's life. She thanked them profusely, and said she'd pay them back. Soon. But she never did.

It wasn't until late 2017, after one of those real estate investors found the blog I started about Mair scamming me, that they figured out she was a con artist. "Does she even have a daughter who had cancer?" one of them asked me over the phone when we first spoke.

"No. That was all a scam," I replied.

Those two real estate investors were grateful to me for outing her. At that point she had not been charged by the police. She was still out and about in Los Angeles scamming new victims, but I was hot on her trail.

"What can we do to help you put her in jail?" the men asked. "Do you need money? We can give you money. How much do you need?"

"I don't need your money," I said, laughing. "I need you both to file a police report in New York. That would really help the criminal case I'm trying to build here in Los Angeles. File a police report and send me a copy."

"I'm sorry," they replied. "We can't do that."

These real estate investors explained to me that filing a police report would make the Mair incident public. And if word ever got out that they were using psychics to help them invest in real estate, they would be the laughingstock of the circles they ran in and would be out of business in no time. So they adamantly refused to file a police report and begged me not to reveal their identities, a request I have honored. They again offered me money to help with my investigation, and again I refused.

By now, I'm sure you realize that this is truly the problem. The vast majority of victims of con artists do not want to go public, and that only helps the con artist get away.

But Mair's days were numbered, even if she didn't know it yet. I wish I could've seen the look on her face the day the LAPD banged down her door and slapped the cuffs on her. She had figured out a genius hiding place forty miles south of Los Angeles.

But I managed to find her. And I led the police right to her.

12. RED FLAG #11: THEY MOVE AROUND A LOT

THIS IS ONLY A RED FLAG IF OTHER RED FLAGS ARE PRESENT. I REALIZE SOME PEOPLE have jobs that force them to move around a lot. And some people are in the military or have spouses who are in the military and move around a lot as well. So in those situations we're not talking about con artists.

But I have noticed that the vast majority of professional con artists do move around a lot. It's not because they like the change of scenery or because they enjoy moving. It's because they have to.

Everything in life has a beginning, a middle, and an end, especially a con. And when a con ends, the jig is up and the con artist has to get the hell out of there. But in most cases the con artist will move away long before people figure out they were conned. And sadly, most people who figure out they were conned never do anything about it. So the con artist can continue scamming at their new address and not worry about being pursued.

Bottom line: If you meet someone new and you notice they've lived in a lot of different places—pay attention. Try and discern if any of the other red flags are present. If there are other red flags waving, you're probably dealing with a professional con artist.

The average person will move approximately eleven times in their lifetime. However, the average con artist will move dozens and dozens of times.

Take convicted con woman Danielle Miller. She's sitting in a Florida jail cell right now and she's only in her early thirties, yet she has had thirty-one different addresses in her short life thus far. And if she hadn't gotten caught a couple years ago, she'd probably have a dozen more.

Danielle Miller is a truly terrifying con artist because she straddles the worlds of "in person" cons and "online" or "virtual" cons with an ease and expertise I have never seen before. Most con artists are either/or. They're either "in person" con artists whom you know and love and develop a relationship with, like Mair Smyth was. Or they're virtual scammers who trick you over the phone or through email; they steal your information and rob you blind, but you never actually meet them in person or know who they physically are.

Danielle Miller is a master of both. This is also a woman who was born with a silver spoon in her mouth, and that's not a con. Her father was a successful attorney and the president of the New York Bar. Her mother was one of the original Rockettes. She grew up in New York's wealthiest circles and attended the best schools. But I have learned that con artists can come from any and all walks of life.

In May of 2021, Danielle Miller was thirty-one years old, living in a glitzy downtown Miami high-rise overlooking beautiful Biscayne Bay. This was actually the thirty-first place she'd lived over those thirty-one years. She was recovering from a *Brazilian butt lift,* a plastic surgery procedure she had had done weeks earlier where they sucked fat from her stomach and injected it into her butt. She had a round-the-clock nurse tending to her every need, as she was completely mummified in bandages and surgical stockings going up and down her legs and torso.

Suddenly there was a knock on her door. Thinking it was a package delivery she was waiting for, Danielle opened the door and a team of federal agents rushed in, threw her up against the wall, and arrested her. She was charged with stealing millions of dollars from the federal government in the form of Paycheck Protection Program (PPP) loans, which provided small businesses with funds to pay up to eight weeks of payroll costs during the pandemic. Danielle had impersonated dozens and dozens of different small business owners and had taken out PPP loans in their names.

Now, you might be asking yourself what I was asking myself when I started investigating this case: How the hell did Danielle Miller get her hands on so many people's names and Social Security numbers and addresses and phone numbers to apply for all those loans?

Two words: data breaches—decades of data breaches.

You see these kinds of stories on the news all the time about big banks like Citibank or Bank of America getting hacked, or the Social Security Administration getting hacked, or giant cellphone companies like AT&T and T-Mobile getting hacked. What the news fails to report is the follow-up story: That all the information those hackers obtain— millions of people's names, dates of birth, Social Security numbers, addresses, cellphone numbers, and even passwords—gets posted on encrypted messaging apps like Telegram and on the dark web.

These entities make up a sort of "secret internet" used for criminal activity, where those in the know use encrypted apps or download a specific internet browser called Tor where they are able to buy and sell drugs or guns or anything illegal—anonymously. Except it's not *that* anonymous. I mean, authorities bust dark web crimes all the time.

So once everyone's stolen personal information that was hacked from banks or cellphone companies or the government is posted on these sites, scammers start collecting it all and selling those collections to other scammers in bulk. It's a whole secret industry.

To get those PPP loans, Danielle Miller bought hundreds of identities from other scammers. Then she meticulously used each piece of "PII"—what authorities call personal identifiable information—to impersonate scores of different people online so that she could get millions of dollars in PPP loans in their names.

But a year or so into that fraud, things ended abruptly for her. The Feds were able to trace the various burner cellphones she'd used and they figured out who she really was and where she was living. That's when they made that May 2021 arrest. The Brazilian butt lift surgery she was recovering from was a $30,000 procedure that she had used proceeds from her scams to pay for. And that was the last big con she would ever pull.

But it certainly wasn't the first. A year earlier, Danielle Miller was at a bank's drive-through window in Sarasota, Florida, trying to withdraw $8,000 from a stranger's bank account. She had been driving from bank to bank impersonating people and successfully emptying their bank accounts all day. She had created fake driver's licenses in the names of those people, and she had even gone through the trouble of porting each victim's cellphone number over to her own cellphone, so that when the bank called to confirm each withdrawal, the call rang to Danielle's cellphone. She answered, pretending to be each victim she was impersonating, and she okayed each transaction.

"And to me, that's not a con artist. That's somebody that's just a straight-up predator," said Carlos Verdoni, an ace detective with the Sarasota County Sheriff's Office.

I've spent weeks working with Detective Verdoni on the Danielle Miller case. What separates him from a lot of other law enforcement agents is that he takes this kind of fraud very seriously and goes above and beyond to try to stop it.

At this particular bank in Sarasota, for some inexplicable reason, the bank teller got a weird feeling and paused before giving Danielle Miller the $8,000 she was trying to withdraw. Even though Danielle Miller's fake ID in the victim's name, Erica Beers, had checked out, and even though the bank had called Erica Beers's phone number listed on the account and gotten confirmation from "Erica Beers" (really Danielle Miller pretending to be Erica Beers), the bank teller felt like something was off. So they proceeded to call the second phone number listed on the account, an older number. And the actual Erica Beers answered. It was her home phone.

But her home was in California. Not Florida.

Immediately the bank teller called the local sheriff's office. Two sheriff deputies showed up minutes later and arrested Danielle Miller.

"We found about $25,000 in the car along with other fake IDs as well," Detective Verdoni said.

But here's what separates Danielle Miller from most other scammers: During a five-hour interrogation by various Sarasota County sheriff's deputies the day of her arrest, including with Detective Carlos Verdoni, she pretended to be Erica Beers the entire time. She recited Erica's birth date, home address, and Social Security number—off the top of her head, again and again under questioning—as if they were her own. A few times she got some of the numbers wrong. But I've watched that five-hour interrogation over and over on video, and if you didn't know better, you would think Danielle Miller was Erica Beers. She was so confident, and so upset that this huge misunderstanding had landed her in handcuffs. "I don't understand why I'm being held, this is nuts. It's like taking money from my own account. I don't understand, I'm suing everybody. This is insane!" she exclaimed to deputies during the questioning. I posted a video highlights clip of this crazy hours-long exchange @QueenOfTheCon on Instagram on January 4, 2023. It's a master class in advanced con artistry and lying.

But as the hours passed, Detective Verdoni was busy going through the twenty-five IDs he had found in her purse and in her car, and he managed to figure out her real identity: Danielle Miller. As soon as he figured it out, he walked back into that interrogation room and confronted her by showing Danielle her actual driver's license—revealing it, almost like a card trick, among a pile of the twenty-four others.

"I just need to know which person you're going to be today so I can write my report correctly," Detective Verdoni smirked.

You can see in the video that Danielle Miller's face completely changed at that point. She was no longer pretending to be upset or shocked that she was in handcuffs. She was no longer pretending to be Erica Beers. She all of a sudden got poker-faced and serious and looked Detective Verdoni dead in the eye. "I want a lawyer," she said coldly.

This was obviously not Danielle Miller's first time being questioned by police. She'd been arrested several times before. She knew the drill all too well.

It was while I was investigating the Danielle Miller case that I decided to freeze my credit so that scammers like her cannot apply for loans or credit cards in my name. Freezing your credit is a somewhat tedious process, but it's free and I'm going to show you exactly how to do it in the last chapter of this book.

Before Danielle Miller became a master at buying strangers' identities from dark web scammers and impersonating them online and in person at banks, she was scamming people she knew. The particular Danielle Miller con I'm about to explain to you completely blew me away because I had never heard of it before. But it's a real thing and it's extremely easy to fall for.

"Danielle and I were roommates," thirty-one-year-old Taylor Firkus reluctantly admitted to me when I got her on a Zoom call back in 2022.

I had been trying to talk to Taylor for months after I found her name listed alongside Danielle Miller's in a set of court records as a coconspirator in a whole other scam she'd pulled. And it didn't make any sense to me. Danielle had always worked alone—now all of a sudden a woman named "Taylor Firkus" was being accused of helping her scam people? Keep in mind, Taylor did not have a criminal record of any kind, so I knew there was something more to the story. Eventually my persistence paid off, and Taylor agreed to talk to me and explain what had happened. And my God, this is a truly crazy con. But hat's off to Danielle Miller for the creativity. I was impressed.

First off, some background: The city of Los Angeles has some of the most pro-renter laws on the books compared to every other city in the United States. If you're a renter who stops paying rent in L.A. and you know how to "work" the system, going to court and filing this motion and that motion, it can take years for a landlord to evict you. Meanwhile, you're living rent free.

One of the most famous examples of this made headlines all over the world in 2023. A Harvard-educated scammer named Elizabeth Hirschhorn had rented a fancy Brentwood guesthouse and just stopped paying rent for two years. For most of that time, the L.A. court system shockingly supported her and advocated for her and kept reaffirming her rights as a renter to live there—rent free. It was an insane case, and it clearly illustrates the gaping loophole that Danielle Miller exploited to scam Taylor Firkus.

In 2014 Danielle Miller was living in Los Angeles and pretending to go to law school at Pepperdine University. At one point, she was actually going to Pepperdine, but she got kicked out and pretended for years that she was still attending.

Danielle met Taylor at a bar in Hollywood in 2014, and the two women hit it off. Danielle regaled Taylor with stories of her wealthy parents in New York. All of it was true, but also Red Flag #5 ("I'm Better Than You"). Of course, Danielle neglected to mention that she'd been scamming people since she was a teenager.

Taylor had just moved to Los Angeles from the Midwest and was looking for a place to live that was closer to where she worked as a bartender in Hollywood. And as soon as Danielle heard that, she offered to be Taylor's roommate (Red Flag #1: "I Just Want to Help").

"Let's move to Hollywood! You'll be able to walk to work instead of using public transportation. It'll be safer," Danielle excitedly told her new friend Taylor. And Taylor agreed.

Now, if Taylor had thought to run one of those $30 internet background checks on Danielle Miller, she would've seen the two dozen or so addresses where Danielle had already lived—and she was just twenty-five years old (Red Flag #11: They Move Around a Lot). She would've also seen Danielle's criminal rap sheet for other scams too.

But running a background check on somebody new in your life is the last thing you think about. Hopefully, after reading this book, it'll be the first.

So Danielle rented a swanky apartment in Hollywood in her own name and Taylor moved in with her, renting a bedroom from her for $1,000 a month, cash. The rent for the entire apartment was actually almost $3,000 a month, but Danielle portrayed herself as a wealthy trust fund baby who wasn't doing this for the money, she was doing it because she really liked Taylor and she wanted to help her out—at least that's what Taylor thought.

As the months passed, Taylor noticed something weird about Danielle. "It kind of like felt like she was never really moving in. There was always boxes everywhere. She was never really unpacking any of her stuff," Taylor told me.

Taylor was paying Danielle $1,000 a month in cash at the beginning of every month, like clockwork. But about six months in, Taylor was shocked to see an eviction notice placed on their door. It appeared Danielle hadn't paid rent in months.

When Taylor confronted Danielle with the eviction notice in hand, Danielle played it off as a clerical error, or a mistake. "My father will handle this," Danielle assured her. And Taylor kept paying Danielle $1,000 a month in cash. But as more months passed, the eviction notices kept coming.

Eleven months in, Taylor got fed up with all the eviction notices and decided to move out. But up until Taylor spoke to me in 2022, it never occurred to her that this was all an elaborate scam and that the reason it looked like Danielle was never really moving in was that she never really did.

Danielle created this roommate ruse to steal $11,000 from Taylor over the course of a year, knowing full well that L.A.'s pro-renter laws would prevent the landlord from throwing them out on the street. Danielle could just keep taking Taylor's cash every month for as long as Taylor was willing to pay her and for as long as she was willing to tolerate all those eviction notices.

Another horrendous thing Danielle did to Taylor was to frame her for an actual crime. Long story short: Danielle stole a checkbook from one of her wealthy friends and wrote a check out to Taylor Firkus for $20,000. Then she asked Taylor to do her a favor and cash the check because this wealthy friend owed Danielle a lot of money but the wealthy friend's mother would supposedly be upset if she saw a check made out to "Danielle Miller," for reasons that only vaguely made sense to Taylor. But she agreed to do it because Danielle assured Taylor she would use some of the $20,000 to pay the rent they owed. And that incentivized Taylor to cash the check.

"And I'll never forget, she did it in the middle of the night. She came up and woke me up from my sleep before I had to go to work. And she was like, 'Here's the check. Like sign it here. I gotta take care of this,'" Taylor recalled.

According to Taylor, it was Danielle who stole the check and framed

Taylor for stealing the $20,000. That's how Taylor's name ended up in a lawsuit against Danielle Miller filed by this wealthy friend, accusing Taylor of conspiring with Danielle to steal that $20,000—because the wealthy friend knew the check was deposited in Taylor's bank account.

"I mean, at the end of the day karma is a bitch, and I hope that it comes and it bites Danielle in the ass. And I hope that she has to be in prison for a very long time for all of the wrong that she has done," Taylor said.

Well, Danielle Miller is now behind bars. She was convicted and sentenced to five years in jail after pleading guilty in that Sarasota bank case in October 2022. She was also convicted and sentenced to five years in federal prison after pleading guilty in that federal PPP loan scam case. Sadly both five-year sentences will run concurrently. So she'll be free soon. Keep an eye out.

Queen of the Con IX

In the four years I knew her, Mair Smyth moved four times. That was a major red flag I did not realize at the time. In her lifetime she has moved at least forty times. She is in fact an inveterate con artist who has to keep moving from place to place to find new victims to scam. It is her life's work.

Mair Smyth has lived in Maine, Tennessee, Florida, Maryland, Michigan, Illinois, and California. And for about eight years, she lived in the UK—more specifically, Northern Ireland. She scammed people, lots of people, in every city that she ever lived in.

"She just bounced from job to job," recalls her daughter Chelsea. "I remember she worked at a pet store for a while. She worked at like a [drug] recovery center. She worked at DENSO, which is a huge manufacturing company in Tennessee. Just any job. She usually worked with temp agencies, but she could never hold a job down." And while Mair Smyth has lived in a bunch of different places over the years and held a bunch of different jobs, "she was actually born in Maine," said Chelsea.

I've gotten to know Chelsea really well over the years. And I will forever be grateful to her for helping me put her mother in jail. I held the final nail that Chelsea hammered into Mair's coffin—irrevocably branding her a "con artist" to the world.

Up until that moment, up until she was convicted in court by a jury of her peers for scamming me, I was viewed by a lot of people as a violent lunatic, as someone who was secretly in love with Mair and who was driven to make up all these crazy things to hurt her because I couldn't have her. A lot of people thought she was an innocent woman and I was a deranged, obsessed paramour trying to get revenge on her for rejecting my affections.

Keep in mind, I'm a happily married gay man. But that's the insane story she would tell people about me to explain why I was accusing her of being a con artist. And make no mistake, she is very convincing. So I don't necessarily blame those people who believed her. After all, I believed all of her crazy stories for four years. So I get it.

"Mair Smyth" was born "Marianne Elizabeth Clark" on July 28, 1969, in Bangor, Maine. She was the middle daughter of Charles and Wilda Clark's five children. But a few years later, Wilda divorced Charles and married a man named Robert Andle. And Marianne Elizabeth Clark became Marianne Elizabeth Andle.

She would go on to have more than two dozen aliases. But when I met her in May of 2013 in Los Angeles, she was Mair Smyth.

I've spoken to former neighbors who knew Mair as a little girl growing up in Bangor, and they all tell me she was a precocious, pathological liar. She'd sneak into neighbors' homes and steal things. She'd pretend she was wealthy; she reportedly told one of her childhood friends that a big, impressive house in the neighborhood belonged to her, and she actually snuck this friend into that house. When she got older, she pretended to have cancer and solicited secret donations from friends and neighbors for her treatment. She would go on to use this cancer scam again and again. In fact, I found out that when we were neighbors in Los Angeles, she got out of paying rent for six months in my building by convincing our landlord she had cancer and was in the hospital, getting treatment.

When Mair was a teenager, according to a former high-school boyfriend I spoke to, she would date college guys and then pretend to get pregnant and summarily shake them all down for abortion money. They all paid, no questions asked.

There are two schools of thought about what causes someone to grow up to become a professional con artist. One posits that con artists are created through childhood trauma or some horrendous experience they had early on that changed them.

The other theory, the one I believe is closer to the truth, is that con artists are just born as psychopaths—genetically different from regular people. Con artists don't feel empathy for other people, they don't care about the difference between right and wrong, and they don't have any inclination or desire to do what is right and ethical. I believe that like other people born as psychopaths, they quickly figure out how to masquerade and act like everyone else to blend in.

Their value system is just different from the rest of us normals. A regular person feels a sense of pride from doing well on a test they studied for, or working hard at a job and getting promoted, or spending years in school to become a doctor or a lawyer. A con artist feels a sense of pride from manipulating people. A con artist gets a godlike sense of satisfaction by creating characters and situations and entire worlds that do not exist—and then watching with unadulterated glee when their victims react to everything they've created as if it's all real.

A professional con artist will never stop conning. It doesn't matter how many times they get busted and go to jail and serve time for their crimes. They are just wired that way. They are made to con.

When Mair was eighteen years old, she got kicked out of the house. Her family had had it with all her lying and cheating and scamming, and they wanted nothing to do with her. At that point, she joined the navy as a corpsman and was discharged a couple years later. But while she was stationed in Florida, she racked up her first felony charges for grand theft, fraud, and forging documents. She was later stationed in Illinois, where she ended up having two children— Chelsea and Courtney—with two different men. But courts awarded full custody of Courtney to Mair's ex-husband, Jeff Welch. So Mair took her other daughter, Chelsea, and moved to Tennessee, where she racked up more felony charges for fraud, passing bad checks, and shoplifting.

After living in Tennessee for a few years, Mair met a guy online named Stephen Smyth—a postal worker living in Northern Ireland. This was in the early 2000s, when internet dating was a new and exciting frontier. Mair essentially kidnapped Chelsea and moved to Northern Ireland for eight years, where she married Stephen Smyth. You see, the courts had ordered Mair to share custody of Chelsea with Chelsea's grandparents (Mair's parents) in Tennessee because they didn't think Mair was a fit mother on her own. But she violated that court order by whisking Chelsea away to Europe for eight years.

While living in Northern Ireland—which is actually a part of the UK, not Ireland—Mair worked for several mortgage companies. And she began scamming up a storm, shockingly drafting her own daughter as an unwitting accomplice.

Chelsea, who was a little girl at that point, had a penchant and a talent for art and strangely, for cursive script. She could duplicate anyone's handwriting effortlessly, and she enjoyed doing it.

"I was obsessed with the movie *Harriet the Spy*," Chelsea told me. "So I had this weird thing about copying people's writing. And that sometimes makes me wonder if the whole con artist thing is like a genetic trait."

But Chelsea is the complete opposite of a con artist. She is kind and loving and has an implacable sense of right and wrong that she firmly adheres to, even in the worst of times.

Mair would bring Chelsea mortgage documents and explain to her that her "stupid" client had forgotten to sign this line or that line. Then she begged Chelsea to forge her client's signature and make it look identical to save Mair from having to drive all over town getting the client to sign something they'd forgotten to sign. And Chelsea did what she was told.

"It was always like on a weekend or like a Sunday night because it was never 'Oh, just casually do this for me.' It was always like an emergency scenario," Chelsea recalled. That is the Red Flag of Scarcity that Mair used to trick Chelsea into complying. But the other reason Chelsea did what she was told was that Mair was brutally abusive to Chelsea, frequently losing her temper and beating her daughter savagely.

"She was violent. But my mom, she's not an idiot. Like, my mom didn't do things like punch me in the face and give me black eyes or break bones. She would like kick me in the head and like kick me like in other places. And you could not tell by looking at me that I was being physically abused. Like, she was not ever doing anything that would have left any traces or signs," Chelsea said.

Over the course of eight years, Chelsea unwittingly helped her mother forge hundreds and hundreds of mortgage documents. Then one day, in 2009, Mair told her husband, Stephen, and Chelsea that they had to leave Northern Ireland immediately. Apparently someone had tipped Mair off that police were coming for her.

The only snag in her escape plan was that Stephen Smyth was an avid greyhound racer who owned more than a dozen dogs.

"We had about fifteen to seventeen dogs in our house, and my mom made my stepdad put all the dogs down because there wasn't time to rehome them," Chelsea shockingly admitted. "And then we packed what we could in suitcases and everything else got left in our house. The house just got completely abandoned. My mom did not communicate with me about what was really going on, but I mean, obviously, you don't put all your animals down and just flee your home."

I can only imagine the magnitude and breadth of coercive control Mair had over Stephen to manipulate him into believing that killing his own dogs was the only solution in this scenario. I mean, why not just leave the dogs in their kennels and let authorities find them and rescue them? Why kill them?

"I'll never forget that day because those dogs, I mean, they were his life, and he had already been through so much of just being married to her and just dealing with her lies, and he had to come with us too, and like, why would you want to be with her?" Chelsea asked incredulously.

Again, repeat after me: Con artists don't outsmart you, they outfeel you. If you're in love with a con artist the way Stephen Smyth was, they have the power to manipulate you into doing unspeakable things.

Chelsea was eighteen years old when the family arrived in Tennessee. And she disowned her mother at that point because she wanted nothing to do with her. She was fed up with all the lies and all the scams, and she was fed up with something else too. For Chelsea's entire life, Mair had never told her who her biological father was. One day she'd say that he was an NFL player, another day that he was a motorcycle bandit, and another day Mair said he had died in the military fighting in Iraq. But none of that was true.

After I interviewed Chelsea at length for the *Queen of the Con* podcast, and after it got millions and millions of downloads from listeners all over the world, Chelsea's biological father contacted me. It turned out that for all those years Chelsea was living in Northern Ireland, her biological father was looking for her and could not find her. I was able to reunite them a couple years ago, and I can't adequately describe to you what a profound sense of satisfaction that gives me.

What Chelsea did not know at the time she flew to Tennessee from Northern Ireland in 2009 with Marianne and Stephen was that her mom was flush with all the money she stole, reportedly hundreds of thousands of dollars. And some very angry and unsavory characters were about to come looking for her.

Marianne and Stephen divorced shortly after landing in Tennessee. And Marianne quickly went into hiding, changed her name to "Mair Smyth," and moved more than 2,000 miles away from Pigeon Forge, Tennessee, to Los Angeles, California, to reinvent herself yet again.

And that's where I met her in May of 2013.

13. RED FLAG #12: STORIES FROM FARAWAY PLACES

PROFESSIONAL CON ARTISTS REVEL IN TELLING STORIES FROM FARAWAY PLACES. IT'S their default in almost every situation, because stories from faraway places are hard to verify and that makes "selling" them much easier.

So if you meet someone new and they're telling you a lot of stories from faraway places, *and* they're waving any of the other red flags at you? You might be dealing with a real-life con artist.

Elizabeth was a super successful airline executive living on the East Coast. At one point she even worked for Homeland Security, so she is extremely smart and wise to the ways of the world. But Elizabeth lost nearly $1 million to a team of diabolical con artists who beguiled her with countless "stories from faraway places."

Elizabeth is not her real name. She's not comfortable sharing her real name at this point, so I assured her that if I ever told her story publicly, I would conceal her identity.

Elizabeth contacted me back in 2020 during one of the darkest times in her life. She happened to have watched an ABC News special called *The Con,* featuring the work I had done to bring Mair to justice, and she began to have some hope that maybe she, too, could flip the script on her own con artists.

"I don't want anyone to go through what we've been through," she said on one of our early calls. Again, this is exactly why victims need to speak out. There is strength in numbers, and you never know who you're inspiring or even just comforting by letting them know that they are not alone—that this horrible thing, this scam they fell for, didn't just happen to them, it happened to a lot of people, and that they're not stupid, they were just not prepared for the experience of meeting a professional con artist.

I mean, unless someone pulls you aside and lays out how these people operate, you will probably fall for all these scams. Because they are ruthlessly engineered to bypass your intellect and tap into your heart.

In 2018, Elizabeth was single and working around the clock as an executive for a major airline. Her best friend thought she needed a little romance in her life, so this friend created a profile on a dating app for her. Elizabeth went on a few dates as a result of the app, but while they were fun and interesting, she just didn't click with anyone—until a message from a man named Michael Lawrence popped up on her phone. His profile had matched with hers. He was an oil and gas engineer, a Stanford grad, and quite the globetrotter.

Now, Elizabeth did her own internet sleuthing and found Michael's LinkedIn page, which confirmed everything he was saying. She also found the website for the company he said he worked for, and lo and behold, he had a profile on that site. He really did work there. Everything checked out. Or so it seemed.

Elizabeth and Michael started chatting like teenagers on that dating app. Soon thereafter they started talking on the phone, every day for hours at a time. Michael told Elizabeth he had a home in the United States and a home in the UK. His daughter was in medical school at Oxford University. And he was always traveling, setting up oil wells in Africa, Russia, South America, Europe, Alaska.

All the while Michael was traveling on all these oil expeditions, he was sending Elizabeth pictures of himself on boats or near oil wells or on planes—even pictures of himself speaking at various industry conferences all over the world. And on a couple of occasions, Michael video chatted with Elizabeth. So she knew he was real, and she was quickly falling in love with him, though they had never met. They talked every day for hours over the course of four months.

Michael was scheduled to be in Elizabeth's city, so they finally made a date to meet in person. But at the last minute he got called away to an emergency. An oil rig exploded and people died. They needed Michael's help immediately. When Elizabeth talked to Michael, she heard fire alarms going off over the phone and she heard people screaming. Michael later sent her pictures of that oil rig on fire. It was all 100 percent real to her. She had no doubt in her mind that everything Michael was saying was true. There were just so many details.

But here's the thing about details: For regular nonpsychopathic people, details are an indicator that people are telling the truth. Professional con artists know this. So they know they have to snow you with details and minutiae of what they're saying and doing to make you believe they are telling you the truth when in fact they are not.

Elizabeth knew so much about Michael's life. And Michael knew a lot about hers. "He had done his homework on me," she said.

You see, Elizabeth sat on the board of a well-known ovarian cancer charity. Ovarian cancer had taken the lives of Elizabeth's loved ones, so it was a cause she felt strongly about. She had never mentioned that fact to Michael. But in one of their conversations, Michael confided in her that his wife had died years ago from ovarian cancer. That struck a chord with Elizabeth. It moved her and made her connect with him on a whole other level. Looking back, that was Michael's absolute intention as he continued to bypass her intellect and go straight for her heart.

"I don't know that I was completely in love. I was enthralled with him. And I thought there could be the possibility of a long-term relationship. And I trusted him," she said.

Four months into their over-the-phone relationship, Michael was in Bangladesh, digging an oil well way out in the middle of the Indian Ocean. He had nearly zero cell service and no internet. But he needed to buy a new oil rig for the Bangladeshi government as part of the job they had hired him to do. It was a $65 million oil rig. He was in the middle of nowhere and didn't have strong enough internet to log into his bank account and transfer the money to pay for the oil rig. So he asked Elizabeth to log into his bank account for him. He gave her his username and his password. She logged onto the bank's website and saw more than $219 million sitting in his account. Add to that, she spoke to a representative of that bank over the phone and confirmed the balance.

Now this speaks to the inordinate sophistication of the scam. Elizabeth was not falling victim to one con artist here. She was falling victim to a team of con artists working in unison to scam her. That bank rep was an actor, and that banking website was not real. But how on earth was Elizabeth to know that? She logged in to it, like you would log in to any bank account, and she saw his bank balance. It was real to her.

Then the plot thickened.

Michael's father suddenly died, and Michael had to fly to Germany to settle his father's estate. But it turned out Michael's father owed $12 million in back taxes, and since Michael was next of kin, the German government froze Michael's bank account—with the $219 million in it—until they got their money. Michael was now in a seemingly full-on panic because he needed to buy that $65 million oil rig for the Bangladeshi government or his business would go belly-up and his reputation in the oil and gas industry would be ruined.

Michael explained to Elizabeth that he needed to pay the $12 million in back taxes. He had started to ask all of his friends in Europe and Japan to contribute toward it, a million dollars here, a million there. Michael said he had assured all of his friends that he would pay them all back as soon as the German government unfroze his bank account—the one with $219 million in it, the one that Elizabeth had logged in to and saw with her own eyes and spoken to the banker about.

"I thought he could be the love of my life. And certainly I wanted to help him," said Elizabeth.

So, wanting to show up for Michael the way his other friends appeared to be doing, Elizabeth wired him close to $1 million.

Red Flag #10: Wires!

When she tried to wire Michael even more money, her bank in the United States called her up and said, "You are being scammed! Do not wire any more money to this man!"

Elizabeth couldn't believe what the bank was telling her. She was deeply offended and upset. The next day she talked to Michael over the phone and told him, "The bank says the money I sent you is fraud and that you are a scammer."

Michael started crying hysterically. He was so upset that he was being accused of being a con artist. And he was even more upset that Elizabeth was entertaining the idea. He said to her he couldn't bear to live anymore.

He told Elizabeth, "I hope one day you will forgive me for what I'm about to do."

"And I heard a gunshot." Elizabeth recalled.

At that point, Elizabeth believed 100 percent that she had just witnessed Michael take his own life. She had heard the gunshot. She had heard the body hit the floor. She was bereft and in utter shock.

The next day, Michael's "attorney" called her. She had actually spoken to Michael's "attorney" a couple times before over the four months she knew Michael. He had an English accent and was very authoritative sounding.

"Hi Elizabeth, do you know where Michael is? We can't reach him anywhere," this "attorney" said. And through tears, Elizabeth explained that Michael had committed suicide and that she had actually borne witness to the gruesomeness of it all over the phone.

Now this demonstrates the absolute inhumanity of con artists. They are not people as we all understand people to be. They have no feelings for anyone. These con artists had already gotten away scot-free with all Elizabeth's money at this point, and now "the attorney" was calling to turn the knife and make her suffer by having her recount Michael's suicide. These cruel con artists clearly enjoyed the power they had over Elizabeth. It wasn't about the money anymore at this point. It was about getting off on witnessing her react to everything they created from thin air—as if it were real. That's what brings these people joy. It's truly disgusting.

A few days later, Elizabeth called her local police department and explained what had happened. In her mind, a man was dead and she felt somewhat responsible, so she wanted to report the incident to the authorities. Sensing the seriousness of the situation, a couple of police detectives got dispatched to visit Elizabeth at her home. They gently explained to her that there was no suicide and that she was actually the victim of a team of scammers who had pulled the same exact elaborate con on several women in California, Tennessee, and Ohio.

All of the pictures that Michael was sending Elizabeth actually came from the Facebook profile of a Russian scholar by a different name who had no idea his image was being used to scam anyone. The "Michael" that Elizabeth saw on those video calls did look similar to the man in those pictures. But if you think about it, there are probably thousands of people who look similar to one another. So clearly, Michael the scammer had just browsed Facebook until he found someone who looked enough like him. Then he downloaded all of their pictures to pass off as himself.

Obviously, the entire banking website was fake. And the lawyer and the banker were other scammers acting to help Michael create the illusion that he was this wealthy oil and gas engineer.

The good news is that three arrests have been made in this case as of late 2023, and the FBI is investigating. So hopefully the authorities will lock them all up and throw away the key. Sadly, though, based on my experience, those SOBs will probably be out scamming again in a couple years. So I'm glad you're reading this chapter and will be able to spot this kind of "stories from faraway places" scam if it comes your way. The con artist may not be an oil and gas man next time. They may use some other profession and some other emergency and some other bank confirmation. But I can guarantee you those three elements will be there. So, keep an open mind and be suspicious. And watch for the red flags.

Queen of the Con X

Over the course of our four-year friendship—or what I took for friendship—Mair Smyth deluged me with stories from faraway places. And I never suspected they were all fake. I just thought she was a really interesting woman from the other side of the world. I mean, I live and work in Los Angeles, I meet a lot of interesting people from all over the world. But knowing what I know now about con artists, I would have spotted Mair as a scammer immediately—strictly by her stories alone—if I had met her today.

And I confess that's a fantasy I entertain frequently. If I had met her today and she had started spouting off all these stories from faraway places, I would have immediately been suspicious and ran a background check on her. And I would have found nothing coming up under the name "Mair Smyth" because that was not her real name. That would have just made me more curious about who she really was. So I probably would have snapped a picture of her license plate. And I would have run her plate and found that her real name was Marianne Elizabeth Smyth. Then I would have background checked that name and found her felonies for fraud, grand theft, forging documents, and passing bad checks in multiple states, and I would have never talked to her again.

But I freely admit, I was naïve back in 2013 when I met her. I fell for it all, hard.

Her elaborate Irish backstory. The framed copy of the Irish Constitution hanging on her living room wall with her great-great-uncle as one of its signatories. Her fight for her inheritance. Her Irish cousins Fintan, Diarmuid, and Tristan who hated her. The story of how when she was a little girl her IRA grandmother used to take her to the top of a bridge and teach her how to hurl Molotov cocktails down on British soldiers. Her great-grandmother, the famous soothsayer of nineteenth-century Europe. Her psychic sister who lived in Germany and helped police find missing children.

There were so many stories from so many faraway places, and they were impossible to confirm. At the time, I really liked her and quickly came to love her, so I believed everything she said.

The intricacies and complexities of her scam protected her in a way—in the beginning. That's true for every con. Professional con artists like to make their scams as detailed and multifaceted and insane as possible because their convolutedness makes it that much harder for victims to (1) realize what's happened to them and (2) try to explain what happened to them to the police.

And if a case is hard for a victim to explain to the police, it's a thousand times harder for a prosecutor to explain it to a jury. And if it's complicated for a jury to understand, "reasonable doubt" can get the con artist off with a "not guilty" verdict if the case goes to trial. But truthfully, the case would never even get that far because no prosecutor wants to prosecute a case that they are not nearly 100 percent convinced they can get a conviction on. They just won't do it. They'll drop the case before that point.

This was the uphill battle I would have to fight, while learning how to fight it.

So, on a Sunday in March of 2017, at five o'clock in the morning, I went down to the local police station in my neighborhood and tried to report what Mair had done to me. I chose that ungodly early hour on a Sunday because the LAPD was open 24/7 and I figured no one would be there at 5 A.M. on a Sunday but me so I would have time to explain this sprawling four-year con that had happened to me.

Keep in mind that at this point "the Irish heiress" Mair Smyth had never been in any news reports. I hadn't even started my blog about her yet, so there was no record on the internet or anywhere calling her a con artist. I had to make the case to the officer from scratch.

It took me about thirty minutes to unpack it all for the desk cop on duty that morning. And his response was a punch to the gut. "I'm sorry, but this is not a crime. You gave her the money," he said to me. "Maybe you can sue her in civil court. Good luck." And he turned me away.

In complete and utter shock, I started stumbling away in a daze.

But as I placed my hand on the glass door to push it open and leave, something in me welled up and shouted in my mind, "No! That just cannot be true."

And I walked back over to that officer. Thankfully, it was still only him and me there at that hour. And I passionately explained why what he was telling me did not make any sense.

"Scammers calling people pretending to be the IRS, the victims *give* them the money—that doesn't mean it's not a crime," I reasoned.

The officer sighed and rolled his eyes. But I continued making my case, getting louder and more animated with each example I was issuing. "When someone points a gun at a cashier in a convenience store that cashier 'gives them the money' that doesn't mean it's not a crime," I argued.

He was clearly getting annoyed with me at this point.

"And even Bernie freaking Madoff, who stole millions and millions of dollars from victims who 'gave him the money,' is sitting in jail now because he was convicted of a crime," I went on. "Clearly lying to people to take their money is illegal!"

I then opened my satchel and started dumping documents on the counter in front of him. "Look, these are bank records, email exchanges, and text messages she sent me over the four years I knew her, that prove she lied to me to steal from me," I implored.

The officer started looking through the documents I was piling up.

"And this is her rap sheet from Florida and from Tennessee for grand theft and fraud. She's a career criminal!" I added defiantly.

At that point there was a noticeable shift in the officer's demeanor. He legitimately seemed impressed by the case I was making, and he suddenly looked curious.

"What do you do for a living?" he asked.

"I'm a television producer," I responded proudly.

"What kinds of shows?" he queried.

So I started rattling off the biggest shows I had ever worked on at that point.

"*UFO Hunters, American Ninja Warrior, Shark Tank* . . . ," I listed.

"*Shark Tank*?" he asked, stopping me mid-ramble.

"I've been trying to pitch something to the Sharks for years," he confessed.

At that point, I knew I had him.

"Look, man, I'll help you if you help me," I said.

And with that, the officer took a police report, admitted all my documents into evidence, and gave me the best piece of advice I have ever received from anyone in law enforcement since.

"You have to call about your case every day," he said.

"Call about my case?" I asked, not fully understanding what he meant.

He explained to me that every time I called to inquire about the status of my case, giving whoever answered the case number to locate it, that piece of paper, aka "my case," got taken from the bottom of a pile of other cases and placed at the top, and re-examined. But by the end of each day, hundreds of other cases got placed on top of it, so it would end up at the bottom of the pile. But if I called about it the next day, it got placed back on top of the pile again and in everyone's consciousness.

So, for the next three weeks, I called about my case every single day. Sometimes I spoke to the officer on duty. Other times I left messages because no one could talk to me. It felt like I was getting nowhere fast.

Then suddenly I got a call back.

14. RED FLAG #13: TMI

AS I WRITE THESE WORDS, I AM SITTING AT MY DESK AFTER JUST GETTING BACK FROM A two-hour meeting with a victim at a downtown Los Angeles coffee shop.

This is a case I started investigating recently. Not only does the con artist in question wave nearly every single red flag proving he is what he is, but the particular Red Flag of TMI is how he got into this victim's life in the first place and how he won her over almost immediately.

TMI, or "Too Much Information," is an extremely effective technique used by most con artists on new marks to get close to them quickly and earn their trust.

When you meet someone new and they start revealing deeply personal, private things about themselves, you immediately get the impression that they must really trust you. And without even knowing it, you start feeling like you can trust them, and you start revealing deeply personal things about yourself. At the end of just a few conversations, you feel close to this new person because of the things you shared and the things they shared. But when you're enmeshed with a professional con artist, the deeply personal things they reveal to you are usually completely made up, designed to extract as much private intel out of you as possible.

"I thought he was an open book. And I really liked that," a woman I'm calling Faith (not her real name) said to me over coffee this morning, about a guy she met on a dating app back in August of 2019, a guy who turned out to be a sophisticated con artist and is now ruining her life.

Dating apps can be great. I know a lot of people who are now happily married with significant others and kids and the whole shebang, who all met on dating apps.

But dating apps are also an effective opening for a con artist to trick their way into your life, because they can portray themselves on that dating app however they want. And it'll usually, by design, be very pleasing and appealing to you.

Faith, a successful Los Angeles attorney and single mother, was looking for romance. She swiped right on the profile of a man we're calling Grayson, not because he was devastatingly handsome or anything like that, but because what he wrote about himself touched her deeply. He was a Stanford grad and the founder of an amazing new app that helped addicts in recovery. That spoke to Faith. She'd seen firsthand how addiction destroys families and relationships and lives, and Grayson seemed to be trying to help people.

"What a great guy," she thought.

On their first date, Grayson came across as the most charming and effervescent man Faith had ever met. Unlike the majority of men Faith had dated in Los Angeles, who were somewhat guarded and seemed like they weren't being themselves on a date, Grayson appeared to be "an open book"—so open, in fact, that he confessed to being a recovering alcoholic who had stopped drinking years ago. He said that's what had inspired him to create this new app of his. Oh, and by the way, this app was worth millions of dollars now and he was being hit up with offers from large companies to buy it.

On subsequent dates as they got to know each other, and as Faith was quickly falling in love, Grayson kept revealing the most personal and specific things about himself that most people would take years to develop enough trust and comfort to reveal to someone new in their lives. Remember, con artists like to use specificity and tons and tons of details to trick you into believing that what they're saying is true. Grayson said he'd been violently abused by his father as a child and sexually molested by his mother. I'm intentionally going to be vague now because the details he used when he was telling these abuse stories were disturbingly vivid and plentiful. He described myriad scenes in graphic, granular minutiae—it was like a horror movie. And these tragic stories made Faith feel a tremendous amount of sympathy for him. They also made her feel like she could reveal personal things to him about herself too: He obviously trusted her, so she could trust him (Red Flag #13: TMI).

"It was a lot of very personal information, very quickly," Faith recalls. "Although it felt like he was oversharing, it made him seem trustworthy and vulnerable. Ironically, I remember thinking that at least I know what I'm getting myself into with him because it's all laid out there. In turn, I shared how much I loved being a mother and how I wanted a family unit. He was able to quickly identify the values and goals that were important to me and then shape his identity around that, i.e., Mr. Family Man."

But none of those stories Grayson told about his horrific childhood were true. They were just powerful TMI ploys he deftly used to get closer to Faith on an expedited timeline. And they worked phenomenally well.

In just the first few weeks, Grayson was waving a lot of red flags that he was a con artist. But Faith never noticed them until we spoke.

Red Flag #1: "I Just Want to Help"

According to Faith, "Grayson was very helpful and very nice to me when we first started dating. He offered to meet repair workers at my condo when I was getting it ready to sell, because I was busy at work. He would go to Costco with me to get groceries. He helped me prepare Lego-themed snack treats for my daughter's Lego-themed birthday party. Very unusual for a guy, especially the kind of white-collar professional guys in my social network who are always super busy with their jobs. He had endless amounts of time to hang out with me and help me with things."

Faith didn't realize it at the time, but Grayson's full-time job at that point was scamming her.

Red Flag #2: Too Kind, Too Quick

Grayson wined and dined Faith and showered her with praise and gifts. He seemed so kind, *so quick*.

"I was unfamiliar with the term *love bombing* when I met Grayson," she said. "But that is exactly what he did to me. When I first met him for a coffee, he was very friendly and warm. He told me that I was the 'love of his life' and was very effusive and affectionate. He was incredibly nice and thoughtful to my daughter. He would frequently bring her Lego presents and play with her, so that she would become emotionally invested in him."

Both Faith and her ten-year-old daughter quickly bonded and felt a deep connection to him. And that was his plan.

Red Flag #3: Drama, Drama, Drama

"Yes, lots of drama," attested Faith. "Grayson was very angry at his app's cofounder. He told me that this guy was a drug addict and sex addict and that he wasn't doing enough for the app because he was having sex parties in his Las Vegas loft."

None of that turned out to be true. But again, it sounded true because he had so many details. In reality, it was just a smokescreen of drama created by Grayson to get sympathy from Faith. And it worked really well. Not to mention all those childhood sex abuse stories. There was just so much drama around this guy.

Red Flag #5: "I'm Better Than You"

Grayson presented himself out of the gate as a Silicon Valley tech genius. This app he'd created was worth millions, according to him. He talked up himself and his app frequently. But in the end, none of that was true. He was actually broke. And he was hitching his wagon to Faith, who was a successful attorney living in Beverly Hills, so that he could get her money and a free place to live.

Red Flag #6: Technology

Grayson's whole entrée into Faith's life was the app he had created to help addicts in recovery. And here's the confusing part—the app was real. It did exist. You could download it on your phone. But it was worthless. Remember, at the end of the day, anyone can create an app and show it to you as evidence of their being a multimillionaire genius. But I'm sure you know by now, just because somebody holds up their phone and shows you something doesn't mean it is what they're saying it is. Be suspicious.

Red Flag #9: A Good Day Job

Grayson presented himself as a Silicon Valley tech genius. His day job was the app he'd created. But it wasn't worth the code it was written with. He claimed to be selling this app for $20 million, but in reality there was no buyer. There had never been any buyers. This was all fiction he spouted to impress Faith and successfully trick his way into her life.

Red Flag #11: They Move Around a Lot

According to Faith, "Yes, Grayson does move around a lot. He originally moved to Los Angeles to live with his sister. He was living in his sister's house in Chatsworth for a while, but then he moved to an apartment in Brentwood. He then moved into my house in Beverly Hills. He then moved to an apartment in Marina del Rey. He then moved into another victim's house in Highland Park, where he has been living for the past two years."

I ran a background check on Grayson and found nearly twenty different addresses for him over the past twenty years. Again, on its own, that's not a huge deal. But based on all the other red flags present in this case, the fact that he moves around a lot just confirms to me that he's a con artist.

Now here's where Faith, as a victim, is in a tough spot: A few months after dating Grayson, she became pregnant. She wanted to have the baby and thought Grayson would be an amazing father. The two planned to get married.

"Why don't I move in with you so I can help with the pregnancy," Grayson said to her in December of 2019.

At this point, Faith was in love with Grayson. She had no idea what she was about to learn after he moved in and after she had her baby.

Faith soon discovered by talking to others in Grayson's life that Grayson was lying about everything. His app was worthless. There had never been any investors. His traumatic childhood was invented. At this point, she's not even sure he's an alcoholic. Faith realized that Grayson had been using her from the beginning. She's a big mover and shaker in Los Angeles legal circles, and Grayson got her to introduce him to the heads of some major companies that he tried to trick into investing in his app as well. None of them ultimately did.

Luckily, they never actually got married. Faith broke up with Grayson and kicked him out of her home. But now she has a son with him, and he sued her for child support because he has no income. So she's paying him thousands of dollars a month in child support! But he's not happy with that. He wants more, so he's suing for full custody, claiming that Faith is an abusive mother. He reported her to child protective services and they conducted a full investigation, but they found no evidence of abuse. Faith is now countersuing for full custody and trying to prove that he made everything up and is using the system to scam her.

But civil litigation can take years to get resolved. In the meantime, Faith is sharing custody of her son with this con artist and paying him thousands of dollars every month.

Since I just started investigating this case, I have yet to find other victims. Faith hasn't tried to locate any herself either. But I am certain once I start digging, calling people from Grayson's past, hitting up his former friends, girlfriends, and neighbors from the past twenty addresses where he has lived, I'll find a pattern of behavior. The fact that he moved in on Faith so quickly and so seamlessly tells me he's done this many times before. And he's really good at it.

Queen of the Con XI

Mair Smyth used the TMI technique on me and on everyone she encountered ad nauseam.

Early in our friendship when we'd just started hanging out, Mair confided in me that her politician boyfriend enjoyed using a *butt plug* during sex. And that he was "hung like a donkey," she said, laughing like a schoolgirl as she held up both her hands about a foot apart from each other to demonstrate the Politician's apparent length.

I laughed at Mair's vulgar confessions. I laughed so hard that tears were streaming down my face and I felt like I was high. My head was buzzing. What a crazy thing to share so early on in our friendship. Mair came across like a woman who told it like it is, a woman with no filter, someone who was *brutally honest* to a fault. Most people would have been offended by the crassness of her stories. But I wasn't in the least. In a weird way, I felt privileged that she would share those kinds of intimate, albeit grossly inappropriate, details with me. I felt like she clearly trusted me. And that made me trust her.

She used the TMI technique on me like a Jedi master and it induced me to share all sorts of intimate details of my life with her. And that was her plan. That was her trap. Snap! I walked right into it. But this was the worst kind of trap. Most traps you fall into give you an immediate heads up, like "Hey, you're really fucked now. Good luck."

But Mair's trap was different. It was like a frighteningly long boa constrictor, slowly and methodically slithering up your legs, torso, arms, and neck, patiently waiting to squeeze the ever-loving life out of you.

Did the politician boyfriend actually use a butt plug during sex? Was he hung like a donkey? I don't know. I've never asked him. And I will never ask him. And since I have already ferreted out a million lies that Mair told me and a slew of her other victims about her personal life, I suspect she was lying about the Politician as well in this instance.

And remember my neighbor Sherry the strip club manager, whom Mair scammed out of $5,000? Well, Mair had "confided" in Sherry that her IRA family back in Ireland had murdered her husband because he routinely beat her. That was not true at all, but it served its purpose. It made Sherry believe Mair was trusting her with that information—and feel obliged to trust Mair in return. That's how she scammed all of us. She used this TMI technique again and again.

If you recall, a couple years into my friendship with Mair I got a frantic call from her when she was stuck in traffic on the 405, asking me to log in to her email and giving me her password. The fact that she trusted me with her email password—talk about TMI—served the purpose of making me trust her even more.

It also demonstrated what little regard she had for me and my intelligence. After all, I was her latest scam victim, yet she was giving me her email password and allowing me to log in to her account. How was she not worried that I would find something incriminating or randomly log in to her account anytime I wanted? Shockingly, she shared her email password with other victims as well.

And here is the paradox: Con artists like Mair are actually very trusting people. That's because they are the ultimate narcissists. Never for a second does a con artist like Mair think a victim they are scamming, like me, would ever double-cross her.

But Mair was dead wrong about that. And it cost her her freedom. Let me explain.

After I realized I'd been scammed and after I started my blog, I had a moment where I remembered the password Mair had given me two years before. It just popped into my head. And I wondered, "Could Mair still be using it?" I ran over to my computer and tried to log into Mair's email account. And I got in!

I felt the *Mission Impossible* theme song pumping in my head as I moved swiftly to change her email password and lock her out of her own account. Success.

And as the ultimate sign from God or the universe or all that is good and great in this world, the law was actually on my side here. Mair had willingly given me her email password years earlier, and to this day she has never communicated to me that she wants me to log out of her account, so from a legal standpoint, I did nothing wrong. I spent the next few weeks going over all of her emails, and it helped me build a compelling criminal case against her.

I discovered she had worked as a "Sugar Baby" for a few years on a website called SugarDaddyForMe.com. Basically, Mair had a dozen guys in Los Angeles, aka Sugar Daddies, paying her a monthly fee for sex. These were all married men who were looking for extramarital affairs. And when each guy would try to end things with Mair, because they didn't want to pay her monthly fee anymore, she blackmailed them. All of them. She threatened to go to their wives and expose their relationship. And all these men paid her tens of thousands of dollars to go away.

I emailed each Sugar Daddy, explaining who I was and what Mair had done to me and urged them to go to the police. And not a single one replied.

I also discovered that Mair had twenty-three other email accounts linked to her main email address that I had taken over. She was impersonating celebrities like Jennifer Aniston and Ashley Judd over email. She was also impersonating wholly fictitious characters like her cousins Fintan, Diarmuid, and Tristan—in addition to lawyers, prosecutors, private investigators, hockey team managers, and a slew of other characters.

And get this: She used that same email password that I already had for every single fictitious account she created. So I logged in in to each of those twenty-three alias accounts and changed the password on her and locked her out.

Legally, I was doing nothing wrong because I was stopping "crimes in progress." It would be like if you were walking past a house in some neighborhood and you heard a child yelling for help and you realized that child had been abducted so you broke into the house to rescue them. Technically you broke into the house, which is normally illegal. But you did it to stop a crime, so there's no way on earth you'd get charged with breaking and entering.

I also used Mair's commandeered email account to locate dozens of other victims she had scammed and encouraged each and every one of them to report her to the police. Sadly, the vast majority of them never did.

But it turned out one of the biggest victims Mair was scamming in Los Angeles, other than me, was her politician boyfriend. She had impersonated a billionaire Irish uncle over email and text to hire the Politician, who was actually a partner at a huge estate-planning law firm, to handle a fictitious billion-dollar estate that this Irish uncle of Mair's was planning to bequeath to his wayward gay son living in California.

The Politician wholeheartedly believed that this billion-dollar estate was coming his way any day, so in the meantime, when Mair would ask him for $25,000 to redo the roof on one of her estates in Ireland because all her money was tied up in CDs, the Politician was only too happy to oblige. I mean, he must have been salivating believing this billion-dollar trust from Mair's uncle was going to be his to handle very soon.

At one point, Mair's "uncle"—aka Mair—sent the Politician fresh lobsters as a thank-you for helping him out with his estate planning. And the Politician sent the uncle—aka Mair—an email on March 1, 2013, saying, "The lobsters arrived alive, and in perfect shape. They were put to an untimely demise later that evening and enjoyed by many. They were absolutely fantastic. Thank you again for your kindness. It was entirely unnecessary, but very generous and very much appreciated." Obviously, there was no billionaire uncle and Mair was the one who sent the live lobsters, but the Politician ate it all up. Literally.

Another insane way Mair scammed that politician happened right before an election. Mair impersonated a former mistress the Politician had told her about when they first met. And this mistress, aka Mair, over email and texts, threatened to go public with evidence of their past affair right before an election.

Now this politician was conservative and married with children. News of an extramarital affair before an election would have cost him dearly. So Mair offered to help him (Red Flag #1) pay off the mistress, whom she was also impersonating, by hand-delivering $50,000 cash that the Politician had withdrawn from his own bank account and packed into a suitcase. The Politician had no idea it was Mair who got that money—until I exposed her as a con artist years later.

Also, while reviewing more of Mair's scammy emails, I uncovered a coconspirator of hers, a woman who lives in Tennessee and helped Mair come up with ways to scam that politician. This coconspirator, who shares her first name with a popular flower, sent Mair an email on April 6, 2011, warning her that her now ex-husband Stephen Smyth, who was back in Northern Ireland at that point, had posted the following on Facebook about police over there looking for her: "If u know the whereabouts of Marianne Smyth or whatever she calls herself these days, please turn her into the Police Service of Northern Ireland. She is wanted for serious financial fraud. tel. 01144 2890650222XXXXXXX."

When I found the email that Mair's coconspirator had sent to warn her, I dropped what I was doing and I called the phone number Stephen Smyth had listed for the police in Northern Ireland. I let them know exactly where Mair was—Los Angeles—and I sent them all the evidence I had that she had scammed me and dozens of others. And lo and behold, a couple months later in late 2017, police in Northern Ireland began official extradition proceedings.

Back in Los Angeles, I got the phone call from the LAPD that I'd been waiting on for weeks. My case had finally gotten assigned to a police detective.

"Yay!" I exclaimed.

But then this police detective called me again days later to tell me that he had been reassigned to another case and that my case was now being assigned to an officer who was working hard to become a detective one day but was not actually a detective yet.

"Great," I responded sarcastically.

This police officer ended up interviewing me a bunch of different times over the course of eleven months. And that blog I started helped me unearth dozens of other victims Mair scammed. Some of whom she tricked by telling them she can get them a spot on *Shark*

Tank! Remember that was the hit TV show I was producing when we met. Every time I found a new victim of Mair's who was willing to go to the police, I would alert this officer who had been assigned to my case, and he would tell me, "This person has nothing to do with your case. They need to go file their own police report."

I fell into the trap of believing what this guy was saying was true because he was a police officer after all. He wore an LAPD uniform and had a badge and everything. He had to know what he was talking about. *But he did not.*

I would find out later from the deputy district attorney in Los Angeles who ended up prosecuting Mair that this police officer was wrong. His unwillingness to investigate and interview Mair's other victims severely compromised the criminal case against her.

Heading into the trial, it did not look good. It was literally a case of "He said, she said." And "she" was a brilliant and believable liar, while I was being painted as an unhinged lunatic with an overactive imagination.

15. RED FLAG #14: THE DALE CARNEGIE TECHNIQUES

HOW TO WIN FRIENDS AND INFLUENCE PEOPLE WAS A BREAKTHROUGH 1936 SELF-HELP book written by Dale Carnegie. More than thirty million copies have been sold worldwide, making it one of the most popular books of all time. Dale Carnegie was a pioneer in behavioral science, and he was a legit self-help guru before that was even a thing.

One of the main principles in his famous book is that it is possible to change other people's behavior by changing your own behavior toward them. A lot of companies and salespeople have successfully employed his techniques to increases their sales. The lessons he imparts were not necessarily intended to teach you how to manipulate or trick people. Rather, they were aimed at getting people to like and accept you and your ideas. But like any tool in the wrong hands, these techniques can wreak havoc. And professional con artists are particularly skilled at using all of them to win and influence their victims. Here are a few of the big ones that stand out.

"Arouse in the Other Person an Eager Want"

This concept speaks to the principle that Mair used on me and that a lot of con artists use on their victims. When our building lost the pool, I took it upon myself to put up flyers everywhere and galvanize a movement with my neighbors to get the pool back. Anonymously reading that flyer was all the information my con artist needed to deduce that I was a "do-gooder," prompting her to create the perfect con for me to want to "do good" for her. She then expertly engineered "an eager want" in me to help her by inventing a wholly fictitious scenario that I, as a gay man who had been recently disowned by his family, would be particularly susceptible to: She portrayed herself as a damsel in distress who had been recently disowned by her family and who was locked in a fight with them over her inheritance. It was the perfect con for me to fall for. And I fell hard.

"When we have a brilliant idea, instead of making others think it is ours, why not let them cook and stir the idea themselves. They will then regard it as their own; they will like it and maybe eat a couple of helpings of it," wrote Carnegie.

Very true, Mr. Carnegie. As much as it pains me to admit this, I feel it's crucial for me to say so you understand how cons work: I was the one who offered to help Mair Smyth clear her name and get her inheritance. She never actually asked me for help. Ever. She made "her con" my idea.

Let that sink in.

"To Be Interesting, Be Interested"

"You can make more friends in two months by becoming interested in other people than you can in two years by trying to get other people interested in you," wrote Carnegie.

When a con artist comes into your life, their first mission is to learn as much about you as possible as fast as they can. The TMI technique I discussed in the previous two chapters helps them do that. Once a con artist knows who you are and what your hopes and dreams and fears are, they can create scenarios that enable them to dangle those hopes and dreams and fears in front of you to get you to act on emotion to give them money.

Remember faux financial manager Peggy Fulford? She got to know her pro athlete victims so well, so fast, that she quickly and expertly figured out the fear that every professional athlete suffers from: How am I going to be able to make a living when I can't play anymore?

That birthed the sprawling con she used on all of them. She told them that if they brought her in to manage their finances, she could create "generational wealth" for them and give them not only enough money to retire on, but enough money to pass down to their children and their children's children. That was what all of these professional athletes wanted more than anything in the world—and Peggy figured that out fast and used it to scam them.

"Dramatize Your Ideas"

"This is the day of dramatization. Merely stating a truth isn't enough. The truth has to be made vivid, interesting, dramatic. You have to use showmanship. The movies do it. Television does it. And you will have to do it if you want attention," wrote Dale Carnegie.

Remember con artist Lizzie Mulder? By dramatizing the hell out of every aspect of her scams, she bilked her close friends and associates out of nearly $2 million. From the fake degree from Pepperdine University hanging on her office wall to the voice-changing apps on her phone, every story she told her victims was backed up with props and drama.

And remember house-flipping con artist Vincent Leli? He flew to Florida so he could send his victim pictures and videos of construction sites and all the houses he and his associates were supposedly flipping to convince the victim that his $365,000 investment was legitimate and was making money. But none of that was true. Leli just showed up to random construction sites and took pictures and videos to "dramatize" his con.

"Remember That a Person's Name Is to That Person the Sweetest and Most Important Sound in Any Language"

Carnegie suggests not only that you try to remember the names of people you meet for the first time but also that you use their names in conversations with them as much as possible to get them to like you quickly.

This is something every con artist does to their victims, so pay attention. Over the four years Mair was laying the groundwork to scam me, she frequently used my name to me in conversations and over text and emails. I always noticed when she did it, but I never assigned a meaning to it. It did strike me as odd, but I dismissed it as just her conversation style. I was wrong. Mair was actively employing this most famous Dale Carnegie technique.

"People are so proud of their names that they strive to perpetuate them at any cost. Even blustering, hard-boiled old P. T. Barnum, the greatest showman of his time, disappointed because he had no sons to carry on his name, offered his grandson, C. H. Seeley, $25,000 if he would call himself 'Barnum' Seeley," wrote Carnegie.

It's important to point out that on their own, these Dale Carnegie techniques are harmless. Just because you meet someone employing them doesn't mean they are a con artist. But if any of the other red flags I talk about in this book are present—and now this new person in your life is using these Dale Carnegie techniques on you? Be suspicious.

Queen of the Con XII

The trial of con artist Marianne Smyth was finally scheduled to begin on January 4, 2019, in a downtown Los Angeles courthouse. She had been charged a year earlier with grand theft by false pretense for scamming me out of close to $100,000. It really appeared that this was it: Justice was finally going to be served. It had taken me nearly a year to convince the police that there was a crime here to begin with, and it took a whole other year to get my day in court. Two years of my life were consumed with bringing this woman to justice. But Marianne "Mair" Smyth still had one more trick up her diabolical sleeve—a checkmate move that nearly destroyed me and the criminal case against her in one fell swoop.

One month before trial, I received a lawyer's advertisement in the mail. "Superior court records indicate that a TRO/Domestic Violence Lawsuit has been filed against WALTON, JOHNATHAN," the first line read.

I quickly dropped what I was doing, logged on to the court's website, and plugged in the case number referenced in that lawyer's advertisement—and I just about fell on the floor. Marianne Smyth had filed a restraining order against me, accusing me of stalking her and violently threatening her life.

I quickly alerted the deputy district attorney prosecuting Mair about this, but he was uncharacteristically reluctant to do anything. "I can't help you with this," he said. "You need to hire a civil attorney ASAP."

"If a judge approves this restraining order," I asked fearfully, "what happens then?"

"Well," he paused. "You wouldn't be allowed in court to testify against her at the criminal trial, but we can have you testify over video monitor."

I was stunned and temporarily lost for words.

"How is that going look to a jury?" I stammered. "Big bad wolf

Johnathan Walton is too dangerous to be allowed into the court-room?"

"I mean, it definitely doesn't help your case," he confessed.

Never underestimate the creative resourcefulness of a professional con artist. Even when, perhaps especially when, they are backed into a corner, they still have the ability to come up with a brilliant and believable con to save their skin.

So I went out and found a civil attorney and paid him $1,500 for a consultation. And thank God, he had the simplest and most effective idea to battle Mair's scammy restraining order: Don't get served.

You see, the only ray of light in this whole dark and depressing restraining order fiasco was the fact that I had not been "served" the restraining order yet. I only found out about it through a lawyer's advertisement in the mail. One of those lawyers who reviews all the new case filings for the day and copies and pastes the addresses of all the defendants listed and then mails out ads offering his law firm's services.

And in the world of civil litigation, until a lawsuit or restraining order is actually "served," it does not really exist and cannot be ruled on by a judge. To serve a restraining order, Mair had to hire a "process server" to knock on my door or accost me in public and hand me a paper copy of the restraining order and say the magic words "You've been served." Until that happened, the restraining order was sort of on pause in the legal system.

"Just don't get served," the civil attorney told me as a smile crept across his face.

"What does that mean?" I asked.

"Your home, do you have a back way in?" he inquired.

"I'm a gay guy, of course I have a back way in," I responded.

He laughed.

But I was serious. I did have a back way in.

And that is exactly what my husband and I ended up doing for the next few weeks. We took the back way in and out of our home.

Avoiding service is technically illegal. But this restraining order was fraudulent, and it endangered the criminal proceeding against the filer that was weeks away. So I decided to take the risk and I actively avoided service.

Sometimes in life, you have to do the wrong thing to do the right thing. This was definitely one of those times.

For an entire two-week stretch leading up to the trial, off-duty sheriff's deputies moonlighting as process servers were pounding on my front door at all hours of the day and night: 5 A.M., noon, 8 P.M., 2 A.M. My husband and I huddled inside, shaking in fear. The few times I did look through the peephole, I saw an angry-looking sheriff's deputy in uniform banging away. I'm sure he was thinking that I was some woman-beating degenerate and that his anger and disgust were justified. Under any other circumstance, I would've opened the door immediately. But the civil attorney I hired warned me that it could very well be a sheriff's deputy working as a process server in his off-hours. So I never answered the door. Eventually, during the course of the criminal trial, that bogus restraining order got dismissed for "lack of service" and it was no longer an issue.

But the fact remains, had she successfully served me that restraining order, a judge would've probably approved it. Nine times out of ten, in our legal system, when a woman is accusing a man of stalking and violently threatening her, the judge believes the woman and wants to protect her—and will not believe the man. That's "chivalry theory" in action. Add to that, Mair is probably the most believable woman that judge would have ever seen to date. So I'm betting he would have believed her.

Out of the twenty-plus victims I provided the deputy district attorney with to testify, the judge approved only four, including me. It was explained that twenty would have been overkill.

And because the police officer who investigated my case had refused to call up and interview any of these other victims—remember he told me all these other victims have *nothing* to do with my case—the deputy district attorney called each victim and interviewed them himself. And that's normally a huge no-no, because Mair's attorney could then call the deputy district attorney as a witness on the stand to testify, and that would have been a disaster. But at this late stage, with the trial about to start, the deputy district attorney had no choice but to do his own police work and call up and interview all the victims to figure out who he wanted testifying.

Newport Beach engineer Bob testified about Mair trying to trick him into adding her name to the titles of his two homes. Another victim named Heather testified about Mair telling her the same Irish inheritance story she told me. Though Mair had scammed Heather out of $20,000 by pretending to be a psychologist, Heather was not allowed to talk about that because the trial was about how Mair had scammed me and not how she had scammed anyone else. "No prior bad acts allowed," said the judge. The only reason Newport Beach engineer Bob was allowed to testify about his scam was that it involved the Irish inheritance story. And the prosecutor got approval from the judge to show that Mair had told this Irish inheritance story to others as well—evidence that I was telling the truth and Mair was lying.

But the star witness of the entire trial was Mair's own daughter Chelsea, who flew in from Tennessee that morning to testify against her mother. But here was the snag: Chelsea was not allowed to testify about all the crazy cons Mair had pulled in Northern Ireland that had involved drafting her young daughter to forge mortgage paperwork to scam people with. Chelsea was allowed to testify only about the fact that her mother had a history of lying, that her mother was in no way Irish, and that there was no Irish inheritance or Irish family in existence whatsoever.

If you listen to Season 1 of the *Queen of the Con* podcast, I play long excerpts from each person's testimony, including my own.

It was truly a crazy and intense experience. I lost my shit on that witness stand several times and was shouting as Mair's attorney accused me of making everything up and inducing dozens of other people to lie about Mair on my behalf. And here's the terrifying thing: It was believable, and it stood to create reasonable doubt in the jury's mind.

Her lawyer skillfully made the argument to the jury that "Johnathan is a television producer." And I am.

"And this whole proceeding is being filmed, you all see the camera there, right? Because Johnathan wants it to be filmed," he said. That again was true. I'd gotten permission to bring cameras into the courtroom to film everything.

"So Johnathan is planning to make a movie about this," he said. Again, that was true. I was planning to make a documentary. So those three statements were 100 percent true.

Then, while he was cross-examining me on the stand, he told the jury that I needed to spice up this movie because I was a "sensationalist." In his closing arguments, he told the jury that this documentary I was making came from my "imagination," implying not only that I was making everything up about Mair but also that I was getting other people to go along with what I was making up.

That was a lie. I hadn't imagined or invented anything. Everything I testified about was 100 percent true. But if you're a juror, you might assume his fourth statement was true because the previous three statements were true. And all any juror needs is "reasonable doubt" to vote "not guilty." Mair's lawyer was making a compelling case for reasonable doubt.

At another point on the stand, I was fighting back tears as the prosecutor had me go over each dollar amount I had given Mair and the story she had told to get it. I felt so stupid and so utterly exposed to a roomful of strangers intensely watching me. That experience forever changed me and changed my understanding of the criminal justice system.

But in my mind, the biggest thing that jurors ended up holding against Marianne Smyth was the fact that here she was at forty-nine years old, and she couldn't find a single solitary person to get up on that stand and testify on her behalf. There was no one she could beg or cajole who could get up on that stand and say good things about her—not a family member, not a friend, not a co-worker. Not anyone. And that, I think, spoke volumes about the type of person the jury perceived her to be: a lying, cheating con artist.

The trial lasted a total of four days, and the jury deliberated for only three hours—which can be a good or a bad sign. But in the end, they found Marianne "Mair" Smyth guilty of grand theft by false pretense, and she was sentenced to five years behind bars for conning me. That was the maximum.

I was over the moon and vindicated. It felt like a huge weight had been lifted. And I felt whole again.

The judge also ordered her to pay me "court-ordered restitution," which sounds powerful and impressive. But the sad reality is—it's impossible for most victims to collect any meaningful restitution, for two reasons:

1. You need to hire a lawyer who can run an asset search and subpoena banks and subpoena employers to ferret out where the con artist has money or assets, and then can file hundreds and hundreds of papers and motions with a court to garnish wages or bank accounts. Conservatively that costs tens of thousands of dollars out of your pocket before the prospect of collecting a single dime. It's just not worth it. You would think I could take that "restitution order" I have that is signed by a judge to her bank or her employer and get my money. But that's not how the system works. Certainly, the implication of a restitution order is powerful. But in reality, it's anything but. It means almost nothing at all.

2. Any con artist knows they can avoid a restitution order simply by creating an LLC or corporation and directing any income they make from any business or scam through that LLC or corporation. That is what Mair did. It's what they all do. The restitution order I have is for Marianne Elizabeth Smyth, not any of the dozen LLCs she has since created to funnel her money through to avoid paying me. Oh, and don't even get me started on how all the laws and rules are different for restitution from state to state and county to county. I came to the sobering realization that the United States is not one country. It's actually fifty different countries with different rules and different laws in each one— especially if you've been scammed. The system makes it impossible to collect restitution—just impossible.

Still, the good news is: Mair went to jail in January 2019 to serve her five-year sentence. And the bad news is: One year and eleven months later, in December of 2020, she got out early because the State of California decided to release thousands of nonviolent inmates to stem the spread of Covid in jails and prisons.

After Mair was released, she disappeared. I had no idea where she was. A few months later, I produced my opus: The *Queen of the Con* podcast, chronicling all her scams, and it was a huge hit. Millions of downloads later, I started getting contacted by people who had heard the podcast and knew where Mair was.

Apparently, she had moved to the state of Maine, the farthest you can get from Los Angeles and still be in the contiguous United States. I guess she was scared and didn't want to be anywhere near me. That kind of made me feel good. Even though she had grown up in Bangor, she had now moved two hundred miles north of her hometown to Madawaska, I suspect because she had scammed a lot of people in Bangor back in her youth and feared crossing paths with them.

Then all of a sudden, avid podcast listeners started giving me a literal play-by-play of her comings and goings.

"She's my neighbor," one woman texted.

"I just saw her at the gas station," another woman emailed.

"She just scammed me out of $800," said a new victim of Mair's who called me up on the "Mair hotline" I had posted on my website.

The new scams Mair was pulling in Maine were next-level. She had successfully infiltrated a Facebook group of military families who were concerned about what was happening in the Ukraine and wanted to help. Mair offered to help by passing herself off as an IRA-connected Irish woman who was working with the U.S. military and NATO to run rescue missions in the Ukraine (Red Flag #1, "I Just Want to Help," and Red Flag #12, Stories from Faraway Places). Mair actually raised thousands and thousands of dollars for that effort. She even went so far as to impersonate Senator Susan Collins of Maine over email and text to convince her victims she was legit (Red Flag #6: Technology).

I worked closely with one of the victims of this Ukraine scam to put an end to it and out Mair as a con artist. And I assisted three other victims with filing police reports. My hope was that since Mair was on parole these new scams would constitute a violation and land her back in jail. But shockingly, that's not how the system works. The only thing her parole officer would consider a violation would be if she was convicted of another crime. And as I'm sure you know by now, convicting a con artist literally takes years and requires a diligent, impassioned, dog-with-a-bone-type victim like me to pursue a case.

Anyway, after her Ukraine scam went south, so did Mair. She moved to a new location, a new city in Maine called Bingham, and started a whole new scam. She began passing herself off as a Satanic high priestess named "Lucia Belia" and she started a Satanic church to scam people.

I wish I was creative enough to make stuff like this up. But I just don't have that ability.

Again, because of the *Queen of the Con* podcast's popularity, all of a sudden I started getting contacted by practicing Satanists telling me that Mair was scamming them and asking for my help and advice.

And while this was all happening, I was constantly sending updates to a police detective in Northern Ireland whom I'd been talking to since 2017. Over that past seven years I had been giving him detailed updates on all her new scams and all her new addresses, and begging him to extradite her already.

I was also able to get my hands on a video of one of Mair's Satanic ceremonies where she's dressed in a black robe, wielding a giant silver knife, and proclaiming her undying love to "Satan my father," as the reflection of candlelight flickers in her eyes. I think that was the straw that broke the camel's back in Northern Ireland, a very religious country, because a few months later, U.S. marshals showed up out of nowhere with guns drawn to the address a podcast listener had sent me that I had sent Northern Ireland police, and they arrested Mair as part of the extradition proceeding against her.

As I type these words now, Marianne Smyth is sitting in a jail cell in Northern Ireland awaiting trial for scamming dozens of victims over there out of hundreds of thousands of pounds sterling when she worked as a mortgage broker from 2002 to 2009.

I hope and pray for justice for the victims of Northern Ireland.

And I want to stress to all who are reading these words: None of this would be happening if I had stayed quiet and let the potential shame of being conned silence me like so many other victims do.

You never know the effect your story will have on the world by speaking up. And that is what I want to encourage each and every one of you to do. Speak up! In the famous words of poet Dylan Thomas, "Do not go gentle into that good night."

Never in a million years did I think I would ever write these words: I am grateful I got scammed. I mean, it certainly felt like the end of the world when it was happening, and I suffered a lot and lost a lot. But over the past seven years I've gained much more than I lost: not just financially, though certainly that's part of it, but intellectually, emotionally, and spiritually.

I am constantly getting emails and Instagram messages and texts from people telling me that my story has helped them avoid getting scammed or that my fervent pursuit of justice has inspired someone who got scammed to seek justice in their case. To know that this is the effect I'm having on people fills me with a sense of purpose that I've never felt before. The mere fact that you are reading these words right now means you now know what I know. And since you're armed with all this information, the chances of your ever getting scammed by a professional con artist just went down considerably. I can't even begin to put into words how happy that makes me. But I'll try: IT MAKES ME VERY, VERY HAPPY!

Oh, and great news. We got the pool back! And Mair had nothing to do with it. Basically, our building sued, and the other building settled. And bam splish splash, we were swimming again.

16. WHAT TO DO IF YOU'VE BEEN CONNED

PLEASE KEEP IN MIND THAT I AM NOT A LAWYER, AND I'M NOT TELLING YOU TO DO OR NOT do anything. I'm merely offering my experience and explaining how things went for me and what I have gleaned over the past few years in the hopes of educating you about the process of seeking justice after getting scammed. Before you engage in any of your own interactions with the law, you should by all means consult your own attorney—though in my experience, if you ask ten different attorneys the same question you'll get ten different answers. But I digress.

A lot of what I'm about to get into here has been hinted at or mentioned in previous chapters. But I wanted to give you all step-by-step instructions on what to do if you've been scammed so you have it clearly and concisely all in one place after you've read the whole book and you can better apply what you've learned to this process.

It ain't easy. But nothing worthwhile ever is.

If you've been the victim of a con artist, I want you to keep this in mind: the last thing in the world that con artist wants you to do is to tell people what happened. They want you to keep quiet. They want you to limp away and never breathe a word about what they did. But I beg you: Do not give them the satisfaction of your silence. Do not help them scam other victims by letting them off the hook for what they did to you. Report them, at least to the police.

But before you go to the police, you have to get your ducks in a row. You have to be prepared. You have to treat it as if you're going to give a twenty-minute presentation to a class of college students, complete with compelling visual aids and props. You can't just walk into a police department empty-handed to tell them your sob story of how you got scammed. They will not care.

And they will turn you away. "It's a civil matter," they'll tell you. "Go hire a lawyer and sue them in civil court."

You would think, as a taxpaying citizen in this country, that you have a right to file a police report if you believe a crime has been committed. But it is 100 percent up to that officer taking (or refusing to take) the report. They are the judge, jury, and executioner on the front lines, solely responsible for determining if a crime has been committed. They are the ones you have to convince.

A lot of police departments, especially in big cities, are overwhelmed with the amount of violent crime happening every day. To them, your con artist case seems trivial by comparison. That is all the more reason you need to be carefully prepared *before* you go to the police.

In chapter 1, I told you that pitching a criminal case to the police is a lot like pitching a television show to a network executive—you have to make it sexy.

Nobody is going to tell a victim what I'm going tell you: The onus for getting justice is 100 percent on you, the victim—not the system, and God knows not that low-level officer writing the initial police report, or refusing to write a report in most cases.

If you suddenly realize that you are the victim of a con artist, the first thing you need to do is create a timeline on paper in the privacy of your own home with details of what happened.

- When did you meet this person?

- How did you meet this person?

- What stories did they tell you and on what dates?

- When did the money change hands?

- Why did you give them money?

- What was the lie or lies they told you?

- How and when did you figure out they were lying?

- How and why did you figure out you were conned?

Then you need to gather up and print out all the emails and all the text messages you have—to and from this person—and download all the voicemails you have that prove what you're asserting in that time-line you're writing is true.

Now you need to do some simple investigative work.

First, run a background check on the con artist. For a few hundred dollars you can hire a licensed private investigator who can do a really professional check and bring up tons of info. Or for around $30 you can go to one of those internet database sites like BeenVerified.com or Intelius.com and bring up criminal records if they exist and bring up all the addresses in the United States associated with that con artist.

Then figure out which counties those addresses are in, google to find the website for the courts in each of those counties, and do a criminal case search and civil case search to see if anyone has sued your con artist over the past few years. In a lot of counties, a civil case search is free. Sometimes they charge a dollar or two per search. And they can charge as much as fifty cents to a dollar to download each page of a lawsuit or a filing. In smaller cities and towns, the courts may not have that advanced a website, so you'll need to call the civil clerk for that court and ask them to search for all the civil filings in your con artist's name. If the clerk refuses to help you—which has happened to me—just use Google or Yelp to find a paralegal in that town to go to the courthouse in person (if you can't go) and search for those records. That can cost you anywhere from $50 to $100.

There's also a government website called Pacer.UScourts.gov. It's for federal cases. You can sign up for an account and search for federal criminal or federal civil cases in the con artist's name for free—though there is a ten-cent-per-page charge if you want to download documents in any of the cases that may come up.

Now, if you are able to locate a lawsuit filed by someone against the con artist, just reading through the complaint will tell you a lot about their past actions. And nine times out of ten, if you call up the party who filed that lawsuit, they will be only too happy to be a character witness in your case.

So after you've created your detailed timeline and done your background checks, you need to start calling around to people you know who know this con artist and tell them you were scammed. Ask if they were scammed or if they know anyone else who says they were scammed by this person.

Keep in mind, the con artist may have already told lies to this person you're calling in anticipation of your call, but at that point offer to share with them the stuff you've found in your own background searches. If you've found criminal records or lawsuits filed against the con artist, offer to email them the records you've found to prove you are telling the truth.

If you manage to find other victims or other character witnesses, ask them to write up a witness statement and get it notarized. Just google "how to write a witness statement." Basically, it's a short one-page essay about what they witnessed in terms of a crime or potential crime, using short, concise sentences, including dates and times.

Now you have your timeline, you have your background check results, you have your court records, and you have at least one or more notarized witness statements from other people. It's time to write up your sworn affidavit and get it notarized too.

An affidavit is a lot like a witness statement. Just google how to write an affidavit. It's a statement of facts that are numbered.

My advice is to write it like a college essay: Tell them what you're going to tell them. Then tell them. Then tell them what you told them.

The first statement needs to be something like:

I, the undersigned, do hereby swear, certify, and affirm that:

1. I am over the age of 18 and a resident of the state of California. I have personal knowledge of the facts in this affidavit and, if called as a witness, could testify competently about them.

2. (Summarize the crime here) From May 2013 to March 2017, a woman by the name of Marianne Smyth, 47, scammed me out of nearly $100,000 using a series of elaborate confidence tricks to steal my money. I have since discovered she has a lengthy criminal record of fraud and grand theft, and I have found several other victims she scammed whose notarized statements I'm including with this sworn affidavit.

Then number each subsequent paragraph and go through your timeline of events, numbering each event 3, 4, 5, 6, 7, and so on.

Ask a friend or family member to read over your affidavit and troubleshoot or correct anything that doesn't make sense or is not abundantly clear to someone reading about your case for the first time.

Now you're ready to go to the police. But before you go, you need to rehearse your speech. You need to be able to sum up what happened to you in a compelling sentence. For example: "My name is Johnathan Walton and I was the victim of an international con artist who scammed me out of nearly $100,000 over the course of four years through a series of elaborate confidence tricks." At this point you pull out your affidavit, your evidence (printed out emails, texts, voicemails on a thumb drive—whatever evidence you have), corroborating witness statements, and court records, and you make your case to the police. Answer any questions the officer might have.

By now this officer will be acutely aware that you are a freaking force to be reckoned with and that you have done a lot of investigative legwork, and they will more than likely take a police report. Make sure to get a copy of that report. Call the police and ask for an update about your case every day thereafter. Badger them. Ask them when it will be assigned to an investigator. You need to become a pain in their ass for them to do anything. And keep in mind, 99 percent of all other victims are not calling about their cases every day, so your case will stand out and get placed on the top of the pile for consideration every time you call.

How to Prevent Scammers from Stealing Your Credit

One super important thing that I think everyone reading these words should do immediately is freeze their credit. It doesn't cost you anything—except a little time and aggravation. But the truth of the matter is: Your name, address, date of birth, and social security number are floating around on illicit websites with millions and millions of others right now. Every time there's a hack at a bank, or the Social Security Administration, or your cellphone company, all of your personal info gets posted on the dark web for scammers to buy and sell among one another. It is only a matter of time before one of these SOBs takes out a loan in your name or charges up credit in your name and leaves you responsible to pay the bill or to try to climb out from under it, because at that point the onus is 100 percent on you to convince the credit card company and the credit reporting bureaus that you were the victim of fraud. It's not an easy thing to do, and doing it can take years of your life and mountains of paperwork.

When you freeze your credit, no one—not you, not a family member, not a scammer, no one—will be able to take out a loan or get a credit card or open a line of credit in your name.

To freeze your credit, log on to the websites of each of the credit reporting bureaus—TransUnion.com, Equifax.com, and Experian.com—and do a search on each site for "Freeze Credit." Create a free online account on each credit bureau's website, navigate to their "freeze credit" option, and click "freeze." And it's done. Then later you can click "unfreeze" if you're trying to get a new credit card or loan of any kind.

Keep in mind, each of those bureaus will try *really hard* to direct you to buy monthly credit monitoring. They throw a zillion popups and links at you. Make sure you decline all of those offers, and pay close attention because they like to sneak them in there. But by law, freezing and unfreezing your credit is *100 percent free.*

Thanks for reading my book. I hope I've armed you with the tools you need to spot the scammer in your life or in the lives of your loved ones. But if you've already been the victim of a scammer, I know how hard it is. I know how impossible it might seem to get justice. I know how embarrassed and ashamed you are that you fell for it all. I've been there too. I think everyone has in some form or another felt that way whether or not they've ever been scammed. In life we all get knocked to the ground at some point by something, whether by a duplicitous con artist, a disease, or some other tragedy.

But getting knocked down doesn't define us. What defines us is how we rise.

ACKNOWLEDGMENTS

This book would not be possible without the unending love and support of my husband, Pablito, and my mom—who brainwashed me from a very young age that I was "*brilliant* and can do *anything*"—so now that's the recording in my head regardless of what all the vocal naysayers are espousing.

Thanks to my brother Jason for his frequent and passionate proclamations over the past two years about what a HUGE hit this book will be. I've never wanted him to be right about ANYTHING more. My sincerest thanks and gratitude to producing impresario Aliza Rosen whose "You want to do a podcast?" phone call to me back in late 2020 forever changed the trajectory of my life in the most spectacular and amazing way and gave birth to *Queen of the Con*.

I am forever in debt to my agent, the magical Jenna Land Free, who read an online article I penned identifying all these *Red Flags* and immediately called me up and implored, "This would make a great book!"

Thank you to my brother from another mother, Evan Goldstein, who's a big-time showrunner in Los Angeles and yet made the time and spent many *hours* reading the chapters I wrote while giving me tons of great ideas and inordinately constructive criticism.

Thanks to my cherished best friends Eileen and Jorge—where would I be on this crazy con-hunting journey without you both always putting the wind in my sail and cheering me on at every turn.

Special thanks to my fellow con hunter Vicki Eckles whose help and kindness I will never forget.

I'd also like to thank some of my fellow victims-turned-vigilantes who continue to inspire me to this day: T. J. Dominguez, Chelsea Fowler, Jeff Quinn, Erik Kramer, Anna Dergan, Carol Porter, Vanessa Spatz, Carmen Hereter, Karen Pfeffer, Caroline D'Amore, Denise Harvill, and Grace Kang. If *every* victim of every con did what you all have done, the world would be a much safer place.

Thank you to my childhood friend Marcos Dabdoub Jr. for your Ponzi scheme expertise and eyewitness account. Thanks to fellow con artist "outer" Javier Leiva of the Pretend podcast for your friendship and guidance over the years.

Thank you journalist Waylon Cunningham for that insightful first print story about Mair back in 2018 where your lede summed up what happened to me so perfectly and gave me the words to explain it quickly to everyone else from that point on: "A former Maryville woman is set to appear in a Los Angeles court on charges of grand theft after she allegedly played an elaborate series of confidence tricks to steal more than $75,000 from a man over the course of years." I've also met some of the most incredible people in law enforcement while investigating con artists over the past seven years who have profoundly moved me by their selfless dedication and compassion. Sgt. Jordan Mirakian, Det. Carlos Verdoni, Sam Fadel, and Det. David Lingscheit— if every cop operated the way you guys do, *there would be no crime.* PERIOD.

I'm also in debt to former federal prosecutor Scott Tenley (now with Tenley Law), former federal prosecutor Paul LeBlanc (now with the San Diego DA's office), Los Angeles deputy district attorney Jeffrey Megee, Los Angeles deputy district attorney Jessica Palasik, former prosecutor and current legal eagle Emily D. Baker (*The Emily Show* podcast), and former FBI criminal profiler Candice DeLong—knowing you all has made me so much smarter and stronger and infinitely more effective at stopping con artists. THANK YOU.

And my deepest gratitude to my editor, the amazing Matthew Benjamin, for making me a better writer than I ever thought I could be.

INDEX

A

affidavit
  as crucial legal document, 64
  preparation of, 225–26
Andrew the Politician, 79–82, 136, 203, 206–7
Arouse in the Other Person an Eager Want, 209–10
artificial scarcity, 7–8. *See also* Scarcity technique

B

background checks, 10–11, 134, 158, 177, 224–25
Baird, Cortney. *See also* Kramer, Erik
  assault accusations by, 21
  background, 16
  court delay tactics, 22–23
  felony charges, 22
  guilty plea, 23
  helping Erik with medical recovery, 16–17
  L.A. County sheriff's detective interview, 19–20
  marrying Erik, 20
  moving in with Erik, 17
Baker, Emily D., 141
Baker Act (Florida), 54, 59
bank wires. *See* Wires technique
Barnum, P. T., 212
Beak Wetting technique
  David Smith and, 126
  Mair Smyth and, 136, 150–51
  overview, 8–9, 122
  scams using, types of, 9, 122
Beers, Erica, 174
Best, Travis, 37
Bloom, David
  arrest of, 120–21
  bonding with Caroline, 117–18
  first meeting with Caroline, 116–17

I'm Better Than You technique used by, 118–19
  Los Angeles District Attorney's Office and, 120
  overview, 115
  scarcity technique used by, 119
  technology use, 117
Bob (victim). *See* Newport Beach engineer Bob
bonding technique, 11. *See also* TMI (too much information) technique
Broward Sheriff's Office
  Carol Porter's case, 63–64, 69–71
  Economic Crimes Unit, 69–71
  Elizabeth Lee and, 63–64
  lack of evidence gathering, 69–70
Broward State Attorney's Office, 71–72

C

Carey, Pam, 35, 36
Carnegie, Dale, 209. *See also* Dale Carnegie Techniques
Chambers, Jonathan, 127
child support scam, 201–2
chivalry theory, 20–24, 215
Clark, Marianne Elizabeth. *See* Smyth, Marianne "Mair"
Cochrane, Mike, 104
con artists
  assessing weaknesses quickly, 76
  Bina Fink (*See* Fink, Bina)
  books about, ix–x
  causes of, 181–82
  complicated scams, benefits of, 141–42
  Cortney Baird (*See* Baird, Cortney)
  Danielle Miller (*See* Miller, Danielle)
  dating apps, use of, 197
  David Bloom, 115–20
  David Smith (*See* Smith, David)
  as easiest to fool, 132

con artists (*cont'd*)
  false beliefs about, xiii–xiv
  fighting back against (*See* Getting Justice)
  Grayson (*See* Faith and Grayson (victim and
    scammer))
  Jen Shah (*See* Shah, Jen)
  justice, bringing to (*See* Getting Justice)
  Lizzie Mulder (*See* Mulder, Lizzie)
  Mair Smyth (*See* Smyth, Marianne "Mair")
  manipulating the legal system, 20–24
  Michael Lawrence (*See* Elizabeth (victim))
  as narcissists, 5, 132–33, 204
  out-feel their victims technique, x, 48,
    112–13, 126, 143, 149, 161, 184
  in person vs online/virtual, 172
  preventing credit stealing by, 175–76, 227
  reliance on technology, 99–100
  revealing themselves, unintentionally, 140
  using human nature to their advantage, 130
  using your emotions, x
  value system, 182
  Wendell Pfeffer (*See* Pfeffer, Wendell)
confidence artist. *See* con artists
conservatorship, 19, 54
contracts, as civil vs criminal case, 166–67
Cooper, Sherry, 31–32, 83, 131, 204
court-ordered restitution, 218
credit freezing, 175–76, 227
credit stealing, 175–76, 227
Cystic Fibrosis Foundation, 96

D
Dabdoub, Marcos, Jr., 125–26
Dale Carnegie Techniques
  Arouse in the Other Person an Eager Want,
    209–10
  Dramatize Your Ideas, 211
  overview, 12–13
  using victims' first names as much as
    possible, 211–12
D'Amore, Caroline
  arranging protest against L.A. Attorney's
    Office, 120
  background, 115–16
  confronting David, 120
  David Bloom meeting, 116–17
  David distracting, 118–19
  David using scarcity to act fast, 119
dark web, 173
data breaches, 173
dating apps, meeting con artists through, 197
DeLong, Candice, 3
Department of Homeland Security, 145
Dergan, Anna, 18, 22
details, power of, 111–12, 157, 188, 193,
  197–98
distracting scam technique, xiii, 5, 118–19,
  122, 147, 148–49
Drama, Drama, Drama technique
  Bina Fink and, 53–54
  Grayson (con artist) and, 199
  Lizzie Mulder and, 102

Mair Smyth and, 73–75, 80–81, 135, 149
  overview, 4–5, 48–49
To Be Interesting, Be Interested, 210–11

E
Elizabeth (victim)
  author and, 186–87
  background, 187
  bank wire scam, falling for, 189–90
  falling victim to a team of con artists,
    188–91
  meeting Michael (con artist), 187–88
  Michael's trust building, 188
  reporting incident to the police, 190–91
  witnessing Michael's death, 190
Escobar de Salcedo, Luz Elvira, 92

F
Faith and Grayson (victim and scammer)
  child support scam, 201–2
  drama sharing, 199
  first date, 197
  Grayson as very helpful and nice, 198–99
  Grayson sharing too much information,
    197–98
  Grayson's entrée into Faith's life, 199–200
  on Grayson's love bombing, 199
  pregnancy, 201
fear, as second most powerful force, 55
financial scams. *See also* Wires technique
  Lizzie Mulder and (*See* Mulder, Lizzie)
  Vincent Leli and (*See* Leli, Vincent)
Fink, Bina. *See also* Porter, Carol
  author's background check on, 50–51
  becoming Carol's best friend, 52
  Carol balking at money requests, 60–61
  Carol's growing reliance on, 60
  Carol's trust in, 55–56
  case reassignment, 69–71
  convincing Carol to move, 59
  creating drama, 53, 54
  Fernando as suspicious of, 55
  isolating Carol, 55–58
  law enforcement's awareness of, 66–67
  LinkedIn profile, 67
  meeting Carol, 52
  modus operandi, 69
  possible connection with state attorney,
    71–72
  rap sheet, 51
  Sun Sentinel article, 71
  victims of, 67–69
Firkus, Taylor, 176–79
Flatley, Joseph L., 142, 144
foreign exchange trading, 123–25
Fulford, Peggy
  background, 33–34
  bigamy of, 36
  civil suit against, 40
  Dennis Rodman and, 40–41
  federal charges against, 41–42
  gaining power of attorney, 38–39, 40

generational wealth investment scams, 38—39, 40—41, 211
getting to know her victims, 210—11
guilty plea, 42
Kristin Williams and, 39—40
Pam Carey and, 36
portraying herself as a financial manager, 37
refusing payment from victims, 38—39
Ricky Williams and, 37—38
son Elkin, 37
Travis Best and, 37
using kindness as a weapon, 34

G
generational wealth promises, 38—39
Getting Justice
affidavit preparation, 225—26
background checks, 224
do not stay silent, 222
finding other victims, 225
information gathering, 224
investigative work, 224
locating character witnesses, 225
overview, xi—xiii
pitching a criminal case, 223
preparations, 222—23
rehearsing your pitch, 226
timeline draft, 223—24
working with law enforcement, 226
GoFundMe scam, 96
Goldstein, Evan, 130
A Good Day Job technique
as con artists' appearance of legitimacy, 139—40
Grayson (con artist) and, 200
Mair Smyth and, 146—47
overview, 9
Grayson (con artist). See Faith and Grayson (victim and scammer)
greed, power of, 126

H
Hawkins, James, 41
Hereter, Carmen, 86. See also Pfeffer, Wendell
building case against Wendell, 92
creating blog about Wendell, 91
reaching out to author, 85—86
suspecting Wendell's scheme, 90
Wendell's meeting with, 88—89
Wendell's ruse to impress, 88—89
Hirschhorn, Elizabeth, 176
How To Win Friends and Influence People (Carnegie), 209. See also Dale Carnegie Techniques
human beings, innately driven to help others, 14—15

I
I Just Want to Help technique
Bina Fink and, 52
Danielle Miller and, 177
David Bloom and, 116

David Smith and, 127
Grayson (con artist) and, 198—99
Lizzie Mulder and, 101—2
Mair Smyth and, 30—32, 43—46, 146—47, 206—7, 219
overview, 3—4
Vincent Leli and, 157—58
I'm Better Than You technique
Danielle Miller and, 177
David Bloom and, 118—19
David Smith and, 127
Grayson (con artist) and, 200
Lizzie Mulder and, 102
Mair Smyth and, 93—96, 97, 147
overview, 6—7, 85
Vincent Leli and, 157
Wendell Pfeffer and, 86
inheritance scams, 73, 111—12, 122, 129, 147—52, 216
investment scams, 8, 9. See also Fulford, Peggy
Isolation technique
Bina Fink and, 55—58
Mair Smyth and, 83—84
overview, 5—6

K
Kaplan, Richard, 56
kindness, 33, 43—46. See also I Just Want to Help technique
King, Elkin, 37
King, Peggy. See Fulford, Peggy
King Management, 37
Kramer, Erik. See also Baird, Cortney
Anna Dergan and, 18
author's assistance to, 22
background, 15—16
Cortney marries, 20
court trial, 22—23
David Lingscheit and, 18—19
diminished mental capacity, 16—17
domestic violence charges, 21—22
healing of, 21
L.A. County sheriff's detective interview, 18—19
source of income, 17—18
The Ultimate Comeback, 23

L
law enforcement
Broward Sheriff's Office, 63—64, 69—71
jurisdictions within, 62
Los Angeles Police Department, 96—97
Orange County District Attorney's Office, 105
pitching a criminal case to, 62—63
police report pushback, 166—67
pushback against victims, 62
unwillingness to investigate, 207—8
working with (See Getting Justice)
Lawrence, Michael, Elizabeth and. See Elizabeth (victim)

Lee, Elizabeth, 63–64
Leli, Vincent. *See also* Wires technique
  background, 157
  bank wire scam, 156–57
  conviction, 160
  dramatizing his con, 158, 211
  trust building with his victim, 157–58
Lingscheit, David, 18–19
Los Angeles Police Department, 96–97
love
  making decisions based on, 4
  as most powerful force in universe, 4, 55, 127
love bombing, 199
love scams
  artificial scarcity use in, 8
  beak wetting in, 9, 122
"Lucia Belia." *See* Smyth, Marianne "Mair"

M
Madoff, Bernie, 125
Mark (not his real name). *See* Wires technique
Mendosa, Geneva, 101
Miller, Danielle
  background, 172
  conviction, 179
  impersonating Erica Beers, 174–75
  Paycheck Protection Program loan scam, 172–74
  roommate ruse, 176–78
  scamming people she knows, 176
  Taylor Firkus, as victim of, 176–79
  withdrawing strangers' bank accounts, 174
mingling victims strategy, 82
Mirakian, Jordan, 105–6, 107
money laundering, 151
Mulder, Lizzie
  account business, 101
  background, 100
  creating drama, 102, 211
  Department of Justice and, 106
  faking client signatures, 104–5
  Geneva Mendosa as victim of, 101
  I Just Want to Help technique, 101–2
  IRS investigation, 106
  Mike Cochrane as victim of, 104
  offering help, 102
  police investigation of, 105–6
  prosecution of, 106
  recast as downtrodden, 100–101
  technology use, 100, 102–3
Mulder Financial, 101

N
Newport Beach engineer Bob, 95, 146–50, 153, 216

O
Occam's razor, 65, 79
OLINT (Overseas Locket International), 124
online texting accounts, 7
Orange County District Attorney's Office, 105
Orchid Psychics, 163

out-feel their victims technique, x, 48, 112–13, 126, 143, 149, 161, 184
oversharing. *See* TMI (too much information) technique

P
Paycheck Protection Program (PPP) loans, 172–74
Pfeffer, Wendell. *See also* Hereter, Carmen
  accomplice of, 92
  background, 86–87
  finance and investing abilities, 86
  fleeing to Spain, 92
  mansion, as a prop, 87–88
  Puerto Rico mansion-hunting expeditions, 88
  purported AT&T expansion, 89–90
  running father-in-law's beverage company, 87
  sister Karen and, 87, 88
phone number spoofing, 103
Pig in a Poke scam, 78–79
Pizza Girl marinara sauce, 116, 118
police. *See* law enforcement
Pollak, Edmund, 20
Ponzi schemes
  beak wetting in, 9
  David Bloom (*See* Bloom, David)
  David Smith and (*See* Smith, David)
Porter, Carol
  background, 51–52
  Bina Fink and (*See* Fink, Bina)
  cash payments to lawyers, 56–58
  contacting the author, 58, 61
  Elizabeth Lee and, 63–64
  Fernando (financial manager) and, 53, 54–55, 60
  preparing an affidavit, 63–64
  reaching out to author, 49–50
  reporting crime to law enforcement, 61–62, 63–64
  susceptible to sunk cost fallacy, 57
  worried over family Baker Act'ing her, 53–54
power
  con artists seeking, 77
  of details, 111–12
  of greed, 126
professional con artists. *See* con artists
Prosper, Inc., 142
publicity, as kryptonite to a con artist, 71, 91, 115
Pucket, Penny, 143–44

Q
Queen of the Con podcast, 92, 153, 219, 221

R
Real Housewives of Salt Lake City (reality series), 139–40. *See also* Shah, Jen
reasonable doubt, 142, 193
rescue merchant, 3–4, 30–32

restitution orders, 218
Rodman, Dennis, 40–41
Rodriguez, Jen, 105
Roosevelt, Teddy, x

S
Scaccia, Lauren, 101
scammers. *See* con artists
scams, complicated
  benefits of, 141–42
  creating reasonable doubt in court, 142, 193
  as detailed and multifaceted, 193
scarcity, effects on human behavior, 114–15
Scarcity Principle, 114
Scarcity technique
  David Bloom and, 119
  Mair Smyth and, 133, 168–69, 183
  overview, 7–8
Shah, Jen
  background, 139–40, 142
  investigation of, 145
  portraying herself as self-made mogul, 140–41
  Prosper, Inc. and, 142–43
  revealing herself, unintentionally, 140
  telemarketing fraud scheme, 142–45
  victims of, 143–44
Smith, David
  arrest of, 128
  author's family investments with, 124–25
  background, 123
  beak wetting use, 126
  as celebrity in Jamaica, 127
  clients' trust and belief in, 127–28
  in foreign exchange trading, 123–25
  investigations into, 127–28
  investors' demographics, 127
  Marcos Dabdoub's doubts about, 125–26
  running a Ponzi scheme, 125
  technology use, 126
  using clients' greed against them, 126
Smyth, Marianne "Mair," 4. *See also* Walton-Smyth relationship
  Andrew the Politician and, 79–82, 136, 203, 206–7
  apparent selflessness, 97–98
  arrest and conviction of, 94–95
  arrest of, 129–33
  background, 182
  bank wire scam, 161
  beak wetting, 136, 150–51
  blackmail activities, 204–5
  Bob and (*See* Newport Beach engineer Bob)
  bonding with her victims, 5
  cancer scam, 168–69, 181
  childhood story, 73–75
  coconspirator of, 207
  crafting scam, 28
  criminal background check, 134
  criminal case, 137–38
  daughter Chelsea, 97, 180, 182–85, 216
  daughter Courtney, 96, 182

day job, 94–95, 131, 146
distracting technique, 148–49
engaging Dale Carnegie techniques, 212
family estrangement, 112
family of, 108–9
far-off places story, 29–30
gaining victim's love and trust, 43–47
GoFundMe scam, 96
husband Stephen (*See* Smyth, Stephen)
impersonating celebrities, 205
inheritance scam by, 129
Irish origin story, xiv, 73–76, 110–11, 192
Jeff Welch and, 182
kindness of, 43–46
as a life coach, 166
living in Northern Ireland, 182–83
lupus story, 27–28
Maine scams, 219–20
mingling victims strategy, 82
moving around a lot, 136–37, 180
Northern Ireland's extradition proceedings, 207, 220
Orchid Psychics business, 163–64
the payoff for, 149–50
Pig in a Poke scam, 78–79
post-jail scamming activities, 219–20
as a psychic, 161–66, 168–69
as a psychologist, 166
as a rescue merchant, 30–32
as Satanic high priestess, 220
scamming, as full time profession, 73
scamming real estate investors, 168–69
Sherry Cooper and, 31–32, 131, 204
stealing from her employer, 131
stories from faraway places, 192
storytelling skills, 95–97
technology use, 108–12
TMI technique, use of, 203–4
trial for (*See* Smyth Trial)
Ukraine scam, 219–20
waving I'm Better Than You flag, 93–96
Smyth, Stephen, 182–85, 207
Smyth Trial
  author avoiding restraining order service, 214–15
  court hearings, 138
  court-ordered restitution, 218
  deputy district attorney's victim interviews, 215–16
  guilty verdict, 217–18
  Mair's restraining order against author, 213–15
  sentencing, 218
  witness testimonies, 216–17
Soho House, 118–19
Stories from Faraway Places technique
  Mair Smyth and, 29–30, 219
  overview, 11, 186
storytelling
  craft of, 95–97
  power of details, 111–12, 157, 188, 193, 197–98

Sun Sentinel (Florida newspaper), 71
sunk cost fallacy, 57, 60, 151

T
Technology (use of) techniques
    con artists' reliance on, 99–100
    David Bloom and, 117
    David Smith and, 126, 127
    fake online texting accounts, 7
    Grayson (con artist) and, 200
    Mair Smyth and, 108–12, 138, 147, 219
    Michael Lawrence and, 191
    overview, 7, 99–100
    phone number spoofing, 103
    Vincent Leli and, 158, 211
    voice-changing apps, 102–3
Tenley, Scott, 106, 132
They Move Around a Lot technique
    Danielle Miller and, 177
    Grayson (con artist) and, 200–201
    overview, 10–11, 171–72
TMI (too much information) technique,
    11–12, 196, 197–98, 210
To Be Interesting, Be Interested, 210–11
Too Kind, Too Quick technique
    David Bloom and, 117
    David Smith and, 127
    Grayson (con artist) and, 199
    overview, 4
    Vincent Leli and, 157–58
trauma bond, 5

U
The Ultimate Comeback (Kramer), 23
U.S. Department of Justice, 106

V
Verdoni, Carlos, 174
victims
    Bob (*See* Newport Beach engineer Bob)
    bonding with, 5
    Carmen Hereter (*See* Hereter, Carmen)
    Carol Porter (*See* Porter, Carol)
    Caroline D'Amore (*See* D'Amore, Caroline)
    con artists out-feeling (*See* out-feel their
        victims technique)
    Elizabeth (*See* Elizabeth (victim))
    Erik Kramer (*See* Kramer, Erik)
    Faith (*See* Faith and Grayson (victim and
        scammer))
    fear of going public, 169–70
    fighting back (*See* Getting Justice)
    Geneva Mendosa, 101
    impressed by con artists, 6–7
    Johnathan Walton (*See* Walton, Johnathan
        (author))
    Mike Cochrane, 104
    not wanting to appear rude or disrespectful,
        90–91
    onus for getting justice, xii
    pay close attention to the small things, 93
    Peggy Fulford (*See* Fulford, Peggy)

protecting credit, 175–76, 227
proving criminal case, 167
Ricky Williams (*See* Williams, Ricky)
shame felt by, xi
Taylor Firkus, 176–79
Villa Carlotta, 116–17
voice-changing apps, 102–3

W
Walton, Johnathan (author). *See also* Walton-
    Smyth relationship
    advising other victims, xi–xii, 22, 50–51
    Andrew the Politician and, 81–82
    apartment building pool project, 24–25
    Bina Fink investigation, 64–66
    Bob (Newport Beach engineer) and, 153
    as building tenants meeting host, 29–30
    commandeering Mair's email account,
        204–6
    family estrangement, 112
    FBI reaching out to, 65–66
    husband's doubts about Mair, 113
    investigating con artists, 64
    Lebanese background, 123
    on Mair's arrest, 130
    on Mair's background check, 134
    Mair's trial (*See* Smyth Trial)
    Melting Pot dinner, 46
    Palm Springs weekend vacation, 46
    Queen of the Con podcast, 92, 153, 219,
        221
    realizing Mair's schemes, 152
    reporting Mair's crime to law enforcement,
        193–95
    as television producer, 24, 129
    as victim, ix–xi
    viewed as a violent lunatic, 180–81
Walton-Smyth relationship
    arranging Mair's bail, 133–35
    bond between, 112
    building tenants meeting, 29–30
    dinner with Mair, 75–77
    dress giveaway, 45–46
    email account, 204–6
    email communications, 24, 26
    face-to-face meeting, 26–29
    Johnathan's offer of publicity for, 137
    loaning money to Mair, 150–51
    Mair's psychic show, 164–65
    offering Mair publicity help, 137
Welch, Jeff, 182
Western Union, 154
Williams, Kristin, 39–40
Williams, Ricky
    failing NFL drug tests, 38
    in *MTV Cribs* predicament, 35, 37–38
    NFL suspension, 38
    Pam Carey and, 35
    Peggy Fulford and (*See* Fulford, Peggy)
    signing power of attorney to Peggy, 38–39
Wires technique, 10, 154–60, 189. *See also*
    financial scams; Leli, Vincent

ABOUT THE AUTHOR

Johnathan Walton is an Emmy-winning former TV reporter and current reality TV producer who has written and produced shows for NBC, ABC, HBO, Disney Plus, the Discovery Channel, and many others. He is also the host, writer, and executive producer of the hit true-crime podcast *Queen of the Con*. In his free time, he helps other victims of con artists get justice.